T0330129

Economy and Society in Europe

Economy and Society in Europe

in Europe

A Relationship in Crisis

Edited by

Luigi Burroni

Associate Professor of Economic Sociology, University of Teramo, Italy

Maarten Keune

Professor, University of Amsterdam, The Netherlands

Guglielmo Meardi

Associate Professor (Reader) of Industrial Relations, University of Warwick, UK

Edward Elgar

Cheltenham, UK • Northampton, MA, USA

Published by
Edward Elgar Publishing Limited
The Lypiatts
15 Lansdown Road
Cheltenham
Glos GL50 2JA
UK

Edward Elgar Publishing, Inc.
William Pratt House
9 Dewey Court
Northampton
Massachusetts 01060
USA

A catalogue record for this book
is available from the British Library

Library of Congress Control Number: 2011936406

ISBN 978 1 84980 365 6

Typeset by Servis Filmsetting Ltd, Stockport, Cheshire
Printed and bound by MPG Books Group, UK

Contents

Figures

Tables

Contributors

Luigi Burroni, University of Teramo, Italy

Roland Erne, University College Dublin, Republic of Ireland

Henry Farrell, Elliott School of International Affairs, George Washington University, US

Ulrich Glassmann, University of Cologne, Germany

Anton Hemerijck, Free University University Amsterdam, Netherlands

Simcha Jong, University College London, UK

María José González López, Universitat Pompeu Fabra, Barcelona

Teresa Jurado-Guerrero, Universidad Nacional de Educació a Distancia, Madrid, Spain

Maarten Keune, AJAS – University of Amsterdam, Netherlands

Patrick Le Galès, Sciences Po – CNRS, Paris, France

Guglielmo Meardi, University of Warwick, UK

Manuela Naldini, University of Torino, Italy

Preface

Over two days in May 2009 an unusual event took place in an ancient Venetian palace. Thirty researchers from nine different countries and three different generations intensively discussed as wide a theme as 'the changing boundaries between economy and society in Europe'. The topics of the presentations were, at first sight, disparate: from housework to university organization, from regional economies to trade unions. In today's ultra-specialised, technocratic academic environments experts on such topics tend to work in separate departments and to attend separate conferences, or at least separate streams within the conferences. Yet in Venice the discussions on the wide-ranging topics were particularly intense and open: regardless of different specialisms and origins, the participants understood each other perfectly; despite lively debate and differences of opinion, they really spoke the same language; and they felt affinities with the entire range of subjects.

The occasion for this meeting was to celebrate Colin Crouch's career in the year of his 65th birthday. The participants had in common the experience of having worked alongside him, whether as doctoral students, research assistants or as colleagues, between the 1970s and the 2000s, whether in the UK, in Florence or somewhere else in Europe. This shared experience is an initial explanation of the strong integration of the debates at the Venice meeting: the influence of common readings, of interlinked projects, or of shared doctoral supervision, all elements of Crouch's teaching that proved to be pedagogically outstanding over a period of three decades.

Yet the intellectual integration of the meeting went beyond 'elective' and 'socialization' factors. Combining economics with political science and sociology is not an easy task. Intimate knowledge of developments in the wide variety of European countries, East and West, is not acquired just by socializing. What had made the integration of the meeting possible was the meticulous development, over decades, of a broader area of study with its own intellectual rigour. Intriguingly, the participants themselves, brain-storming over a long coffee in the palace's canal-side garden, struggled to put the right label on this area of study: 'economic sociology' was a fair approximation, 'socio-economics' as well, but these were both too vague and at the same time not comprehensive enough. But that did not matter because the participants were concerned with contents more than with labels; with in-depth discussion more than with catchwords.

The integrated study of economy and society, over the years, has allowed us to overcome the limits of mono-causal explanations (whether market, politics or class-based) and to highlight linkages between different institutions and previous studies by different people: family, associations, government, corporations. One of the examples Crouch likes is that you can't understand the long job tenure in the Italian labour market without the role of severance pay, but you can't understand severance pay without its role in the Italian financial and real estate markets, which themselves cannot be understood without the role of the family, including parents buying houses for their children, which itself cannot be understood without looking at the labour market, and so on.

It would be a theoretical contradiction to ascribe this area of research, interested in complex linkages, networks and hierarchies, to a single person. Yet, at the more 'approximate' level of actual academic debates, the contribution by Colin Crouch cannot be overestimated. It is not a contribution that may be called a theory or a school of thought, as it is more pluralist than that. Crouch's work is not in the style of the *maîtres-penseurs*. It is based on a broader methodological approach that combines historical sensitivity to unique causal links with social sciences theory. Other theorists have also highlighted the interdependence and complementarity between institutions, but Crouch has also studied how these institutions change, and avoided any determinism in doing so. For instance, when trying to comprehend the variety of industrial relations in Europe (*Industrial Relations and European State Traditions*, 1993), Crouch employed rational-choice concepts and political science typologies, but also engaged in a fine-grained historical reconstruction that led him back to the Middle Ages.

The wide scope of multidisciplinary knowledge that such an approach requires reminds us, rather than of contemporary *grand philosophes* or management gurus, of the Renaissance man (but Crouch would rename him Renaissance woman), a qualification which is in many ways exemplified by his ten years of polyhedric work at the EUI in Florence. These were also the years in which he wrote, among others, *Social Change in Western Europe*, a book covering developments in labour markets, family, religion, ethnicity, politics, industrial relations and welfare state, across the whole of Western Europe over a period of 50 years. The theoretical and methodological breadth combines with the geographic one: Crouch's avoidance of methodological nationalism, while remaining interested in the nation, may explain why students and colleagues from so many different countries have been influenced by him. His role in the broader scientific community has been inspirational across disciplines and has been particularly visible in the growth of the Society for the Advancement of Socio-Economics.

Finally, Crouch's work has clear policy and political implications without, however, falling into the straitjacket of a program or an ideology. That is visible from his role as president of the Student Union of the London School of Economics in 1968, to his most recent book, *The Strange Non-Death of Neo-Liberalism* (2011), his latest example of application of knowledge to the current crisis, going beyond the common simplistic accounts of 'neo-liberalism'. At the time of the Venice meeting, Crouch had just finished a critical assessment of the privatization plans for the British Royal Mail. Renaissance men do not distinguish between pure and applied sciences.

This book is the outcome of that meeting in Venice, which took place under the Mediterranean sun, but also in the shadow of the global economic crisis. We opted for a book written exclusively by Crouch's former PhD students and research assistants to underline his contribution to the education of two subsequent generations of broadly oriented social scientists who continue to work in his spirit. Besides the authors of the chapters, the comments from other participants were significant inspiration: Franca Alacevich, Arne Baumann, Andrea Hermann, Ann-Louise Holten, Dawn Lyon, Ulrike Mühlberger, Jackie O'Reilly, Ida Regalia, Philippe Schmitter, Catherine Spieser, Simona Talani, Alessia Vatta and Elke Viebrock. The organizational and financial contributions of the University of Warwick made the meeting physically possible. Yet the greatest contribution and inspiration is from Colin Crouch himself, and the book is dedicated to him.

LUIGI BURRONI
MAARTEN KEUNE
GUGLIELMO MEARDI

1. Introduction

Luigi Burroni, Maarten Keune and Guglielmo Meardi

THE RELATIONSHIP BETWEEN ECONOMY AND SOCIETY

One of the classical ways in which the social sciences have studied the emergence and consolidation of capitalism has been through the analysis of the relationships between social institutions and economic institutions. As a pioneer in this respect, Max Weber contributed two major insights. One is the importance of individual beliefs, evidenced by the effects of the Calvinist version of protestant ethics on entrepreneurial attitudes. The other is the relevance of associations, demonstrated by the analysis of the relationship between the development of capitalism and the presence of protestant sects in American society. Religious beliefs and religious associations for Weber constituted crucial factors that underline the deep social and institutional roots of economic development processes (Weber 1978). Karl Polanyi, building on these insights, showed that the market, often seen as the economic coordination mechanism *par excellence*, is only one of the mechanisms regulating economic exchanges. Other such mechanisms include redistribution, including a key role for the state, and community relations, with the community playing a fundamental regulating role also in contemporary societies (Polanyi 1957). And also Albert Hirschmann underlined how the analysis of social variables like *exit* and *voice* has important explanatory power in the study of the functioning of economic phenomena and relationships (Hirschmann 1970).

The relationship between economy and society has been important also in more recent work by, for example, Mark Granovetter or Margaret Grieco, who show how the workings of the labour market and the labour market success of individuals are influenced by social, relational resources in the form of strong and weak social ties (Granovetter 1973; Grieco 1987). They underline that a person's labour market position does not depend solely on his or her competencies but also, or rather, on the social networks of which he or she forms part. Others have demonstrated the relevance of interest representation organizations in determining the shape contemporary capitalist models have taken (Crouch 1993; Schmitter and Streeck 1999). The presence of a small number of large and strongly inclusive organizations geared towards representing not only the interests of their members but also the general interest has favoured the emergence of neo-corporatist models of capitalism. In these models the state shares political space with these organizations which use internal discipline to supplement government authority to bring order to the economy and in exchange see certain private arrangements virtually acquire the status of public authority. They are contrasted with pluralist models in which a high number of fragmented organizations representing specific interests compete to influence politics. Other research has highlighted other examples of social variables playing an important role in the functioning of the economy, such as the family or social capital.

CAPITALIST DIVERSITY AND INSTITUTIONAL CHANGE

This volume addresses the relationship between economy and society and the influence of social institutions on economic processes, examining this relationship from a variety of perspectives. It highlights in particular two dimensions. One is comparative. From a comparative point of view different mixes between economy and society can be observed that produce a range of capitalist diversity, that is, different national models with deep historical roots and different competitive capacities. This diversity concerns a wide variety of institutional arenas, ranging from industrial relations systems and labour market and training policies, to education systems and the role of the families, to corporate governance architectures and corporate financing structures, and so on. Based on the exploration of these institutional arenas, many recent studies have developed typologies of models of capitalism, often largely reflecting the extent to which market mechanisms are central to the coordination of economic and social processes. Main examples of such typologies are the distinction between Anglo-Saxon capitalism and Rhenish-continental capitalism (Albert 1991), between models based on diversified quality production, flexible specialization and flexible mass production (Crouch and Streeck 1997; Piore and Sabel 1984), between Asian and Western economies (Dore 1987; Whitley 1999), or between coordinated market economies and liberal market economies (Hall and Soskice 2001). Whereas these studies mainly deal with national models of capitalism, others have also identified major differences in the relationship between economy and society, as well as of the role of market mechanisms at the sub-national level, that is, at the level of sectors (Hollingsworth and Lindberg 1985; Crouch et al. 2004) or regions (Crouch et al. 2001).

Identifying different models of capitalism, often based on the different extent to which economies and societies are exposed to market mechanisms, is one of the major research questions in the study of capitalist diversity. Another is the question to what extent this diversity corresponds to differences in economic performance. Since the 1990s there have been four main lines of research concerning this question. The first has shown that there are multiple routes towards economic competitiveness and that different mixes of economic and social institutions can have similar outcomes in terms of the overall performance of the system (Berger and Dore 1996). The second, influenced by the contributions of major international organizations, has adopted a more neo-liberal vision and has tried to demonstrate that countries that are more exposed to market mechanisms are also more competitive. The third has underlined rather that institutional constraints to market forces can have beneficial effects on economic competitiveness, fostering in particular the development of models based on high levels of quality and diversification (Crouch and Streeck 1997). And finally, there are a series of contributions that argue that certain models of capitalism are more competitive in economic activities centred on incremental innovation, whereas others, more exposed to market regulation, are more competitive in activities based on radical innovation (Hall and Soskice 2001; Hancké et al. 2007). Clearly, these groups of studies take distinct views on the relationship between types of capitalism and performance. They coincide however in their observation that social institutions play a determining role in the functioning of capitalism and that if we exclude such social institutions from the analysis we will not be able to properly understand the workings of these models.

The second dimension, next to the comparative one, is the observation that the various models of capitalism are not necessarily stable over time but that they can change, and that the results of such change can be small adaptation but also radical transformations. For example, the New Right of Margaret Thatcher radically altered the institutional make-up of the United Kingdom of the 1970s, dramatically increasing the role of the market. In more recent years, in many European countries, changes have been made to the welfare state, which then also affect the functioning of the capitalist model (Ferrera et al. 2001). The same could be said for reforms of the labour market (Esping-Andersen and Regini 2000). What these examples indicate is that apart from the characteristics of different models of capitalism, it is of great importance as well to study how capitalist economies and societies change (Streeck and Thelen 2005; Campbell

2004). This includes the study of the relationships between economy and society, which are also not necessarily stable over time, as well as of social causes of economic change. Among the elements that lead to such changes of major importance are contradictory interests that lead to conflicts between (groups of) actors; such conflicts can then result in institutional change (Crouch 1993). Through the confrontation of diverging interests, enterprises, interest representation organizations, local and national governments, EU level entities and others contribute to incremental or radical changes in the prevailing institutional features of capitalist models (Crouch 1993; Schmitter and Streeck 1999). Apart from interests, the confrontation of different ideas can also play a prominent role in causing such changes (Boltanski and Chiapello 1991). A good example of this has been the widespread promotion of privatization and liberalization, and the accompanying efficiency rhetoric, in most European societies. These processes have affected strategic sectors like local public services, telecommunications, transport, and so on. In many cases these reforms were advanced following the belief that private management of public goods would bring higher quality services and more efficiency expressed in lower prices. However, in many cases the increased role of the private sector has not automatically resulted in cheaper and/or higher quality services (Keune et al. 2008). Similarly, labour market flexibilization has often been forwarded as a solution to competitiveness problems, unemployment or the growth of the informal economy. Also in this case the results of ongoing flexibilization have often not matched the expectations. Interests and ideas are however not always easy to disentangle: ideas play a key role in the definition of interests, while interests may lead certain actors to promote corresponding ideas. Also, gradual and radical changes are not always easy to distinguish: multiple moments of gradual change may in the end add up to radical changes (Streeck and Thelen 2005). Finally, a major factor that can spur actors to seek changes is an altering context in which a national or regional model operates. Indeed, many such changes are justified by actors referring to factors such as globalization, technological change or European integration.

THE GOVERNANCE APPROACH

We have highlighted two major dimensions of the study of contemporary capitalism here: (i) the prevalence of a variety of models of capitalism with different relationships between economy and society; and (ii) the occurrence of changes in these models as actors confront their ideas and interests and react to changing contexts. These two dimensions guide the analysis in the chapters in this volume, as they lead us to take a broad analytical approach, taking into account the direct and indirect relationships between multiple institutional arenas as well as the role of a range of modes of regulation. We take much of our inspiration from what is sometimes defined as the 'governance approach', that is, a strand of research that studies the role of and interaction between various forms of governance pertaining to society (such as the community, the family, social networks or associations), to the economy (such as corporate hierarchies or the market) and to public actors (the state at its various levels) (Hollingsworth et al. 2002; Crouch 2005). This strand does not aim to fit empirical cases to predefined typologies but rather considers to what extent these forms of governance are present in different empirical realities and how they interact. This allow us to draw up the 'chemical composition' of empirical cases (Crouch 2005) and to make social analysis more scientific following the analogy of chemical and biological analysis, by, instead of asking to what type a case corresponds, asking what types of governance can be found in the case, in what proportions and how this changes over time (Crouch 2007). This helps us not to define a case by a sole dominant characteristic but to approach it as a complex of various modes of governance with different weights that can change over time (Crouch and Keune 2005). In this way, we can, for example, determine if the UK model of capitalism is indeed dominated by market regulation or if oligopolistic competition between large enterprises plays an important role as well (Crouch 2005). Or we can study if the Germany model of the 1980s still persists today or if it is progressively transformed into something profoundly different (Streeck 2009). It also allows us to show the role of social institutions in explaining processes that in the first instance seem to have only economic causes, for example, the recent crisis (Crouch 2008).

Hence, this approach is broad and dynamic and provides a more complex and realistic image of contemporary capitalism than the simplistic view of neo-classical economics. It also helps us to formulate more credible and accurate explanations for changes we observe. This may be the reason why in recent years more and more economists have started to introduce social institutions in explaining phenomena such as economic transactions (Williamson 1985) and the functioning of the labour market (Solow 1992).

THE CONTRIBUTIONS IN THIS VOLUME

Based on the above outlined approach, the contributions to this volume expose the characteristics and transformations of the institutional architectures of contemporary European societies, covering a wide range of themes that are strongly interrelated. Focusing on different arena, from European integration to welfare reforms, from labour market and gender relations to the university system, from industrial relations to the role of the central state, from local and regional regulatory mechanisms to the views and interpretations of economic crisis, it will be possible to see how the mobile boundaries between economy and society have changed in European countries during the 2000s. The reaction to global pressures such as the 9/11 in 2001 or the 2007 financial crisis, the consequences of European political integration and endogenous variables and mechanisms triggered a series of processes of restructuring that modified the basic functioning of many institutional arenas considered in this book.

In particular, in Chapter 2, Keune examines the social content and social effects of European integration, both in terms of the development of European social standards and in terms of domestic social policy capacity. Following Hooghe and Marks (1999) European integration is pictured as a contested process between groups of actors with projects based on different ideas and interests: one is the neo-liberal project pursuing European-wide market integration while at the same time trying to insulate the market from political interference by resisting the creation of a European polity and rejecting the development of positive market regulation; and the other is the project for regulated capitalism, which wants to see market integration accompanied by positive market enhancing and market-supporting regulations to create a social democratic dimension to European governance. It is first of all demonstrated that although European integration was originally solely of an economic nature, over the years an important body of labour market and social Directives has been adopted and, since the late 1990s, there has also been a growing use of experimental forms of governance in the labour market and social field. At the same time these regulations are fragmentary, largely complementary to national regulations, and they fail to make up a coherent or comprehensive social or labour market model. The core regulatory level for social and labour market issues remains the national level. This is in stark contrast with the deep and comprehensive economic integration that has dominated the European project. Overall, then, it seems that the social dimension of European integration is quite limited, especially where its function of limiting the role of the market is concerned.

Where the effect of EU integration on domestic social policy capacity is concerned, the Internal Market and European Monetary Union (EMU) may have positive and negative effects. On the one hand, they may lead to higher economic dynamism and growth, and to more macro-economic stability. In this way, they may help safeguard the welfare state. On the other hand, they foster regime competition, affect the power balance between workers and employers in favour of the latter, foster wage moderation and put limits on social expenditure. These developments clearly put social standards and policy-making capacity under pressure and undermine achievements of the past. This effect differs substantially between countries, however, depending on domestic institutions, power constellations and actor strategies. Also, the character of the integration process itself has changed over time and may do so again in the future, acquiring new directions. In Chapter 3, Hemerijck provides a detailed analysis of how ideas concerning the role and development of the welfare state have changed in Europe since World War II and how this resulted in profound institutional change. After the war, the 'Golden Age' of organized welfare capitalism, class compromise and embedded liberalism began, buttressing democratic governance and complementing the market economy with human solidarity. Far from being polar opposites, open markets and organized solidarity prospered together. However, in the wake of the oil shocks of mid- to late1970s, a period of welfare retrenchment and neo-liberalism took off with the elections of Margaret Thatcher and Ronald Reagan, which epitomized the revival of self-regulating markets. They were inspired by monetarist and neo-liberal ideas voiced by increasingly influential neo-classical economists. Together, the supply-side revolution in economics and the politics of neo-liberalism fostered a deliberate change in the hierarchy of social and economy policy objectives in favour of the latter. Also, where the postwar welfare state was designed essentially to provide the institutional underpinning for an economy organized around stable industrial employment relations, the common quest in the wake of the two oil shocks became that of enforcing more flexible employment relations. The key policy recipe of neo-liberalism was to free markets, institutions, rules and regulations from the collective political decision-making that had been the norm under embedded liberalism.

Finally, by the end of the 1990s, political disenchantment with neo-liberal policy measures began to generate electoral successes for the centre-left that believed that most European welfare states had to be transformed from passive benefits systems into activating, capacity building, social investment states. They were soon joined by the Organisation for Economic Co-operation and Development (OECD) and the European Commission. This policy platform was inspired intellectually by Giddens, Esping-Andersen and like-minded academics who argue that the 'passive' male breadwinner policy legacy frustrates a more adequate response to the 'new' social risks of the post-industrial economy. At the heart of the social investment paradigm lies a re-orientation in social citizenship, away from *freedom from want* towards *freedom to act.* Citizens have to be endowed with capabilities and high levels of employment for both men and women should be the key policy objective. And whereas neo-liberal doctrines demanded a trade-off between these goals, the social investment paradigm sees improved social equity go hand in hand with more economic efficiency. Key social policy provisions can be viewed as investments, potentially enhancing both social protection and productive potential. While social investment advocates share the neo-classical critique of the postwar welfare state when emphasizing the supply-side, they do see a key role for the state.

Based on this analysis, Hemerijck argues that each phase of welfare state development can be conceptualized as a distinct policy advocacy, designed to effectively respond to impending socio-economic challenges and to achieve shared policy objectives, supported by fairly robust political compromises. The moments of fundamental policy change are often associated with successive waves of economic adjustment and deep economic crises especially provide important political windows for policy redirection by newly-elected politicians with radically different ideas. He also underlines the importance of intellectual developments in developing new policy paradigms by offering political actors convincing analyses of the problems of the day and direction to new policy approaches.

Although the European Union repeatedly proclaims a commitment to gender equality, and indeed equal opportunities regulations are among the most important aspects of 'Social Europe', the common definitions of 'European Social Model' are gender-blind. If the vague 'European Social Model' is, for the sake of economic rigour, to be redefined as 'a specific case of "mid-century social compromise"' (Crouch 1999), then it has to be added that this was not just a political and industrial relations compromise between state, employers and employee organizations. It was also, as Jurado-Guerrero, González López and Naldini point out in Chapter 4, a gender compromise between men and women, especially in the distribution of labour. O'Reilly and Spee (1998) proposed an analytical framework to integrate three interdependent arenas of exchanges that have been all too often studied separately: welfare state, industrial relations and gender relations (especially with regard to childcare). Indeed, it is impossible to understand the developments in one of these arenas without considering simultaneous changes in the other ones. In their chapter, Jurado-Guerrero, González López and Naldini propose an empirical application to the case of housework sharing between men and women. Given that the most important change in the labour markets of industrialized societies in the last 30–40 years has been the near-doubling of female employment in the formal economy, they expect major changes to emerge also in the sharing of unpaid work. However, the data indicates that the share of men performing an equal share of housework is still very low. This finding has two important implications. First, it confirms the importance of social embeddedness of the economy: what happens in the formal economy depends largely on what happens in non-monetary social relations. Second, a gender approach suggests a much deeper insight in the meaning of 'crisis'. The 'crisis' of social models, first of organized capitalism and, with the latest financial crisis, of 'privatized Keynesism', may well have deeper roots in unresolved contradictions not just in capital–labour relations, but also in gender relations.

A blind spot in the analysis of models of capitalism is constituted by universities. This is surprising since they play a critical role in cultivating social-political elites, in educating members of various modern professions, and in forming society's technological knowledge base. Moreover, academic scholarship at universities shapes cultural debates as well as political, social, and esthetic categories. As a result, the way institutional systems of higher learning are set up has fundamental implications for the organization of capitalist systems, touching on many of the critical institutional outcomes with which scholarly debates in the political economy literature have been concerned. Yet, scholars in the political economy literature have to date shown little interest in examining how the national frameworks governing these institutions affect the capitalist enterprise beyond their role in vocational training. In Chapter 5, Simcha Jong addresses this blind spot by examining how national systems of higher learning work together with other institutions in national political economies in producing social and economic outcomes. He focuses his analysis on the Conservative university reform movement of the 1980s and 1990s. He shows how the relationship of universities to the state and the economy in Britain has changed over the past decades as part of the broader neo-liberal shifts in the political economy of the United Kingdom. Based on his analysis, Jong identifies three dimensions along which the institutional set-up of national systems of higher education shape contemporary capitalist societies. First, like other civic institutions, autonomous scholarly communities at universities form a potential counterweight to the power of the central state and forces of free marketeering. British scholarly communities played such a role up until the dawn of the Thatcher era. The Conservative university reform movement was in part an attempt to quell political dissent that was linked into a broader political agenda to weaken the position of civic institutions, and reassert the power of central government. Second, the set-up of academic institutions plays a role that complements the role of labour and financial institutions in the governance of economic life in capitalist systems. These shifts were integral to a broader shift in the British capitalist system towards a greater reliance on private, market-based governance models in the economy. The re-orientation of the academic system towards more utilitarian goals was explicitly linked by the Conservative reform movement to the empowerment of private enterprising at the expense of coordinated models of governance in the British economy. Third, the institutional set-up of national systems of higher learning potentially plays a role in supporting the competitive advantage of firms in certain industries. As universities have come to play an increasingly important role over the past decades in cultivating the expertise and skills firms require in gaining a competitive advantage in today's so-called knowledge-based societies, the world of academia has become critical in supporting the economic performance of firms in a range of high-tech sectors.

Moreover, the reforms promoted by the governments of Margaret Thatcher and John Major are not only relevant for the study of the British political economy but had an impact well beyond the United Kingdom. In fact, the Conservative university reform movement has probably introduced the most important institutional changes to institutions of higher learning since the rise of the American research university and the transformation of universities into institutions of mass education during the postwar decades. The institutional changes pushed through by this movement have guided university reforms in countries around the globe, leading to a transformation of the relationship between universities and the national political economies of which they are a part.

Contrary to universities, the labour market has always been a privileged focus for studies of the boundaries between economy and society, because of its unique nature. As institutional economists (Kerr, Solow, Commons) have pointed out, a market, in theory, requires four prerequisites: an anonymous good, exchange between equals, price leading to equilibrium, and economic rationality. The labour market clearly fails on all four tests, and therefore does not deserve the definition of 'market'. This point has been best outlined in Polanyi's (1944) critique of labour as a 'fictitious commodity', an idea that has been adopted by the Philadelphia Declaration of the International Labour Organization (ILO), declaring that 'labour is not a commodity'.

Among the contributions of social theory to the understanding of the labour market, that by Claus Offe (1985) is particularly important, including the analysis on the logics of association of employers and employees, and the observation of the indispensible role of the state. Both associations and state have been the focus of a large 'industry' of 'corporatism' studies, launched in the 1970s by Schmitter and Crouch in particular. Since the late 1980s, as capitalism was apparently being 'disorganized' to an unprecedented level, and even more later on as the idea of 'globalization' came to the fore, corporatism and the state have received less attention. In Chapter 6, Meardi reassess the relevance of some classic ideas of national industrial relations and national state traditions, against a background of increased internationalization and, specifically, Europeanization of employment policies.

Internationalization and Europeanization have often taken the form of a search for a 'one best way' of regulating labour markets. This was evident in the 'flexibility' recipe of the OECD Jobs Study of 1994, which has been the object of systematic criticism by sociologists and institutional economists: flexibility does not guarantee a more efficient equilibrium and may well have negative effects on training, commitment and equality (Esping-Andersen and Regini 2000). Indeed, labour market reforms in the 1980s and 1990s have been associated with major changes in equality: in France, a country which under successive socialist governments intensified regulation, especially through the minimum wage, inequality fell, while in the UK and the US, liberalization led to the opposite result (Koeniger et al. 2007). As Marx and Weber had equally pointed out, the labour market is a privileged arena for social stratification.

More recently, in Europe internationalization of 'one best way' employment policies has taken the form of the promotion of the more ambiguous 'flexicurity' by the European Commission. Again, attention to institutions and social effects has raised a number of criticisms (Keune and Jespen 2007; Burroni and Keune 2011). In his chapter, Meardi indicates that although there is a converging trend among European countries, it is more towards flexibility than security and its timing and forms do not correspond to EU initiatives. Therefore, the weight of supranational institutions should not be overstated. By contrast, there is evidence of national variations and of resilience of national styles of labour markets and industrial relations, which had been described in historical depth by Therborn (1986) and Crouch (1993) before the beginning of the European Employment Strategy and the OECD Jobs Study. Indeed, the recent financial crisis has provided further evidence of the relevance of national institutional arrangements: similar falls in economic output have had very different effects on employment depending not only on economic structures (e.g. the weight of the construction sector), but also of institutional arrangements of different countries. Hyper-flexible labour markets of Ireland, Spain, US and the Baltic states witnessed a major jump in unemployment, while Germany, through social-political agreements on short working time, avoided it, and other countries such as Italy, France and the UK had a more mixed result.

However, the evidence of enduring national traditions must not be confounded with deterministic path dependency and lack of change. Some institutionalist approaches, and in particular the 'Varieties of Capitalism' approach (Hall and Soskice 2001), have been criticized for their excessive functionalism, stressing complementary coherence between institutions. As Chapter 4 by Jurado-Guerrero, González López and Naldini indicates, the same variety of capitalism may well hide huge differences in how work is actually organized, and in particular contradictions between female and male work. Moreover, as argued before, national systems do change, and not just in an incremental, specializing way (Streeck and Thelen 2005; Crouch 2005). The chapter by Meardi deals with this issue by developing a critique of typologies of industrial relations 'models', and adopting instead the less rigid concept of 'styles', noticing that industrial relations actors have different, contradictory and changing strategies within each 'model'.

The balance between 'structure' and 'agency' in studies of society and economics is indeed particularly problematic as the role of actors generally receives too little attention. In Chapter 7, Erne addresses this issue most directly by looking in particular at the role of trade unions in Europe in the light of the recent of economic crisis. This is not a new concern: during the crisis of the 1970s, following the oil shock, Crouch and Pizzorno (1978) produced an exemplary comparative analysis of trade union activities throughout Western Europe. A historical perspective is therefore very useful, as well as caution on making any prediction – not exactly the main task for social scientists. Erne provides in his chapter is a critique of dominant economic ideas from the point of view of democracy, an idea that also appeared in the works of Crouch (2004, 2011). The economic crisis has indeed highlighted new contradictions between economy and society, and therefore, Erne argues, opened up more scope for social actors' action. The relationship between economy and society comes to the fore possibly most clearly when examining the role played by the state and in particular the process of state restructuring. Even if the ongoing process of recasting the state led to important changes in the nature and features of the policy instruments adopted by the state, there is a general agreement that the state continues to be one of the most important governance mechanisms and its action strongly influences the relationship between economy and society in contemporary capitalism. Chapter 8 by Patrick Le Galès is particularly important in understanding these changes and relationships. Le Galès stresses that the state continues to be a very important actor and that the withering away of the state is not a central issue anymore. Politics makes an important contribution to the definition of the boundaries between economy and society (Polanyi 1957; Streeck 2010) and for this reason the focus on the 'action' of the state in terms of policies and policy instruments is useful to understand socio-economic change in contemporary societies. By this point of view, the two examples that Le Galès underlines in his chapter are particularly useful: on the one hand, he focuses on the pervasive use of new public management practices and, on the other, on the set-up of participatory practices of government at local level.

An example of the first trend is given by the attempts of the Blair and Brown governments to regenerate the public sector, providing better services with a strategy that had many elements in common with the previous Conservative governments: they are all based on the importance of statistical measures, indicators and objectives for evaluating the results or improvements in performance, largely inspired by public choice economics. From this point of view, New Labour simply systematized a way of steering policies on the basis of performance objectives and strict financial control, developing a large series of synthetic indicators. In a few years, universities, schools, hospitals and local governments were subjected to a system of incentives and sanctions based on aggregated indicators, whereas the logic of auditing and inspection progressively led to more standardization, with a growing attention to pursuing a good performance according to the system of evaluation and a minor attention to the creation of public goods.

Auditing practices have now a high legitimacy in the UK and affect a large part of the society and influence the way of organizing public policies, political parties, agencies, schools and associations. They are also notable instruments of power for governments that can modify the indicators relatively easily, obliging individual and collective actors to 'run along behind instruments that are constantly changing in the name of efficiency and rationality'. Focusing on these instruments it is possible to note how the culture of auditing influenced the relationship between economy and society promoting specific behaviour and policy approaches and influencing the contents of public policies.

The second example is related to the new instruments of governance that triggered the mobilization of actors in the making of collective goods. Le Galès stresses the importance of practices set up by the state that favour deliberation and participation and the emerging of a quasi-contractual policy making based on agreements and pacts among individual and collective actors. These processes are evident in many cities and regions reacting to the pressures of globalization, where local and regional governments decided to share political space with other economic and civic organizations to regulate the territory. Even in this case, the action of the state directly contributes to creating opportunities and constraints as well as to promoting new forms of participation that modify the equilibrium between economy and society at local level.

The role of the state and the importance of the territorial level of regulation emerge also in the contribution of Ulrich Glassmann (Chapter 9). He focuses on the responses of coordinated market economies to increasing international competition. Glassmann emphasizes that these responses are based on a twofold process of fragmentation, caused on the one hand by a policy shift towards exclusively regional support of traditional manufacturers (spatial fragmentation) and, on the other, by domestic deregulation furthering a dual labour market (institutional fragmentation). Spatial fragmentation is increasingly affecting countries such as Germany that until the 1990s were characterized by a relatively homogeneous production regime across regions. In recent years traditional manufacturing activities strongly declined and many local economies specialized in technological activities typical of liberal market economies, such as life sciences, biotechnologies, communication technologies, and so on. To support this kind of specialization, regions need support in terms of collective competition goods (Crouch et al. 2001, 2004), but the public infrastructure is designed to support production for traditional markets. For this reason, there is space for regional institutions to deviate from the national regulations, leading to the emergence of political entrepreneurialism that promotes territorial specialization and differentiation. At the same time, this differentiation is also reinforced by the action of many Länder governments that abandoned their equalizing spatial support measures to reinforce competitive advantages of dynamic areas. Thus, economic restructuring and public policies promoted a rising territorial fragmentation. Institutional fragmentation is caused by the progressive erosion of industrial relations with a decline in coverage and decentralization of collective agreements and the spreading of atypical employment (part-time, temporary and self-employment).

According to Glassmann, territorial fragmentation emphasizes the divide between rich and poor regions, while institutional fragmentation leads to a rising income inequality: these two processes overlap, reinforcing competitiveness of traditional markets and prosperous regions, but also creating social exclusion and regional decline of weak regions. Thus, the role of the state in terms of public policies and the action of collective organizations contributed in recent years to modify the architecture of social inequalities in coordinated market economies.

Even if the role of the state continues to be important, the analysis of local and regional governance shows that also others governance forms are playing a very important role. Chapter 10 by Luigi Burroni compares local governance models in the United Kingdom, France and Italy. It shows that these cases have different regulatory architectures, where firms, interest organizations, development agencies, local communities, the voluntary sector and local governments interact to produce competitive advantages for local firms. In the United Kingdom large firms, development agencies and public–private partnerships are the dominant forms of governance; this model finds its roots in a process of reorganization of public policies aimed at weakening the power and the autonomy of local councils, and in the growing legitimization of new public management practices. Thus, even if relevant changes in urban policies occurred in the last 20 years, it is possible to identify some pillars that continue to be the key feature of the UK model during this period: the promotion of competition in the provision of local services, the reinforcement of local and regional agencies and the encouragement of private–public partnership.

The French model of urban governance continues to be characterized by the dominant role played by the state, both at central and local level: the local coalitions of actors/organizations of this governance architecture tend to be mono-centric, with the local state monopolizing the political space devoted to the creation of common goods and the participation of local associations or private organizations is promoted directly by the local government and regulated by formal instruments (such as contracts and plans). Development agencies and partnerships are led by state actors. Together with the state, large firms play a very important role in the provision of collective competition goods directly providing them and influencing the strategies of local and regional governments.

The Italian case is more heterogeneous, as it is characterized by very relevant territorial disparities between northern and southern regions in terms of economic performance, governance structures and outcomes. Burroni shows that in Italy a model of local neo-corporatism prevails in industrial districts. This model is based on social concertation and is characterized by development-oriented coalitions formed by local governments, trade unions and employers' associations that produce mainly sectoral competition goods aimed at promoting economic development. At the same time, many cities are characterized by a more deliberative process of planning, where an incremental negotiation promotes the rise of heterogeneous groups of actors composed of experts, politicians and practitioners who share a common vision of the world: the outcome of this process is a plan that delivers a 'vision for the city', based on the identification of long-term needs, priorities, objectives and measures. In this case, the process of negotiation is more similar to a sort of experiment of deliberative democracy than to local corporatist pact and it aims to promote economic competitiveness but also many other kinds of common goods.

All this shows that in these three countries there is an important relationship between economy and society at local level: single firms, local political actors such as the local government, local organization such as unions and employers' associations and organization representing civil society directly contribute to the set-up and distribution of local competitive advantages that influence the competitiveness of local firms.

As many of the above-mentioned chapters have shown, to understand the changes of contemporary capitalism it is important to take into account the role played by economic actors and organizations, such as firms or interest organizations, but also to focus on the role of non-economic institutions, such as families or the voluntary sector. This path of research helps to explain which kind of regulation characterizes contemporary societies, and how, why and when a specific model emerges in some places and not in others. However, overlooking one of these dimensions may give rise to relevant misunderstandings of the processes and changes that characterize modern society. This is what happened with the recent economic crisis: as Chapter 11 by Henry Farrell shows, research approaches based on mainstream economics became highly path dependent and were not able to predict the crisis, and had little useful to say about it in its early stages. According to Farrell, these difficulties are related to the impoverished view that mainstream economics has of institutions, as a result of which it is not well suited to deal with changing societal conditions. This may also explain why economists converged on the solution of neo-Keynesianism, even if it did not provide a clear understanding of the origins of the crisis, instead of engaging in a costly and difficult search for alternative explanatory frameworks. According to Farrell, this is unsurprising given the distance between mainstream economics and those fields in the social sciences that include the role of social institutions in their analysis and that therefore have had alternative explanations to offer. Furthermore, as has been shown recently (Streeck 2010), the focus on the interplay between economy and society may help to identify the main features of contemporary capitalism and to understand its recent changes.

REFERENCES

Albert, M. (1991), *Capitalisme contre Capitalisme*, Paris: Editions du Seuil.
Berger, S. and Dore, R. (1996), *National Diversity and Global Capitalism*, Cornell: Cornell University Press.
Boltanski, L. and Chiapello, E. (1999), *Le nouvel esprit du capitalisme*, Gallimard: Paris.
Burroni, L. and Keune, M. (2011), 'Flexicurity: A Conceptual Critique', *European Journal of Industrial Relations*, **17**, 75–91.
Campbell, J. (2004), *Institutional Change and Globalization*, Princeton: Princeton University Press.

Crouch, C. (1993), *Industrial Relations and European State Traditions*, Oxford: Oxford University Press.

Crouch, C. (1999), *Social Change in Western Europe*, Oxford: Oxford University Press.

Crouch, C. (2004), *Post-Democracy*, Oxford: Polity.

Crouch, C. (2005), *Capitalist Diversity and Change: Recombinant Governance and Institutional Entrepreneurs*, Oxford: Oxford University Press.

Crouch, C. (2007), 'How to "do" post-determinist institutional analysis', *Socio-Economic Review* **5**(3), 527–37.

Crouch, C. (2008), 'What will follow the demise of privatised Keynesianism?', *Political Quarterly* **79**, 476–87.

Crouch, C. (2011), *The Strange Non-Death of Neo-Liberalism*, Oxford: Polity.

Crouch, C. and Keune, M. (2005), 'Changing Dominant Practice: Making Use of Institutional Diversity in Hungary and the United Kingdom', in W. Streeck and K. Thelen *Beyond Continuity: Institutional Change in Advanced Political Economies*, Oxford: Oxford University Press, pp. 83–102.

Crouch, C. and Pizzorno, A. (eds) (1978), *The Resurgence of Class Conflict in Western Europe since 1968*, New York: Holmes and Meier.

Crouch, C. and Streeck, W. (eds) (1997), *Political Economy of Modern Capitalism: Mapping Convergence and Diversity*, London: Sage.

Crouch, C., Le Galès, P., Trigilia, C. and Voelzkow, H. (2001), *Local Production Systems in Europe. Rise or Demise?*, Oxford: Oxford University Press.

Crouch, C., Le Galès, P., Trigilia, C. and Voelzkow, H. (2004), *Changing Governance of Local Economies. Responses of European Local Production Systems*, Oxford: Oxford University Press.

Dore, R. (1987), *Taking Japan Seriously: A Confucian Perspective on Leading Economic Issues*, London: Athlone.

Esping-Andersen, G. and Regini, M. (eds) (2000), *Why Deregulate Labour Markets?* Oxford: Oxford University Press.

Ferrera, M., Hemerijck, A. and Rhodes, M. (2001), 'The future of the European "social model" in the global economy', *Journal of Comparative Policy Analysis: Research and Practice*, **3** (2), 163–90.

Granovetter, M. (1973), 'The Strength of Weak Ties', *American Journal of Sociology*, **78** (6), 1360–80.

Grieco, M. (1987), *Keeping it in the Family*, London: Tavistock Publications.

Hall, P. and Soskice, D. (2001), *Varieties of Capitalism. The Institutional Foundations of Comparative Advantage*, Oxford: Oxford University Press.

Hancké, B., Rhodes, M. and Thatcher, M. (2007), *Beyond Varieties of Capitalism. Conflict, Contradictions, and Complementarities in the European Economy*, Oxford: Oxford University Press.

Hirschmann, A.O. (1970), *Exit, Voice, and Loyalty: Responses to Decline in Firms, Organizations, and States,* Cambridge, MA: Harvard University Press.

Hollingsworth, J.R. and Lindberg L.N. (1985), 'The Governance of American Economy: The Role of Markets, Clans, Hierarchies and Associate Behavior', WZB Discussion Paper **85** (8).

Hollingsworth R., Hollingsworth E.J. and Müller, K.H. (2002), *Advancing Socio-economics: An Institutionalist Perspective*, Lanham: Rowman & Littlefield Publishers.

Hooghe, L. and Marks, G. (1999), 'Making of a polity: The struggle over European integration', in H. Kitschelt, P. Lange, G. Marks and J. Stephens (eds), *Continuity and Change in Contemporary Capitalism*, Cambridge, UK: Cambridge University Press, pp. 70–97.

Keune, M. and Jespen, M. (2007), 'Not Balanced and Hardly New: The European Commission's Quest for Flexicurity', in H. Jørgensen and P.K. Madsen (eds) *Flexicurity and Beyond*, Copenhagen: DJØF, pp. 189–211.

Keune, M., Leschke, J. and Watt, A. (2008), *Privatisation and Liberalisation of Public Services in Europe. An Analysis of Economic and Labour Market Impacts*, Brussels: ETUI-REHS.

Koeninger, W., Leonardi, M. and Nunziata, L. (2007), 'Labor Market Institutions and Wage Inequality', *Industrial and Labor Relations Review*, 60, 340–56.

Offe, C. (1985), *Disorganized Capitalism*, Cambridge, MA: MIT Press.

O'Reilly, J. and Spee, C. (1998), 'The Future Regulation of Work and Welfare: Time for a Revised Social and Gender Contract?', *European Journal of Industrial Relations*, 4, 259–81.

Piore, M. and Sabel, C.F. (1984), *The Second Industrial Divide*: *Possibilities for Prosperity*, New York: Basic Books.

Polyani, K. (1944), *The Great Transformation*, New York: Rinehart.

Polanyi, K. (1957), *The Great Transformation*: *The Political and Economic Origins of Our Time*, Boston: Beacon Press.

Schmitter, P. and Streeck, W. (1999), 'The Organisation of Business Interests. Studying the Associative Action of Business in Advanced Industrial Societies', WP 99/1, Cologne: Max Planck Institute for the Study of Societies.

Solow, R.M. (1992), *The Labour Market as a Social Institution*, Cambridge: Basil Blackwell.

Streeck, W. (2009), *Re-forming Capitalism. Institutional Change in the German Political Economy*, Oxford: Oxford University Press.

Streeck, W. (2010), *Taking Capitalism Seriously. Toward an Institutionalist Approach to Contemporary Political Economy*, Cologne: MPIfG Discussion Paper 10/ 15.

Streeck, W. and Thelen, K. (eds) (2005), *Beyond Continuity: Institutional Change in Advanced Political Economies*, Oxford: Oxford University Press.

Therborn, G. (1986), *Why Some People Are More Unemployed than Others?*, London: Verso.

Weber, M. (1978), *Economy and Society*, Berkeley: University of California Press.

Williamson, O.E. (1985), *The Economic Institutions of Capitalism*, New York: Free Press.

Witley, R. (1999), *Divergent Capitalisms The Social Structuring and Change of Business Systems*, Oxford, Oxford University Press.

2. The social dimension of European integration

Maarten Keune

1. INTRODUCTION

European integration has been advancing steadily since the establishment of the European Coal and Steel Community (ECSC) in 1951, the predecessor of the European Economic Community (EEC, later European Community or EC) established in 1967, which later turned into today's European Union (EU). One remarkable feature of this process has been its geographical extension, from the six original ECSC countries to the present 27 EU member states. The other is the broadening and deepening of integration. Where the ECSC initially concerned the creation of a common market for coal and steel, in the present EU the Single Market concerns most economic activities and the scope of integration has been broadened to common policies in a wide range of other issues, one way or the other touching upon most economic, social, political and environmental aspects of life.

Few would contest that economic integration forms the core of the integration process and that it is here that integration is most advanced. The Single Market consists of a very extensive body of European level economic regulations and national governments have transferred much of their sovereignty in this field to the European level. Also, already 17 EU countries have joined the Economic and Monetary Union (EMU), sharing a common currency, a European Central Bank and a common macro-economic policy framework. But to what extent has negative integration been matched by positive integration and what have the social effects of European integration been, both in terms of the development of social standards and in terms of domestic social policy capacity? The literature is strongly divided on this issue with both Euro-pessimists and Euro-optimists claiming their case, as will be discussed below. The present chapter aims to discuss some of the key elements of this controversy.

It should be underlined, however, that it is not an easy exercise to come to a straightforward answer to such a question. European integration is a complex and multidimensional process that can be sometimes incoherent or contradictory. Also, over time it has dramatically expanded its geographical scope and the policy areas it concerns, and has seen new actors emerge. In addition, it has had a differentiated impact in different national and local contexts (Crouch 2002). Finally, on the one hand, European integration can be seen from a national viewpoint as an 'external constraint'; at the same time it is also shaped by domestic actors and 'used' by these for their purposes (Dyson 2002). As a result, it is not easy to single European integration out as a straightforward causal factor.

This chapter is structured as follows. In the next section two diverging views on European integration, those of the Euro-optimists and the Euro-pessimists are confronted with each other. Section 3 discusses the contested nature of the European project. In section 4 the character of the social dimension of European integration is examined, while in section 5 the social effects of economic integration are reviewed. Section 6 presents conclusions.

2.   EURO-PESSIMISTS AND EURO-OPTIMISTS

The Euro-pessimists take the view that European integration is characterised by a fundamental asymmetry between negative integration and positive integration (Scharpf 2010, 1996, 2002). 'Negative integration', that is, measures that serve to increase market integration by eliminating national restraints on trade and distortions of competition, has been the dominant feature of European integration, while 'positive integration', that is, the development of common European policies to shape the conditions under which markets operate and to promote social protection and equality, has been much more limited. Also, European social policy is of largely voluntaristic character which allows circumvention by national actors (Streeck 1995). Negative integration has been aimed principally at deregulation and eliminating national level obstacles to the 'four freedoms' (free movement of capital, goods, services and people), at the fostering of competition and at the creation and expansion of EMU. As a result, the rule of the market has become stronger and stronger and threatens to trump social justice. And whereas initially, in the 1960s and 1970s, national welfare states could develop and grow independently from this process of market making, gradually it started to limit the range of policy instruments available to national policy makers and to restrict their control over their by now semi-sovereign welfare states (Leibfried and Pierson 1995, 2000). As a result, domestic welfare states are undermined and social standards are under pressure.

Different factors are put forward to explain this asymmetry. One is institutional. The Treaty of Rome of 1957 had a strong bias towards economic integration and politically decoupled economic integration from social protection and labour regulations: the responsibility and autonomy to shape the development of the welfare state remained at the national level. Clearly, negative integration has been strongly institutionalised in the European Treaties from the outset and subsequently it has been extended consistently by interventions of the European Commission against Treaty obligations and through rulings by the European Court of Justice (ECJ) (Scharpf 1996, 2010; Höpner and Schäfer 2010). Positive integration, by contrast, depends upon the agreement of national governments in the Council and is subject to a series of impediments facing European intergovernmental decision making. This is particularly so since in many areas related to positive integration decisions are based upon unanimity. Hence, in institutional terms, negative integration faces fewer obstacles than positive integration.

A second factor is the heterogeneity between European countries in terms of their institutional characteristics, traditions and interests, in particular concerning their welfare states, industrial relations systems, labour market regulation and other areas of positive regulation. This heterogeneity has spurred strong desires to preserve national sovereignty on these issues and has made it hard to reach agreement on elements of positive integration (Scharpf 1996, 2002). Heterogeneity has increased dramatically with the 2004 and 2007 rounds of European enlargement which substantially increased both the number of member states and the extent of their diversity, further complicating the development of positive integration.

Thirdly, it is argued that the dominance of negative over positive integration derives from the power of transnational capital that successfully manages to influence European integration (van Apeldoorn and Hager 2010). Through, for example, the European Round Table of Industrialists (ERT) capital manages to get its interests reflected in European policy making, adding to its focus on market making instead of market correction (ibid.). From this perspective, the content of policy initiatives stemming from European institutions and the shape EU integration takes are not interest free or politically neutral but reflect political strategies and power constellations.

Finally, European integration can also be viewed as an advanced version of more general processes of globalisation and increasing international competition. European market making is then argued to lead to heightened competition between countries and the need for national economic and social regimes to be competitive. The welfare state and wages are then seen as the likely losers in this quest for competition as they determine to a large extent labour costs and hence competitiveness. In this view, efficiency concerns overrule equity concerns.

The Euro-optimists look very differently at these issues. First of all, they argue that the threats and negative effects of globalisation and EMU on national autonomy and welfare systems, although they play a role, have been exaggerated (Ferrera et al. 2001). Generous welfare policy does not necessarily inhibit economic progress, social protection can be an effective productive factor and there remains ample scope for political choice within the nation-state (ibid.).

Secondly, they focus less on the capacity of welfare states to maintain their traditional shape or resist challenges and more on their adaptive capacity. Welfare states are subject to external challenges like globalisation, but, possibly more importantly, also to internal challenge creating new social risks that the traditional welfare state does not adequately cover (Bonoli 2007, Taylor-Gooby 2004). These internal challenges include ageing and related rising pension and health care costs, problems in the reconciliation of work and non-work activities, and the difficulty for the low skilled to be successful in the labour market. They create the need for a profound and constant adaptation of welfare state arrangements. Hence, welfare state change is not necessarily a problem but a necessity and the real issue is how well they adjust to the new requirements.

Thirdly, they argue that negative integration has not been the only game in town and that, in particular during the Delors era and with the start of the Lisbon Strategy in 2000, European integration has acquired a genuine social dimension. Over the years an important set of EU Directives has been developed in the labour and social field, playing an important role in correcting the market (e.g. Weiss 2010). Also, in 2009, the Charter of Fundamental Rights of the EU became a legally binding part of the Lisbon Treaty, putting social policy, in principle, on equal footing with economic policy (ibid.).

In addition, the EU has developed a broad range of experimental forms of governance that diverge from traditional, legally binding regulations, including in the social field the Open Method of Coordination (OMC) (Sabel and Zeitlin 2010). These experimental forms of governance can be characterised as directly-deliberative polyarchy (ibid.), as they are arguments-based, involve concrete experience of actors, and form a system in which local units learn from, discipline and set goals for each other. The OMC involves processes of debating, learning and benchmarking on labour and social issues, and allows member states to reform their welfare state 'in ways that grow out of their own traditions and allow them to pursue their own best judgments for innovative advance. Similarly, it is encouraging the Member States to reconfigure their systems of social protection, and obligating them to learn from one another how best to retain their distinctive forms of solidarity in a radically new context' (Sabel and Zeitlin 2008: 272). Hence, according to the authors, the OMC both motivates and assists member states in making the necessary adaptations of the welfare state.

The fact that there are two so very diverse views on the social effects of European integration results to some extent from the diverging analysis of the challenges faced by contemporary welfare states. Where the pessimists focus on the preservation of the welfare state, the optimists underline the need for adaptability and change. But there are also genuinely opposed views on the question of the significance of the social dimension of European governance, on the market-constraining character of European labour and social policy and regulations, and on the social consequences of the expanding Single Market and EMU. Below we will discuss these questions in some more detail. First however we need to underline the political and contested character of the integration project.

3. A CONTESTED PROJECT

As we can already read from the contradictions between the pessimist and optimist views on European integration, the integration project is a politicised process in which various political and social actors pursue their interests and ideas. The broad direction of the integration process, its particular policy goals and instruments as well as its institutional setup and decision-making structures are subject of contestation and conflict and are not set in stone. Contestation over European integration has two fundamental dimensions (Hooghe and Marks 1999): (i) an ideological dimension taking the shape of the classic divide between left and right or social democracy and market liberalism; (ii) a distinctive European dimension of nationalism versus supernationalism, largely concerning the question to what extent national sovereignty can or should be transferred to the European level.

Hooghe and Marks argue that European politics is to a large extent an interplay between two political projects, that is, two comprehensive packages of institutional reform around which broad coalitions of political actors at European, national and sub-national level have formed. These two projects have diametrically opposed positions on the two dimensions identified above. One is the neoliberal project pursuing European-wide market integration while at the same time trying to insulate the market from political interference by resisting the creation of a European polity and rejecting the development of positive market regulation. The neo-liberal agenda argues for the maintenance of national sovereignty since this will keep authority fragmented and will generate competition among national governments in providing regulatory climates that are attractive for capital. The other concerns the project for regulated capitalism which wants to see market integration be accompanied by positive market-enhancing and market-supporting regulations to create a social democratic dimension to European governance. This project calls for the provision of collective goods through European regulations to improve the functioning of the European economy and to allow it to compete internationally based on quality, productivity and technology. It also calls for the strengthening of the regulative capacity at the European level, for various types of partnerships, including Social Dialogue between unions and employers' organisations, and for social solidarity to empower those who are less well off to compete more effectively in the market (Hooghe and Marks 1999).

The composition of the coalitions of actors supporting these two projects is variable over time. Social-democratic parties, a number of Christian-democratic parties and national and European trade unions are likely to support the regulated capitalism project. Conversely, liberal parties, many conservative parties, financial interests, multinationals and national and European employers' organisations generally support the neoliberal project. But their positions are not necessarily fixed over time.

The same counts for the position of supranational actors. For example, the political colour of the Council of Ministers depends on the national political situations and over time we see that sometimes social democratic governments dominate while at other times liberal governance has the upper hand. This has implications for the policies pursued by the Council. Variable also is the role of the ECJ. It clearly has been a staunch guardian of the four freedoms, supporting the dominance of the market. At the same time the ECJ has played a role in expanding the scope for social regulations at the European level by proposing broad interpretations of some of the Treaty texts, health and safety and equality issues but includes also certain aspects of the access to health care and of the portability of welfare entitlements (e.g. Martinsen 2005).

Possibly most important has been the role of the European Commission. The Commission has the right to initiative where European legislation is concerned and also clearly plays the role of agenda setter where the European debate on economic and social integration is concerned (e.g. Keune 2008). As will be discussed in more detail below, until the mid-1980s the social dimension of European integration was very limited and largely conceived as a contribution to creating the common market, fostering cross-border mobility or creating a level playing field for competition. With the entry of the Delors Commission in 1985, however, this changed. Delors was a major proponent of regulated capitalism and assured that new areas were opened for European social regulations and that unanimity voting was reduced. Also, it successfully promoted a stronger role for the social partners in Europe through 'Social Dialogue'. In this way, the Delors Commission played an important role in the expansion of 'social Europe'.

Also other additions to social integration, successful or not, have seen an important role for the Commission. This includes the introduction of the European Employment Strategy, including the respective OMC, in the late 1990s and the expansion of such experimental types of governance to other social areas in the 2000s (see below). This does not mean however that the Commission is necessarily favouring or promoting a strong social dimension to European integration. Indeed, it is often criticised for not pursuing a better balance between negative and positive integration.

4. THE SOCIAL DIMENSION OF EUROPEAN INTEGRATION

4.1 Social Directives

As emphasised above, economic integration has from the outset been at the core of the European project and has advanced at high speed, constructing the Internal Market by transferring much of national sovereignty to the European level and by developing a comprehensive apparatus of European level economic regulations and policies. Where the social field is concerned, the situation is rather different. The Treaty of Rome (1957), with its strong bias towards economic integration, left social policy and labour market regulations basically to the member states. Initially the legislative competences of the Community in the social field were oriented towards facilitating the building of the market. As such, they were largely limited to the free movement of workers and equal treatment and equal pay. Indeed, the first four social Directives concerned the free movement of workers. The possibility of adopting social Directives was further restricted by the fact that they were subject to unanimity voting.

Over time, however, this picture has changed substantially (Falkner et al. 2005, Goetschy 2006). First of all, the competences of the Community in the social area were gradually expanded. In the 1970s decisions in the Council of Ministers, as well as creative and broad interpretations of the principle of equal treatment by the ECJ, extended these competences to other areas, especially elements of health and safety, initially not envisaged by the Treaty. Nonetheless, these competences remained closely related to the establishment of the common market. Competences were further extended, again largely concerning health and safety, following the proactive role played by the European Commission in the context of the 1986 Single European Act, in which health and safety Directives became subject to qualified-majority voting (QMV) and received increased legitimacy through the close involvement of the social partners in their design. Health and safety thus became the major area that came under Community competence and has been the subject of no less than 38 Directives between 1978 and 2006, around 50 per cent of the total amount.

A new milestone in the process of social integration was the 1992 Maastricht Treaty, one of the main achievements of the Commission under the presidency of Jacques Delors. In the previous period social provisions had been conceived largely as contributions to creating the common market, fostering cross-border mobility or creating a level playing field for competition. Delors, however, was a major proponent of regulated capitalism and enjoyed support from the social democratic parties, from a number of Christian Democrats, including, most importantly, German Chancellor Helmut Kohl, and from most trade unions (Hooghe and Marks 1999). Delors took the view that a stronger European social dimension was required to ensure acceptance of economic integration by the European public and to offset its harmful consequences. At the same time, there was strong opposition to this view from the neoliberal coalition, spearheaded by the conservative British government and including also parts of the Commission itself.

The result was a skilfully designed but somewhat paradoxical strategy (Goetschy 2006: 53–5). The Commission did indeed open up new possibilities for European social regulations by ensuring that the Maastricht Treaty was broadened by the annexed Social Policy Agreement (SPA); but it was accepted that the UK did not ratify this agreement. Catering to the wishes of the coalition favouring regulated capitalism, the SPA widened the range of social issues subject to Community competence and extended the number of social issues subject to QMV. At the same time, however, more in line with the neoliberal project, the Treaty restricted the possibility for new social Directives to be adopted. Some issues, most importantly wages, the right to strike and the right of association, were explicitly singled out as falling outside Community competence. What is more, the Treaty introduced the principles of subsidiarity and proportionality, thus formally recognising and respecting national diversity in relation to social issues. Since then, subsidiarity has regularly been invoked by member states and by the major European employers' organisation, BusinessEurope, to justify their rejection of new Community social measures (ibid.).

A further important innovation made by the Maastricht Treaty is that the SPA marked the start of a series of measures aimed at strengthening the role of the social partners in Europe through 'Social Dialogue'. With adoption of the SPA the European social partners received the competence to become, in principle, co-regulators of the European labour market. They have the right to negotiate framework agreements and then jointly request the Commission to convert these agreements into Directives so that they become formally incorporated into European law. Additionally they can make so-called autonomous framework agreements, the enforcement of which is their own responsibility and which depends on their national member organisations. Initially social dialogue concerned the inter-sectoral European social partners BusinessEurope, the European Association of Craft Small and Medium-Sized Enterprises (UEAPME), the European Centre of Employers and Entreprises providing Public services (CEEP) and the European Trade Union Confederation (ETUC).

Inter-sectoral European Social Dialogue has so far played only a minor role in the production of social Directives: only three such Directives, dealing with parental leave (1996), part-time work (1997) and fixed-term work (1999), have resulted from the inter-sectoral social dialogue. Several other attempts were made to negotiate such framework agreements but to no avail. This should come as no surprise considering that whereas the ETUC, in line with the regulated capitalism project, supports the further development of European level labour market regulations, the basic position of the main employers' organisation, in line with the neoliberal project, is that there is no further need for such regulations and that European integration should centre on economic integration. Also, the employers have alternative channels to influence European policies and are not dependent on European Social Dialogue in this respect (Schäfer and Streeck 2008, van Apeldoorn and Hager 2010). Trade unions have fewer options at the European level and are more dependent on Social Dialogue. They do however not have a sufficiently strong power position to muscle reluctant employers into concluding framework agreements.

An additional explanatory factor here is the changing role of the European Commission. While the more social democratically oriented Commissions of the 1990s would to some extent use the 'threat of a Directive' to overcome the employers' position and to ensure a more productive Social Dialogue, in recent years, the present, more liberal Commission has ceased to apply such pressure.

At the same time, however, in recent years, the Commission has very actively been promoting European Social Dialogue at the level of sectors, through the financing of meetings and the chairing of committees. This European Sectoral Social Dialogue (EESD) has grown explosively and today covers almost 40 different sectors (Weber 2010, Léonard 2008). And in 2009 the first sector Framework Agreement was concluded in the hospital and health care sector on prevention from sharp injuries, which was subsequently implemented through an EU Directive in 2010. Hence, potentially (although not necessarily) the growth of the EESD might lead to the resurgence of social Directives originating in social dialogue in the future.

As mentioned above, the ECJ has also played a role in expanding the scope for social regulations at the European level by proposing broad interpretations of some of the Treaty texts, especially in the area of 'traditional' health and safety and equality issues but includes also certain aspects of the access to health care and of the portability of welfare entitlements (e.g. Martinsen 2005). The role of the ECJ in developing positive rights may, however, increase substantially in the near future with the Charter of Fundamental Rights of the EU becoming a legally binding part of the Lisbon Treaty, which means they can be defended before the ECJ. It remains to be seen how the ECJ will interpret the Charter.

For the moment, however, although in the last two decades a number of innovations were introduced that in principle provide opportunities to increase and broaden European level social and labour market regulations, European integration in this area has been limited in number and scope. By 2006, a total of 78 social Directives had been adopted, a huge contrast with the numerous economic ones. Also, the 'traditional' issues of health and safety, working time, the free movement of workers and gender equality and non-discrimination are the subject of 80 per cent of these Directives, indicating their limited scope. At the same time the rate of adoption of social Directives has been reasonably constant over time, without a clear upward or downward trend (Falkner et al. 2005): of these Directives 35 date back to before 1992, while 43 were adopted afterwards.

From the above we can conclude that since the 1960s an important body of Directives concerning labour market and social issues has been adopted. At the same time these regulations are fragmentary, largely complementary to national regulations, and they fail to make up a coherent or comprehensive social or labour market model (Goetschy 2006, Keune 2009). The core regulatory level for social and labour market issues remains the national level. This is in stark contrast with the deep and comprehensive economic integration that has dominated the European project.

However, since the late 1990s, attempts have been made to strengthen the social dimension by introducing (additional to the 'traditional' governance through Directives) new experimental forms of governance.

4.2   Experimental governance of social Europe

Two major forms of experimental governance have been introduced in the social field since the late 1990s: the Open Method of Coordination (OMC) and autonomous agreements by social partners. Both these forms of governance are non-binding in the traditional legal sense of (and are therefore often characterised as) voluntaristic (Schäfer and Leiber 2009). They were introduced to overcome the difficulties in decision making on social issues at the EU level, which, as shown above, has strongly limited the expansion of social Europe.

The OMC was first introduced under the flag of the European Employment Strategy (EES) in the late 1990s. The EES emerged in a context of widespread unemployment throughout the 1990s and great uncertainty on how to deal with this problem. Also, in the eyes of the proponents of regulated capitalism as well as in the eyes of much of the public, the lack of European attention to unemployment more and more contrasted with the EU's drive for further economic integration. As a result, a European advocacy coalition committed to a more active role for the EU in employment policy consolidated. This advocacy coalition consisted of key actors within the Commission, the European Parliament, and member state governments, especially recently acceded countries such as Sweden but also newly elected centre-left governments like the Blair government in the UK and the Jospin government in France (Zeitlin 2007, Mailand 2006). This pressure resulted in the inclusion of an employment chapter in the 1997 Amsterdam Treaty and in an extraordinary European Council meeting on Employment (the so-called Jobs Summit) in Luxembourg in that same year where the EES was launched.

The EES as a new, experimental type of governance does not impose specific rules and regulations at national level. Instead, the European Council is obliged to regularly adopt a series of common objectives, guidelines and indicators for monitoring, based upon proposals from the Commission. The member states each have to develop their National Action Plans for Employment (NAPs), outlining how the general guidelines will be put in practice. Hence actual policy decisions are left to national authorities and adaptation to the EES guidelines is voluntary. The EES is to a large extent based on the Open Method of Coordination (OMC), a multilevel process of benchmarking, multilateral surveillance, peer review, exchanges of information, cooperation and consultation. In subsequent years the OMC was also introduced in other areas such as social inclusion, health care, education and training and pensions, but it is most developed within the EES.

The OMC as a new European mode of governance aims to strike a balance between European integration and deep-rooted and legitimate national diversity by encouraging convergence of objectives, performance and broad policy approaches, but not of specific programmes, rules or institutions (Zeitlin 2005: 448). Also, 'the OMC has been acclaimed as a promising mechanism for promoting experimental learning and deliberative problem-solving insofar as it systematically and continuously obliges member states to pool information, compare themselves to one another, and reassess current policies against their relative performance' (Zeitlin 2005: 448). Additionally, the OMC aspires to the incorporation of a broad range of actors in its processes, thus increasing their legitimacy and effectiveness. Moreover, the Commission regards the EES and its OMC as a means to frame and structure the debate on employment policies in Europe by disseminating concepts, comparing the performance in the different member states and identifying 'best practices' (Keune and Jepsen 2007). From this perspective the EES is an instrument in disseminating a cognitive model that aims to alter the beliefs and expectations of national actors. From this perspective, and as is often ignored in the literature, the EES and the other OMCs can be considered as a political instrument in the hands of the European Commission (Keune and Jepsen 2007, also van Apeldoorn and Hager 2010).

There is little agreement however concerning the extent to which the EES is achieving its objectives and concerning its actual influence on national policies and policy-making processes, not in the least because such effects are methodologically hard to research. The OMC influence could be differentiated as to its discursive, substantive and procedural effects. As to the discursive influence that the European Commission has had through the EES, it has been quite successful in using the EES to disseminate new concepts and objectives related to employment policy, to some extent achieving cognitive shifts at the national level and setting a policy framework for domestic policy makers (Zeitlin 2007, Keune and Jepsen 2007). There is evidence, however, that suggests that in a number of cases these cognitive shifts are limited to the elites directly involved in the OMC machinery and that the EES hardly has a place in public debate (de la Porte and Nanz 2004, Mailand 2006).

The substantive and procedural effects of the EES are subject of clear controversy in the literature and are evaluated in very different terms. Zeitlin argues that there is 'evidence from both official reports and interviews that OMC objectives, guidelines, targets, and recommendations have contributed to changes in specific national policies (policy shifts), in areas such as activation/prevention, tax-benefit reforms, active ageing/lifelong learning, gender equality, child care, social assistance, and pension reform' (Zeitlin 2007: 5). He also sees a positive influence in terms of procedural shifts in governance and policy-making arrangements, including better horizontal coordination and cross-sector integration of interdependent policy areas, enhanced vertical coordination between levels of govern-ance, improved steering and statistical capacity; increased consultation and involvement of non-state actors and the development of horizontal or diagonal networks for participation of non-state and sub-national actors in EU policy making (Zeitlin 2007: 5).

In a much more sober fashion, Mailand rather argues that the EES has had a generally weak but differentiated effect: 'the EES has only to a limited extent had a direct impact on the employment policies of the member states, but the impact varies between countries' (Mailand 2006: 174). The factors determining the differentiated impact of the EES include the extent to which employment policy was already in line with the EES, the extent to which there is a national consensus on the main lines of employment policy, Euroscepticism, labour market performance, and economic and dependence on the EU (Mailand 2006). Also, according to a number of authors the participation of social partners and other non-state actors in the OMC employment remains weak and its dynamic is top-down rather than bottom-up (de la Porte and Nanz 2004, Mailand 2006).

Hence there is no agreement in the literature on the success or failure of the EES. In any case, it is questionable to what extent the EES can be considered an example of positive integration. Although full employment is formally among the EES objectives, the cognitive model it promotes has emphasised supply-side problems on the labour market. Its aim is to increase the flexibility, employability and activation rate of the labour force in the light of the claim that labour market problems originate largely in the individual characteristics of the unemployed or inactive. In this sense, it can be considered an approach that focuses on the obstacles to the smooth functioning of markets rather than one that conditions markets.

Experimental types of governance have also emerged from the inter-sectoral European Social Dialogue and the European Sectoral Social Dialogue. At both levels, a large amount of legally non-binding, voluntar-istic 'new generation texts' have emerged (Weber 2010, Pochet et al. 2009). They concern a wide variety of texts including autonomous agreements, codes of conduct, joint opinions, declarations, guidelines, and so on. Like the OMCs, they aim to achieve a certain convergence between national policy goals through exchange of information and learning. These joint texts elaborated by European social partners, apart from being legally non-binding, are not directed at the EU institutions but rather at the national members of the social partner organisations, with their imple-mentation also depending on the social partners themselves (Weber 2010).

The impact of the new generation texts is still largely uncharted territory and is even less clear than that of the OMCs. They often lack comprehensive and transparent follow-up and monitoring procedures (Pochet et al. 2009) and have been less subject to research. Implementation often seems to be incomplete and patchy, and differs widely between countries both where the extent and the instruments of implementation are concerned (Pochet et al. 2009, Larsen and Andersen 2007, Visser and Ramos Martin 2008, Weber 2010). Implementation tends to be less complete in the countries with the weakest industrial relations systems, while the choice for implementation through collective agreements and guidelines or through legislation (spurred by social dialogue) depends to an important extent on national institutions and traditions (Visser and Ramos Martin 2008). Also, in the countries without comprehensive coverage of workers by collective agreements, if no legislative backup is present, large parts of the workforce will be excluded from social partner agreements (Schäfer and Leiber 2009).

The growing resort to new generation texts has often been interpreted as a sign of an increasing autonomy of the social partners from the European institutions (Branch 2005). However, it also increases the dependence on national level actors, both national social partners and governments, for the implementation of these texts. And since there is no clear mechanism of articulation between the European social partners and these national actors, this so-called autonomy may well point to new dependencies.

5.   THE SOCIAL IMPACT OF ECONOMIC INTEGRATION

A last question to briefly discuss here is what the (potential) social effects of the advancing economic integration itself are. We will address this question by discussing the role of the Single Market and of EMU.

5.1   The Single Market

The Internal Market is the core of the European project and is pursued through the liberalisation and deregulation of the national economies, the 'four freedoms' (free movement of capital, goods, services and people) and the fostering of competition. The main argument for this is the supposed positive effects on economic dynamism and growth, which can then result in higher incomes and social standards. At the same time, however, the Internal Market has also had a number of (potential) negative social side effects. It has created the conditions in which private capital is, at least in principle, extremely mobile, in an age when the creation of employment more and more depends on private investment. While countries and workers have therefore become increasingly dependent on private capital, the latter has at the same time seen its exit options being strengthened. As a result, negative integration has increasingly brought countries and workers into competition with each other for capital.

At the macro level this results in regime competition, that is, competition between countries for private investment. It has also been further fomented by enlargement and most new member states have centred their economic development strategies on attracting foreign direct investment (FDI), seen as the motor of economic growth and a source of technology and know-how. European regulations allow for only a limited number of ways of conducting regime competition. Direct investment subsidies, tax incentives or other direct benefits offered to investors have progressively been banned, insofar as they are classified as unfair competition. As a result, regime competition has turned more and more into pressure to offer investors a context that enables firms to be flexible and lower costs. Where the labour market is concerned, this translates increasingly into a drive towards a cheaper and more flexible labour force, expressed in wage moderation, and flexibilisation of labour regulation, as well as in reductions of social contributions, eventually weakening the financing of the welfare state.

At the micro level, the competition for capital is related to the exit options of capital. Capital has always had more scope to pursue its interests by choosing exit options than labour and this 'mobility differential' has strongly increased in the last two decades (Hoffmann 2006). The increased exit options for capital have strengthened its power position towards labour. At the level of companies and especially multinationals this has led to the relocation of a certain activities, especially labour intensive manufacturing activities, from higher wage countries to lower wage countries, although the weight of such relocations in total foreign direct investment for the moment remains limited. Possibly more important is the increased use that companies make of the threat of relocation. By threatening to relocate their present activities or to make their future investments elsewhere, companies increasingly and successfully demand concessions from workers in terms of wage moderation, increased flexibility and extension of working time, in exchange for not exercising the exit option. As a result, we can observe a shift in income from labour to capital over the years (Keune 2008).

Finally, the predominant role of the four freedoms in the Treaty has led the ECJ to judge in favour of economic freedoms over social rights in a series of recent verdicts (Blanpain and Swiatkowski 2009, Bücker and Warneck 2010). The Laval and Viking cases set limits on collective action if it stands in the way of the freedom of movement of businesses or labour. The Rüffert and Luxembourg cases limit the policy options of public authorities in using public procurement conditionality and in setting minimum standards for posted workers.

5.2 Economic and Monetary Union

Today, 17 EU countries have joined EMU. The effects of EMU on social standards and policy-making capacity are not unidirectional. On the one hand it can be argued that EMU makes countries and their welfare states less vulnerable to turbulent financial markets (Rhodes 2002). The Euro is a much more stable currency than many of the national currencies that preceded it and is less vulnerable to speculation or to uncertainty caused by de- or revaluation of currencies by national governments.

At the same time, EMU constitutes a limit to domestic policy-making capacity. Individual countries entering monetary union lose a number of major instruments for adjustment to economic imbalances and shocks, in particular the exchange rate and the interest rate. Under EMU these issues fall under the competences of the European Central Bank (ECB) which sets a common policy for all EMU members. This puts much more emphasis on wage flexibility, labour market mobility and/or fiscal policy as adjustment mechanisms (Dyson 2006: 20). Indeed, under EMU wage moderation and flexibilisation gain in importance as macro adjustment instruments, adding to the earlier discussed pressure for wage moderation and flexibilisation stemming from increased capital mobility.

Another effect of EMU is that it sets criteria for inflation, public expenditure and public debt. For all three indicators maximum levels are defined and although experience has shown that the enforcement of these requirements is not always as stringent as originally intended, they do put important limitations on countries. The inflation criterion adds important further weight to the pressure for wage moderation. Wage growth is often seen as the main factor leading to inflation and hence wage moderation is considered the key to the low levels of inflation allowed under EMU. For the public sector this pressure is further increased by the deficit and debt criteria. And, indeed, it is in the EMU area where wage growth in Europe has been lowest in recent years. The budgetary and debt criteria also further limit the policy responses of countries through fiscal policy and public investment, and put serious pressure on social expenditure. Hence, decreasing social expenditure and a subsequent increase in poverty and inequality are some of the possible effects of EMU.

It should be emphasised however that EMU pressures on social stand-ards and expenditure has differed substantially between countries. Indeed, in some countries EMU entry has required major adjustments, especially in welfare state, while in others it has not. For example, for the Netherlands the start of EMU largely meant a continuation of business as usual, possibly only accelerating ongoing reforms. In Italy, however, EMU entry spurred major reforms of the welfare state, including first and foremost the pension system (Natali 2003, Della Sala 1997). More recently, in Slovakia preparation for EMU entry resulted in dramatic welfare state retrenchment (Bohle and Greskovits 2010). Similar EMU-related attempts to reform and reduce the welfare state in Hungary resulted in widespread social unrest, leading the government, for the moment, to postpone EMU (ibid.).

6.   CONCLUSIONS

Two different views on the social dimension of European integration prevail in the literature: the Euro-pessimists and the Euro-optimists. The Euro-pessimists underline the minimal social character of the integration process, expressed in a relatively insignificant set of social Directives, voluntaristic new forms of governance that pose no effective limits to the market, and the loss of national level policy capacity to maintain the welfare state caused by the predominance of economic integration. The Euro-optimists, instead of maintaining the welfare state, stress the need to adapt it to the external and internal challenges of today. They argue that the experimental forms of governance developed at the European level assist and foster such adaptation through learning, benchmarking and deliberation. Also, they argue that these experimental forms of governance, together with, in their view, the important set of social Directives and the recently revamped status of the Charter of Fundamental Rights do give European integration a genuine social dimension.

Indeed, both the direction that European integration should take and the interpretation of its actual character and achievements are contested issues. Where the desired direction of integration is concerned, it was discussed that roughly two main factions can be identified, pursuing respectively a neoliberal or a regulated version of capitalism. Where the interpretation of the character of the integration project is concerned, the discussion presented in sections 4 and 5 leads to a number of conclusions.

One is that an important set of social Directives exists but that these Directives are concentrated in a limited number of social areas and that they are of little significance in number and scope if compared with the development of economic Directives. Secondly, a number of experimental forms of governance have developed in the social field in the past two decades, that is, the OMCs (and in particular the EES), now covering most major social issues, and the new generation texts in the inter-sectoral and sectoral European social dialogue. Where the OMCs are concerned, their discursive influence has been quite strong, providing the European Commission with a key role in agenda setting and politically steering the European debate about labour market and social reforms. Their substantive and procedural effects are however subject of controversy in the literature, with some assigning them substantial influence on national policy making and others downplaying this same influence. This not least because of methodological difficulties. Hence, to some extent the judgement on the OMCs seems to remain a matter of belief. As far as the new generation texts are concerned, their numbers are growing fast but their implementation often seems to be incomplete and patchy. However, this is still quite a new phenomenon where both practice and research on its impact are in their initial stages. Overall, then, it seems that the social dimension of European integration is quite limited, especially where its function of limiting the role of the market is concerned. One sign of this is that European level social policies have not played any role in softening the social impact of the present economic crisis.

In itself this is not necessarily a problem, provided that the integration process does not affect social standards and policy-making capacity at the national level. It was argued in section 5 that the Internal Market and EMU may have positive and negative effects in this respect. On the one hand they may lead to higher economic dynamism and growth, and to more macro-economic stability. In this way, they may help safeguard the welfare state. On the other hand they foster regime competition, affect the power balance between workers and employers in favour of the latter, foster wage moderation and put limits on social expenditure. Also, the predominant role of the four freedoms in the Treaty has led the ECJ to place economic rights over social rights in recent years. These developments clearly put social standards and policy making capacity under pressure and undermine achievements of the past.

It should be stressed, however, that the above analysis differs substantially between countries, depending on domestic institutions, power constellations and actor strategies. For example, in the UK, social Directives concerning leaves, part-time employment and fixed-term contracts have had a bigger impact than in most continental countries where labour law has been more developed. Also, as discussed, in the Netherlands membership of EMU had a much more limited impact that in Italy or Slovakia. Equally important, the character of the integration process itself changes over time. It is not set in stone and can, in principle, be given new directions if sufficiently strong coalitions can be built and institutional obstacles overcome.

REFERENCES

Apeldoorn, B. van and S.B. Hager (2010), 'The social purpose of new governance: Lisbon and the limits to legitimacy', *Journal of International Relations and Development*, **13** (3), 209–38.

Blanpain, R. and A. Swiatkowski (eds) (2009), *The Laval and Viking cases: Freedom of services and establishment v. industrial conflict in the European Economic Area and Russia*, Alphen aan de Rijn: Kluwer.

Bohle, D. and B. Greskovits (2010), 'Slovakia and Hungary: Successful and failed Euro entry without social pacts', in P. Pochet, M. Keune and D. Natali (eds) *After the Euro and Enlargement: Social Pacts in the EU*, Brussels: ETUI, pp. 345–70.

Bonoli. G. (2007), 'Time Matters: Postindustrialization, New Social Risks, and Welfare State Adaptation in Advanced Industrial Democracies', *Comparative Political Studies*, **40** (5), 495–520.

Branch, A. (2005), 'The Evolution of the European Social Dialogue towards Greater Autonomy: Benefits and Possible Challenges', *International Journal of Comparative Labour Law and Industrial Relations*, **21** (2), 321–46.

Bücker, A. and W. Warneck (eds) (2010), *Viking – Laval – Rüffert:Consequences and Policy Perspectives*, Brussels: ETUI.

Crouch, C. (2002), 'The Euro, and labour markets and wage policies', in K. Dyson (ed.), *European States and the Euro*, London: Oxford University Press, pp. 278–305. de la Porte, C. and P. Nanz (2004), 'The OMC – a deliberative-democratic mode of governance? The cases of employment and pensions', *Journal of European Public Policy* **11** (2), 267–88.

Della Sala, V. (1997), 'Hollowing out and hardening the state: European integration and the Italian economy, *West European Politics*, **20** (1), 14–33.

Dyson, K. (2002), 'Introduction: EMU as Integration, Europeanization, and Convergence', in K. Dyson (ed.), *European States and the Euro*, London: Oxford University Press, pp. 1–29.

Dyson, K. (ed.) (2006), *Enlarging the Euro Area. External Empowerment and Domestic Transformation in East Central Europe*, Oxford: Oxford University Press.

Falkner, G., O. Treib, M. Hartlapp and S. Leiber (2005), *Complying with Europe. EU Harmonisation and Soft Law in the Member States*, Cambridge: Cambridge University Press.

Ferrera, M., A. Hemerijck and M. Rhodes (2001), 'The future of the European "social model" in the global economy', *Journal of Comparative Policy Analysis: Research and Practice*, **3** (2), 163–90.

Goetschy, J. (2006), 'Taking stock of social Europe: Is there such a thing as a Community social model?', in M. Jepsen and A. Serrano (eds) *Unwrapping the European Social Model*, Bristol: Policy Press, pp. 47–72.

Hoffmann, J. (2006), 'The relevance of the exit option: The challenges for European trade unions of Post-fordism, internationalisation of the economy and financial market capitalism', *Transfer, European Review of Labour and Research*, **12** (4), 609–20.

Hooghe, L. and G. Marks (1999), 'Making of a polity: The struggle over European integration', in H. Kitschelt, P. Lange, G. Marks and J. Stephens (eds) *Continuity and Change in Contemporary Capitalism*, Cambridge, UK: Cambridge University Press, pp. 70–97.

Höpner, M. and A. Schäfer (2010), 'A New Phase of European Integration: Organised Capitalisms in Post-Ricardian Europe', *West European Politics*, **33** (2), 344–68.

Keune, M. (2008), 'Flexicurity: A contested concept at the core of the European labour market debate', *Intereconomics*, **43** (2), 92–8.

Keune, M. (2009), 'EU Enlargement and Social Standards: Exporting the European Social Model?', in J. Orbie and L. Tortell (eds) *The EU and the Social Dimension of Globalisation*, GARNET 'Europe in the World' series, London and New York: Routledge, pp. 45–61.

Keune, M. and M. Jepsen (2007), 'Not balanced and hardly new. The European Commission's quest for flexicurity', in H. Jørgensen and P.K. Madsen (eds) *Flexicurity and Beyond*, Copenhagen: DJØF Publishing, pp. 189–214.

Larsen, T. and S. Andersen (2007), 'A New Mode of European Regulation? The Implementation of the Autonomous Framework Agreement on Telework in Five Countries', *European Journal of Industrial Relations* **13** (2), 181–98.

Leibfried, S. and P. Pierson (1995), 'Semi-sovereign welfare states: Social policy in a multi-tiered Europe', in S. Leibfried and P. Pierson (eds) *European Social Policy: Between Fragmentation and Integration*, Washington DC: The Brookings Institution, pp. 43–77.

Leibfried, S. and P. Pierson (2000), 'Social policy. Left to courts and markets?', in H. Wallace and W. Wallace (eds) *Policy Making in the European Union*, Oxford: Oxford University Press, pp. 267–92.

Léonard, E. (2008), 'European Sectoral Social Dialogue: An Analytical Framework, *European Journal of Industrial Relations*', **14** (4), 401–19.

Mailand, M. (2006), *Coalitions and Policy Coordination – Revision and Impact of the European Employment Strategy*, Copenhagen: DJØF Forlagene.

Martinsen, D. (2005), 'The Europeanisation of welfare – the domestic impact of intra-European social security', *Journal of Common Market Studies*, **43** (5), 1003–30.

Natali, D. (2003), 'The Role of Trade Unions in the Pension Reforms in France and Italy in the 1990s: New Forms of Political Exchange?', EUI Working Paper SPS No 2003/3.

Pochet, P., A. Peeters, E. Leonard and E. Perin (2009), *Dynamics of European Sectoral Social Dialogue*, Luxembourg: European Foundation for the Improvement of Living and Working Conditions.

Rhodes, M. (2002), 'Why EMU is – or may be – good for European welfare states', in K. Dyson (ed.), *European States and the Euro*, London: Oxford University Press, pp. 305–35.

Sabel, C. and J. Zeitlin (2008), 'Learning from Difference: The New Architecture of Experimentalist Governance in the EU,' *European Law Journal*, **14** (3), 271–327.

Sabel, C. and J. Zeitlin (eds) (2010), *Experimentalist Governance in the European Union. Towards a New Architecture*, Oxford: Oxford University Press.

Schäfer, A. and S. Leiber (2009), 'The double voluntarism in EU social dialogue and employment policy' in S. Kröger (ed.) 'What we have learnt: Advances, pitfalls and remaining questions in OMC research', *European Integration online Papers (EIoP)*, Special Issue 1, **13**, Art. 9, http://eiop.or.at/eiop/texte/2009-009a.htm.

Schäfer, A. and W. Streeck (2008), 'Korporatismus in der Europäischen Union', in M. Höpner and A. Schäfer (eds) *Die politische Ökonomie der europäischen Integration*, Frankfurt a.M. and New York: Campus, pp. 203–40.

Scharpf, F. (1996), 'Negative and positive integration in the political economy of European welfare states', in G. Marks, F. Scharpf, P. Schmitter and W. Streeck (eds) *Governance in the European Union*, London: SAGE Publications, pp. 15–39.

Scharpf, F. (2002), 'The European social model: coping with the challenges of diversity', *Journal of Common Market Studies*, **40** (4), 645–70.

Scharpf, F. (2010), 'The asymmetry of European integration, or why the EU cannot be a "social market economy"', *Socio-Economic Review*, **8** (2), 211–50.

Streeck, W. (1995), 'Neo-Voluntarism: A New European Social Policy Regime?', *European Law Journal*, **1** (1), 31–59.

Taylor-Gooby, P. (ed.) (2004), *New Risks, New Welfare: The Transformation of the European Welfare State*, Oxford: Oxford University Press.

Visser, J. and N. Ramos Martin (2008), 'The implementation of autonomous European Framework Agreements – the example of the 2002 Telework agreement', *International Journal for Comparative Labour Law and Industrial Relations*, **24** (4), 511–48.

Weber, S. (2010), 'Sectoral social dialogue at EU level – recent results and implementation challenges', *Transfer: European Review of Labour and Research*, **16** (4), 489–507.

Weiss, M. (2010), 'European Labour Law in Transition from 1985 to 2010', *The International Journal of Comparative Labour Law and Industrial Relations*, **26** (3), 1–16.

Zeitlin, J. (2005), 'The Open Method of Coordination in Action. Theoretical Promise, Empirical Realities, Reform Strategies', in J. Zeitlin, P. Pochet and L. Magnusson (eds) *The Open Method of Coordination in Action: The European Employment and Social Inclusion Strategies*, Brussels: Peter Lang, pp. 447–504.

Zeitlin, J. (2007), 'A Decade of Innovation in EU Governance: The European Employment Strategy, the Open Method of Coordination, and the Lisbon Strategy', Paper prepared for the Portuguese Presidency of the European Union, June 2007.

3. The political economy of social investment

Anton Hemerijck

1. INTRODUCTION

Most comparative welfare state researchers divide the postwar era into two periods: a phase of construction and expansion, from 1945 to the mid-1970s, and one of consolidation and retrenchment, from the mid-1970s to the first decade of the twenty-first century (Pierson 2002). I wish to put forward an alternative periodization by subdividing the postwar period until the early twenty-first century into three distinct phases of welfare state reconfiguration. These are: (1) the era of welfare state expansion and class compromise, starting at the end of World War II; (2) the period of welfare retrenchment and neo-liberalism, which took shape in the wake of the oil shocks of mid- to late 1970s; and (3) the more recent epoch since the mid-1990s in which social investment policy prescriptions took root. Each phase of welfare state development can be conceptualized by distinct policy expert advocacy, designed to effectively respond to impending socioeconomic challenges and to achieve shared policy objectives, supported by fairly robust political compromises (Hemerijck 2012). It should immediately be emphasized that no single country specific change experience maps neatly onto the suggested three-pronged developmental sequence. Moreover, the social investment perspective has not yet been fully accepted as a hegemonic policy paradigm. Rather, it is an emerging welfare edifice and its institutional fate very much lies in the aftermath of the current financial crisis.

Moments of fundamental policy change are often associated with successive waves of economic adjustment. Especially deep economic crises provide important political windows for policy redirection. At such junctures social policy redirection was often guided by economic and social policy analysis innovation, better suited to the predicament of the day. In the first episode after 1945 economic security transformed from a 'charity' into a 'right' for which potentially every citizen was eligible. Keynesian economic theory, the brainchild of the 1930s, provided the intellectual ammunition for the postwar construction and expansion of the modern welfare state, based on demand stabilization through income-transfer social insurance provision with male-breadwinner full employment as the prime objective. Second, the aftermath of the oil crises of 1970s revealed the practical limitations of Keynesianism in fighting stagflation. In its wake a new economic policy consensus took root, inspired by neoclassical economics, favoring price stability, budgetary discipline, flexible labor markets, and retrenched welfare commitments.

In the absence of deep economic crisis, on a par with the Great Depression of the 1930s or the Great Stagflation of 1970s, the social investment turn is far more difficult to delineate than either the postwar era of Keynesian welfare expansion or the neo-liberal epoch of retrenchment. Whereas the two preceding periods, economic turmoil critically influenced the realm of politics and, subsequently, the direction of welfare state adaptation to new social and economic realities, the social investment rise to prominence was primarily political, triggered by growing disenchantment with neo-liberal policy prescriptions, long before the financial meltdown in the autumn of 2008.

The intellectual reception, collective expression and political acceptance of any novel set of economic ideas and social policy expertise are colored by many factors, ranging from power resources, political ideology, state structures and institutional capacities to enact social policy innovation, and processes of political coalition formation and interest intermediation. In this chapter special attention will be given to the intellectual resources of the emerging social investment perspective.

I proceed in five steps. The next section, to begin with, compares the ideas of social and economic policy analysis of the first two waves of postwar welfare expansion and retrenchment. Section 3 reveals how social investment ideas were triggered by the rise of new inequalities and growth deficiencies and broader political disenchantment with retrenchment and deregulation. Section 4 is devoted to the social policy analysis of social investment, based on the recognition of a shift from old industrial risk management to new post-industrial social risks, associated with intensified economic internationalization, demographic ageing, gender and family change, the shift to services, and labor market transformation. Next, section 5 discusses the economics of social investment. The social investment policy paradigm rests on the fundamental idea, similar to Keynesianism, that social policy can in fact be a productive factor, potentially producing positive sum outcomes in which increased social equity goes hand in hand with increased economic efficiency, higher employment participation and significant labor productivity growth. Beyond the underlying objective of providing effective capacitating resources, tailored to the different needs of individuals and families at risk of social exclusion, social investment expert economists and social policy thinkers, do not share a singular theoretical core, on a par with Keynesian macro management and neoclassical micro-economics. If we wish to say anything profound about the relative economic proficiency of social policy, this diverse group of thinkers and experts obliges us to direct our attention closely to the particular combinations of institutions and policy choices under different problem constellations. Section 6 concludes.

2.   THE ECONOMICS OF WELFARE STATE EXPANSION AND RETRENCHMENT

The postwar European welfare state represents an unprecedented historical achievement. As Fritz Scharpf puts it, never before in history, 'has democratic politics been so effectively used to promote civil liberty, economic growth, social solidarity and public well-being' (Scharpf 2003: 7). Almost all western European countries launched sweeping social reforms in the 1940s and 1950s. Basic systems of social universal security were developed that included effective systems to combat poverty, social insurance to protect people in the event of illness, disability, unemployment, or old age, and high-quality provisions of health care, housing and education to encourage equality of opportunity. The main objective of the postwar welfare state was to provide social security. A full range of income-transfer programs – unemployment insurance, workers' compensation, disability benefits, old age pensions, survivors' benefits, children's allowances, and social assistance, financed largely out of progressive taxation and/or social contributions from workers and employers were introduced to protect citizens from the social risks associated with modern industrialism.

With the memory of the Great Depression fresh in mind, policymakers from all political persuasions found that the public sector had a key role to play in 'taming' the capitalist economy, through a wide range of regulatory, redistributive, monetary, fiscal, and conflict-management institutions. The postwar welfare state fundamentally redrew the boundaries between politics and economics. The extent of public intervention differed from one country to the next, but all advanced democratic governments assumed an active and strategic role in the economic management of the *mixed economies* of postwar Western Europe.

Through the path-breaking analysis of John Maynard Keynes of the Great Depression, macroeconomics became the key economic policy guide to postwar welfare state innovation and expansion. Keynesian macro-economic policy analysis allowed democratic governments to assume political responsibility for achieving full employment and comprehensive social protection without affecting the primacy of the free market economy (Hall 1989, Scharpf 1991). In his *The General Theory of Employment, Interest and Money*, Keynes introduced a completely new brand of economics that focused on the macro behavior of economic systems as whole rather than the micro behavior of individual actors (Keynes 1936). Fundamental to Keynesian economics is the idea that much economic activity is governed by 'animal spirits', best understood as waves of optimism and pessimism (see also Akerlof and Shiller 2009). Left to their own devices, capitalist economies will therefore experience manias, followed by bouts of panic. Animal spirits grip investors and consumers, endogenously generating self-fulfilling prophesies with severe macro consequences for employment, output and investment (De Grauwe 2008). To curb such fluctuations, Keynes argued, the modern state must sail into the wind of these behavioral excesses: when the population over-spends, governments must over-save, and vice versa. Tools of counter-cyclical aggregate demand management such as discretionary monetary and fiscal policy were to be employed to help maintain long-term economic stability and productive capacity. If monetary and fiscal policy proved insufficient to smooth the business cycle, the state should resort to increasing or decreasing its own expenditures, in part through the expansion of social-welfare programs. Welfare spending was considered inherently counter-cyclical, automatically compensating for recessionary declines and expansionary booms in private spending.

Keynes did concede that a combination of full employment and sectional wage bargaining was likely to produce inflationary spirals which could ultimately undermine the very policy objective of full employment that macroeconomic demand management made possible. For much of the 1950s and 1960s, managing the wage bargain acquired a new and strategic importance to the larger pattern of macroeconomic stabilization, and all governments supported the active role of unions in wage determination and income policy, often anchored in effective tri- and bipartite social partnership institutions (Marglin and Schor 1990, Crouch 1999). In this respect, the paradigm shift to Keynesian macroeconomic policy analysis represents much more than simply the acceptance of a new body of economic theory. It implied a fundamental recasting of the social order by envisioning a historic compromise between the contending ideologies of opposing class interests.

Within the wider geopolitical and economic international context, the postwar compromise was structured by two interlinked commitments: first, a dedication to international trade liberalization; and second, a commitment to domestic compensation for the social costs associated with economic change and dynamism. At the Bretton Woods Conference of 1944, again the towering economist Keynes advocated a rules-based global system of pegged-but-adjustable system of exchange rates, to be overseen by the IMF, to allow national policymakers the freedom to pursue relatively independent social and employment policies without undermining international economic stability and trade liberalization. With the establishment of Bretton Woods, the twin objectives of full employment and welfare state expansion were anchored in what John Ruggie has described as a regime of 'embedded liberalism' at the level of the international political economy (Ruggie 1982, 1994). In Ruggie's words, 'governments asked their publics to embrace the change and dislocation that comes with liberalization in return for the promise of help in containing and socializing the adjustment costs' (1994: 4–5, Scharpf and Schmidt 2000). The regime of embedded liberalism thus allowed for the simultaneous pursuit of openness and substantial domestic welfare policy autonomy, predicated on the shelter of capital controls. Free trade, also one of the key objectives of postwar European integration, was hereby made socially sustainable through the welfare state.

Measured by any yardstick of social institution building, the 'Golden Age' of welfare capitalism, class compromise and embedded liberalism was a tremendous success. It buttressed democratic governance and complemented the market economy with human solidarity. Affluence contributed to a high standard of living, full employment, decent wages, universal access to education and health care, rights to income for the elderly, ill, disabled, unemployed and poor, and a significant reduction of poverty and inequality. Far from being polar opposites, open markets and organized solidarity prospered together. With the help of Keynesian macroeconomics and Bretton Woods supranational cooperation, national political economies were, moreover, adequately shielded from too much foreign competition.

The 'goodness of fit' between welfare expansion and market liberalization was put to the test by the breakdown of the Bretton Woods monetary system and, subsequently, by the steep rise in oil prices in the 1970s. In March 1971 the Bretton Woods system of fixed exchange rates was replaced with a system of floating currencies, triggering considerable currency adjustments and economic instability. The oil shocks of 1973 and 1979 simultaneously accelerated inflation and pushed unemployment to unprecedented levels, triggering a dramatic increase in social security outlays. By the early 1980s European political economies no longer seemed capable of guaranteeing industrial full employment while preserving generous social protection. The coexistence of economic prosperity, full employment, income equalization, expanding welfare provision, had, in the words of Peter Flora, 'grown to limits' (Flora 1986). By the late 1970s and the early 1980s, high inflation, mass unemployment, and sluggish growth exhausted public patience with neo-Keynesian demand management and deadlocked corporatism. This created a critical opportunity, intellectually, for the rise to hegemony of supply-side economics, from monetarism to rational expectations macro-economic modelling, and, politically, the welfare state crisis set the stage for electoral ascendance of neo-liberalism and neo-conservatism.

If Keynesian macroeconomics was the brainchild of the Great Depression, then neoclassical economics in various guises was the intellectual product of the crisis of stagflation, the malignant combination of cost-push price inflation, economic stagnation and rising demand-deficient unemployment (Scharpf 1991). Among academic economists, monetarism gained ground over Keynesianism by being better able to explain the predicament of stagflation as resulting from ineffective stop-and-go fiscal demand stimulus measures by governments. Monetarists argued that governments are best advised to keep money supply growing steadily at a rate equal to the growth of aggregate supply, so as to suppress inflationary expectations. Economists in the tradition of rational expectations claimed that economic cycles are not the result of endogenous 'animal spirits', because people form rational expectations. They returned to the theoretical models based on perfectly competitive and perfectly clearing markets.

The elections of Margaret Thatcher and Ronald Reagan epitomized the revival of self-regulating markets. On the European continent changes in government from the centre-left to conservative coalitions followed in a large number of other European polities. Together, the supply-side revolution in economics and the politics of neo-liberalism fostered a deliberate change in the hierarchy of social and economic policy objectives: the erstwhile primary objective of full employment was traded for balanced budgets, low inflation, stable currency, central bank independence, privatization and the drive towards labor market reregulation and welfare retrenchment (Hay 2004). Where the postwar welfare state was designed essentially to provide the institutional underpinning for an economy organized around stable industrial employment relations, the common quest in the wake of the two oil shocks became to enforce more flexible employment relations in order to encourage private sector expansion, falling prices, and output demand growth. The key policy recipe of neo-liberalism was to free markets, institutions, rules and regulations from the collective political decision-making that had been the norm under embedded liberalism. With due caution, neo-liberalism was bent on a broad-based process of 'institutional liberalization' of the form of 'organized capitalism' that was established after 1945.

At the core of neo-liberalism and neoclassical economics was a deeply 'negative theory of the state'. Many neo-liberal commentators came to argue that the normal operation of democratic institutions – democratic governance, electoral competition, parliamentary debate, and interest group bargaining – had consistently produced ineffective, inefficient and unstable outcome, since the 1960s, triggering a crisis of ungovernability (Crozier et al. 1975), which was in large part attributed to perceived contradiction of welfare capitalism. In the course of the 1980s questions of real economy business profitability, international competitiveness, and structural reform jumped to the forefront of the policy debate. Economists turned to diagnosing high unemployment and low growth as the consequences of labor market rigidities. Economic cycles were largely understood as outcomes of exogenous shocks – the oil shocks of the 1970s being the clearest cases in point – combined with slow transmission through the real economy as the result of labor market rigidities, including distortions related to welfare provision. Unemployment thus came to be seen as a microeconomic problem of market distortions, and no longer as a macroeconomic problem of insufficient demand. Blanchard and Summers (1987) offered the paradigmatic explanation of 'hysteresis' to explain why wages did not fall and unemployment remained high in Europe in the 1980s: the structural rigidities of job preservation for employed workers was achieved at the expense of labor market outsiders, and this prevented real wages from falling enough to restore full employment. It was argued that because all other markets were becoming increasingly liberalized (including goods, services, and financial markets) labor markets had to follow suit. Dismissal protection, collective bargaining, highly interdependent wage-benefit systems and minimum wage regulations – were increasingly believed to undermine the labor market's efficiency in allocating economic resources. Also the welfare state, by trying to reduce inequality through a politics of income redistribution, created many labor market distortions, ranging from lower labor supply, less training, wage compression and higher levels of unemployment among the old and the low skilled. Long-term unemployment came to be seen as a consequence of poor motivation and low search intensity resulting from the generosity of the welfare state, creating negative 'moral hazard' and 'adverse selection' externalities. If unemployment is fully insured, workers are less likely to take good care of their employability, while high-skill groups would prefer to opt out.

In the early 1990s the OECD received a mandate to examine the labor market performance of its member countries. The OECD Jobs Study, published in 1994, launched a critical attack on the 'dark side' of double-digit unemployment of many of its European members (OECD 1994,

1997, 2006a). These reports proved highly influential in terms of the debate on welfare state reform, if not on actual policy. The fight against unemployment came to be seen as the quest for flexibility (Dolado et al. 2002). Among the central policy recommendation of the OECD we find making wage and labour costs more flexible by removing restrictions to better reflect local economic conditions and labour productivity, keeping the minimum wage low, reducing non-wage labor costs, restricting the duration of unemployment insurance, reforming employment security provisions that inhibit employment growth in the private sector, loosening employment protection and expanding fixed term contracts. The OECD thus portrayed the fundamental dilemma of Europe's mature welfare states in terms of a trade-off between welfare equity and employment efficiency. From this perspective comprehensive welfare provision and economic security undermine the logic of the market. Well-functioning markets were seen as the best guarantee for wellbeing, self-reliance and autonomy. Inequality is inherent in markets and even necessary to motivate self-sufficient individuals as economic actors.

Important qualifications notwithstanding, the neo-liberal transformation in the 1980s and 1990s has indeed made European capitalism more market-driven and market-accommodating. The strongest liberalization has taken place in capital and product markets. The neo-liberal policy shift to hard currency and balanced budgets also managed to contain wage-price inflation. Neo-liberalism's willingness to tolerate greater income inequality in the name of free markets has had an even more dramatic impact. The 1980s and 1990s were indeed decades of greater inequality and more income poverty, including since the 1980s in the more egalitarian and stronger welfare states in Scandinavia and continental Europe (OECD 2008). On account of welfare retrenchment, labor market deregulation, and the disengagement of deadlocked corporatism, the achievements of neo-liberalism are more elusive. The same study of the OECD on rising incomes inequality, testifies to the staying power of the welfare state. Today, OECD governments 'spent more on social protection than any time in history' (OECD 2008).

3.   NEO-LIBERAL RETRENCHMENT DISENCHANTMENT AND THE SOCIAL INVESTMENT TURN

By the end of the 1990s political disenchantment with neo-liberal policy measures began to generate electoral successes for the centre-left. Newly elected European social democrats such as Tony Blair, Gerhard Schröder,

Wim Kok, and Poul Nyrup Rasmussen strongly believed that most European welfare states had to be transformed from passive benefits systems into activating, capacity building, social investment states. This policy platform was inspired intellectually by Anthony Giddens' 1998 book *The Third Way. The Renewal of Social Democracy*. By the late 1990 Third Way ideas made their way to the European Commission. But intellectually, and very surprisingly, it was the OECD who made the first about-face turn-around, away from the neo-liberal advocacy that had characterized their *Jobs Strategy* publications of the 1980s and 1990s, to spearhead the social investment perspective at their 1996 high-level conference, 'Beyond 2000: The New Social Policy Agenda' (OECD 1996). Recent OECD studies such as *Starting Strong* (2006b), *Babies and Bosses* (2007a), *Understanding the Social Outcomes of Learning* (2007b), and *Growing Unequal* (2008) are perhaps even more exemplary of the OECD's full-fledged endorsement of the 'social investment paradigm' (Jenson 2009).

The EU, meanwhile, developed its own version of the social investment paradigm, beginning under the Dutch EU presidency in the first half of 1997 (Hemerijck 1997), when the Dutch Ministry of Social Affairs and Employment staged a high-level conference in cooperation with the European Commission, entitled 'Social Policy as Productive Factor'. The central tenet of the EU's turn to social investment is that social policy can be a productive factor. Whereas neo-liberal doctrines demanded a trade-off between these goals, the social investment paradigm sees improved social equity go hand in hand with more economic efficiency. Key social policy provisions can be viewed as investments, potentially enhancing both social protection and productive potential.

In 2000 the Portuguese presidency of the EU further raised the social and economic policy ambitions of the EU by putting forward an integrated agenda of economic, employment and social objectives, committing the Union to becoming the 'most competitive and dynamic knowledge-based economy in the world, capable of sustainable economic growth with more and better jobs and greater social cohesion'. The so-called Lisbon Strategy represented an attempt to re-launch the idea of the positive complementarities between equity and efficiency in the knowledge-based economy, in which value creation depends increasingly on innovation and human capital improvement. In addition to the objective of raising employment rates throughout Europe, the Lisbon Agenda placed human capital, research, innovation and development at the centre of European social and economic policy. This broadened the notion of social policy as a productive factor beyond its traditional emphasis on social protection, to include social promotion and improving the quality of training and education. The Lisbon Strategy also prefigured a re-focusing of equal opportunity policies with an eye on raising the employment rates of women and elderly workers.

4. NEW SOCIAL RISKS MANAGEMENT

During the Belgian presidency in the second half of 2001 Frank Vandenbroucke, then Belgian Minister of Social Insurance and Health Care, eager to build on the Lisbon Agenda's social ambitions, invited a group headed by Gøsta Esping-Andersen, including myself, to draft a report on a 'new welfare architecture for 21st century Europe', later published under the title *Why We Need a New Welfare State* (Esping-Andersen et al. 2002). For Vandenbroucke, a towering intellectual of the active welfare state movement in European social democracy, the shift towards a knowledge-based society called for path-breaking social policy change. In *Why We Need a New Welfare State*, Esping-Andersen et al. contend that the prevailing inertia in male-breadwinner welfare provision will result in increasingly sub-optimal life chances in labor market opportunities, income, educational attainment, and intra- and intergenerational fairness, for large shares of the population. European societies are confronted with problems of cumulative welfare failure because labor markets, families, and existing social policy repertoires are still rooted in male-breadwinner passive transfer-oriented social insurance of workers with stable job biographies. The staying power of the 'passive' male-breadwinner policy legacy, according to Esping-Andersen et al., frustrates a more adequate response to 'new' social risks of the post-industrial economy, which adversely affect low skill workers, youngsters, working women, immigrants, and families with small children. Most troublesome is the polarization between work-rich and work-poor families. Top income households are increasingly distancing themselves from the middle as a result of rising returns to skills, exacerbated by marital homogamy. At the bottom of the pyramid less educated couples and especially lone-mother families face (child) poverty and long-term joblessness. As inequality widens, parents' capacity to invest in their children's fortunes will become ever more unequal (Esping-Andersen 2009).

Perhaps the most important conceptual contribution of *Why We Need a New Welfare State* is that it adopts a 'life course perspective' in rethinking twenty-first century welfare provision. Through the lens of the life course, Esping-Andersen et al. are able to identify and explicate better the intricate relationships that link care for children, the elderly and other vulnerable groups, to female employment and changing family structures.

It also makes a case for emphasizing the interaction between social policy and factors determining the future tax base such as education and fertility. From a life course perspective, the real litmus test for future welfare state success will be the ability to resolve the tension between women's new career preferences and the continued desire to form families. In terms of public policy this implicates an institutional realignment of the boundaries between work and family life which, during the heyday of male-breadwinner welfare state, were viewed as functionally differentiated public and private spheres. Parenthood in the post-industrial economy has become difficult to reconcile with career objectives. The lack of affordable childcare and labor market rigidities are the major obstacles to fertility and family wellbeing.

According to Esping-Andersen et al. social policy should actively mobilize the productive potential of citizens in order to mitigate the new social risks. The new welfare state must focus on improving the quality of life of workers and families by strengthening *ex ante* their long-term human capital and employability. Citizens have to be endowed with capabilities, through active policies that intervene early in the life cycle rather than later with more expensive passive and reactive policies (Esping-Andersen et al. 2002). At the heart of the social investment paradigm, in more normative terms, lies a re-orientation in social citizenship, away from *freedom from want* towards *freedom to act*, prioritizing high levels of employment for both men and women as the key policy objective, while combining elements of flexibility and security, under the proviso of accommodating work and family life and a guaranteed *rich social minimum* serving citizens to pursue fuller and more satisfying lives. In other words, new social risks policies should no longer merely follow the postwar social logic of 'decommodification', that is, reducing people's dependence on labour market participation.

Distancing themselves from the neo-liberal 'negative' theory of the state, Esping-Andersen and his colleagues view the state as a key provider for families and labour markets, playing an important role in ensuring adequate social services, for example, childcare, family services, education and training, and active labor market support. The social investment edifice directs our attention to the imperative of enabling services. Charles Sabel aptly refers to *capacitating services* that are not self-evidently supplied by private markets. Capacitating services must increasingly be customized to individual needs across the life cycle to be effective. Increasing societal differentiation, such as rapid changes in labor market supply and demand, family structure and labor market behavior, educational attainment, changes in migration patterns, all entail new demands for social service diversification and coordination.

Because the heaviest burden of new social risks falls on the younger cohorts, in terms of policy redirection, the welfare effort should privilege the active phases of the life course. This entails reallocating social expenditures away from pensions and social insurance towards services such as family policy, active labor market policy, early childhood education and vocational training, ensuring productivity improvement and high employment for both men and women in the knowledge-based economy. Maximizing employment is the key to securing effective, sustainable, and equitable welfare states. Access to paid work is families' single best welfare guarantee. Higher participation rates increase the tax base and hence the sustainability of the welfare state. Moreover, labor market participation is a crucial source of identification and self-respect. Because the health conditions of each elderly cohort is better than that of the cohort preceding it, and also the education gap between the old and the young is rapidly narrowing, supporting flexible retirement, increasing the retirement age to at least 67, and introducing incentives to postpone retirement could greatly alleviate the pension burden. Throughout their contribution, Esping-Andersen et al. acknowledge the paramount importance of passive income transfers, often associated with 'old' social risk management, to make up for the fact that not all labor market incomes are sufficient to meet family needs, especially in the areas of pensions. It remains imperative to have an even more tightly woven welfare safety net of minimum income support below the social investment policy repertoire, even in the best designed, productivist welfare state (Esping-Andersen 2001: 446).

5. THE ECONOMICS OF SOCIAL INVESTMENT

The economic policy analysis of social investment, however, is far from self-evident. Unlike the Keynesian welfare state and the neo-liberal retrenchment movement, the social investment turn is not founded on one unified body of economic thought. Nonetheless, over the past decade both policymakers and scholars have started to re-think the interaction between education and social policy: from trade-offs to mutual reinforcement, with the aim of advancing the knowledge economy. The economics of social investment is, however, ambiguous because, as its protagonists argue, the relationship between substantive social policy and economic performance is critically dependent on identifying institutional conditions, at the micro, meso and macro levels, under which it is possible to formulate and implement effective social and economic policy. There are no 'quick fixes' comparable to the kind of straightforward micro or macro solutions dreamt up by general economic theorists of neoclassical or post-Keynesian academic

planks. The economic and institutional policy analysis of social investment, therefore, relies heavily on empirical data and case-by-case comparisons than on the simple theoretical constructs of more general economic
theories. It is crucial to consider the 'fine' structures of the welfare state.
Social policy is never a productive factor *per se*. One cannot turn a blind
eye to the negative, unintended and perverse side effects of excessively
generous social security benefits of long duration, undermining work
incentives, raising the tax burden and contributing to high gross wage
costs, and, by the same token, rigid forms of dismissal protection making
hiring and firing difficult with the unnecessary consequence of high levels
of inactivity.

Beyond this caveat, social and political institutions have been brought
back into the equation as a potentially positive contributor to growth,
competitiveness, social progress and overall resilience. Largely in agreement with the Keynesian welfare state, the social investment paradigm
makes a virtue of the argument that a strong economy requires a strong
welfare state. Social protection and budgetary expenditures are powerful
stabilizers of economic activity at the macro level, because they help to
stabilize effective demand during recessions. This kind of Keynesianism
through the back door is still operative today as we have experienced from
the early days of the 2007–2010 financial crisis. In addition, institutions of
social partners permit macro-economically responsive wage setting while
encouraging employers and trade unions to jointly invest in and administer vocational education and training programs and thus contributing to
the competitiveness by human capital upgrading at the meso level. Social
insurance, by way of compensating workers and families who contribute
to the common economic good by exposing themselves to periodic market
contingencies, the welfare state encourages private initiative and economic
progress at the micro level. Social security against the adverse effects of
illness, disability, unemployment, old age, divorce or child-bearing is of
value to the citizens who are protected by social policy. Unemployment
insurance and active labor market policies help citizens overcome temporary deprivations. High unemployment benefits of shorter duration are
not dysfunctional, if and only if they are tied to job placement and training
obligations, combined with strong competition in the goods markets and
active labor market policies (Blanchard 2006, Blanchard and Tirole 2007).
By curtailing uncertainty in times of economic downturn, comprehensive
social policy increases citizens' ability and willingness to take on risks and
acquire more specialized skills. This boosts productivity and encourages
high-quality investment decisions in both the public and private sectors.
If successful, social insurance-supported active labor market and vocational training and education policies not only contribute to lowering

unemployment and raising productivity levels by upgrading skills, they also have a moderating effect on wage increases. Adequate levels of social protection help reduce poverty: poverty is bad for any economy, especially when it is passed down the generations, which as we know excludes disadvantaged groups from economic progress.

In line with the neo-liberal critique of the welfare state, the economics underlying the social investment paradigm focus on the supply side, including an emphasis on individual responsibility and self-development. There is a clear orientation towards the future, with a deliberate emphasis on 'early action' and 'early identification' of vulnerable new risks groups, on active prevention rather than passive compensation. Extensive comparative empirical research has revealed that there is no trade-off between macro-economic performance and the size of the welfare state. The presence of a large public sector does not necessarily damage competitiveness; there is a positive relationship between fertility and high levels of female participation in most Scandinavian countries; and, finally, high numeracy and literacy rates can be achieved with educational policies that abide by the principles of equal opportunities (Hemerijck 2002, Lindert 2004, Sabel and Zeitlin 2003).

Central to the notion of social investment is that the economic sustainability of the welfare state hinges on the number and productivity of future taxpayers. Investments today generate private and public dividends in the mid- to long term (Jenson 2009, 2010). In terms of substance, three dimensions of the economics of the social investment paradigm stand out, bearing on human capital improvement, the family's relationship to the economy, and employment pattern. The role of human capital, ensuring learning abilities during the life course, and its interaction with the welfare state perhaps is the central characteristic of the social investment paradigm. In an ageing economy with widening inequalities, increased investment in human capital is imperative to sustain generous and effective welfare states, beginning in early childhood. The 'productivist' human capital investment strategy is everybody's favorite because as it is seen to offer a means of raising economic efficiency, by boosting individuals' productive capacity, as well as narrowing the gaps in wages and employment opportunities between high- and low-skilled workers. There is a widespread consensus among policymakers and academic experts that advanced welfare states have to maintain and reproduce a highly skilled and highly productive work force in order to maintain living standards and to secure a competitive advantage in the world economy. In economics the case for human capital enhancement goes back to endogenous growth theory of the 1980s, suggesting that long-term growth is determined more by human capital investment decision than by external shocks and demographic change (Lucas 1988, Agell et al. 1997). It should however be emphasized that education and training as a means of raising the quality of the work force takes many years. The case of high-quality pre-school early childhood education is most powerfully argued by the economic Nobel laureate James Heckman. Since cognitive and non-cognitive abilities influence school success and, subsequently, adult chances in working life, the policy imperative is to ensure a 'strong start', that is, investment in the training of young children (Heckman 2000, Heckman and Lochner 2000, Heckman and Carneiro 2003). *Ex ante* high-quality early childhood investments and pre-school education are more effective in addressing the perpetuation of social inequalities, reflecting the effects of skill-biased technological change and school segregation, than *ex post* more remedial policies.

As parenting is crucial to child development, and thus the shape of future societies, policymakers have many reasons to want to support robust families, which under post-industrial economic conditions implies helping parents find a better balance between work and family life. The economic reasoning of the OECD in their *Babies and Bosses* (2007) studies is that when parents cannot realize their aspiration in work and family life, including the number of children they desire, not only is their wellbeing impaired, also economic progress is curtailed, through reduced labor supply and lower productivity, which ultimately undermines the long-term fiscal sustainability of universal welfare systems (Esping-Andersen 2009: 133). Moreover, we know that vanguard social investment provision, such as family services and education, are chronically underprovided by the market. To the extent that low levels of education in less well-off groups depress productivity, under-investment in education will engender stunted economic growth and decreased tax revenue. Over-investment by work-rich families in their offspring does not compensate for this.

In the post-industrial context of new social risks and flexible careers, the goal of full employment has come to require far more differentiated inclusion in the labor market over the life course, access to social services and capabilities that ensure employability at critical moments of transition and the ability to participate fully in other relevant spheres of social life (Schmid 2008). There is no inherent contradiction between these objectives of employment flexibility and social protection. A new model of employment relations is in the making whereby both men and women share working time, which enables them to keep enough time for catering for their families. Günther Schmid advocates that in an environment where workers are likely to experience more frequent labor market transitions, which relate not only the transition from unemployment to employment but to a wider set of opportunities of training, full and part-time work, self-employment, family care, parental leave, child-rearing and gradual retirement, institutional structures are needed to put in place the right conditions for individuals to successfully manage these transitions, in line with productivity enhancing flexibility and higher levels of employment. Higher employment of women typically raises the demand for regular jobs in the areas of care for children and other dependants as well as for consumer-oriented services in general. If part-time work is recognized as a normal job, supported by access to basic social security and allows for normal career development and basic economic independence depend-ence, part-time jobs can generate gender equality and active security of working families. Hereby the neo-liberal mantra of 'making work pay' is replaced by the adage of 'making transitions pay' over the life cycle by social policy supports that provide for 'active securities' or 'social bridges' so as to ensure that increasingly non-standardized employment relations, for instance, become 'stepping stones' to sustainable careers. Opportunity structures of making transitions that accommodate critical life course transitions reduce the probability of being trapped into inactivity and welfare dependency. This in turn harbors both individual and economic gains (Schmid 2008, Kok 2004, European Commission 2006, 2008).

While social investment advocates share the neoclassical critique of the postwar welfare state when emphasizing the supply side, it is criti-cally important to stress that they harbor a far more positive role of the state and a less sanguine and benign understanding of efficient markets, especially in key areas of welfare provision. Because citizens often lack the requisite information and capabilities to make enlightened choices, many modern life course needs remain unmet because of market failure. Here social investment economics hark back to the original economic rationale for modern social policy as measures to provide insurance, offering col-lective insurance mechanism for redistribution over the life cycle. This is what Nicholas Barr has coined as the 'piggy-bank' function of the welfare state (Barr 2001). For Charles Sabel social investment economics goes far beyond 'piggy-bank' economic rationality. One of the fundamental reasons why the 'active' welfare state today must provide enabling and capacitating social services he believes is inherently related to the declin-ing effectiveness of the social insurance since the 1980s (Sabel et al. 2010). When the risk of male-breadwinner industrial unemployment was still largely cyclical, it made perfect sense to administer collective social insur-ance funds for consumption smoothing during spells of demand-deficient unemployment. However, when unemployment becomes structural, caused by radical shifts in labor demand and supply, intensified interna-tional competition and skill-biased technological change, unemployment insurance can no longer function as a reserve income buffer between jobs in the same walk of industry. For the effective mitigation of new social risks across the life course, such as skill depletion and tension between work and family responsibilities, against which they cannot be reliably insured, the new welfare state must provide, as noted above, capacitating services tailored to particular social needs caused by life course disruptions. Both the 'piggy-bank' and capacitating services logics are absent in the neo-liberal critique of the welfare state. Neo-classical economics, based on perfect information and market clearing, theoretically rules out the kinds of social risks and market failures that the welfare state seeks to address. Moreover, because neo-classical economics remains focused only on the cost side of the welfare state, it theoretically rules out the welfare state's key macro- and micro-economic benefits (Atkinson 1999: 8).

However, an overriding critical constraint on the part of the state willing to push social investment, especially in the wake of first crisis of twenty-first-century global capitalism, lies in public accounting. Public finance routines and macro debt and deficit constraints, embedded in the Maastricht criteria and the Stability and Growth Pact, remain firmly anchored in the neo-liberal doctrine of balanced budgets and price stability as sufficient conditions for overall macro-economic stability. While all the available evidence suggests that investments in childcare and education will, in the long run, pay for themselves, existing public finance practices consider any form of social policy spending only as pure consumption. This may be true for the modus operandi of the postwar welfare state, which was indeed income-transfer biased. Today, as the welfare state is in process of becoming more service based, there is a clear need to distinguish social investments from consumption spending. A new regime of public finance that would allow finance ministers to (a) identify real public investments with estimated real return, and (b) examine the joint expenditure trends in markets and governments alike, has become imperative. This would be akin to distinguishing between current and capital accounts in welfare state spending, just as private companies do, as Esping-Andersen argues (2006).

6.   CONCLUSION

In a deliberately stylized manner, this chapter has traced the evolution of the welfare state since the mid-twentieth century through three periods, each marked by distinct combinations of socioeconomic conditions, economic analysis and social policy prescription, shaped, in turn, by political contestation and compromise. Over the long-run history of the modern welfare state we can observe how welfare Keynesianism and neo-liberal policy prescriptions, in part, sowed the seeds of their own demise. Although neo-liberal policy prescriptions helped to improve monetary stability, budgetary restraint, together with micro-level labor market flexibility and social insurance activation, conservative governments turned a blind eye to the political correlates of new social risks associated with the feminization of the labor market, family change, and the new demography of low fertility, ageing populations, and the obvious market failures of private social service provision. As the epoch of welfare retrenchment gave rise to new inequalities and growth deficiencies, the social investment perspective, with employment participation, human capital formation, family and childcare servicing at its core, emerged from the widespread disenchantment with neo-liberal retrenchment and deregulation over the 1990s.

The rise of the social investment perspective thus exemplifies how political and economic developments are not tied together in any straightforward 'functional' or 'materialist' manner. Over the 1990s it also became clear that dramatized neo-liberal forebodings of the demise of the welfare state were much exaggerated. To wit, some of the most generous welfare states, with large public sectors, allocated to human capital and family services, outperformed many of the most liberal political economies (Lindert 2004). Especially the Nordic countries, in the words of André Sapir, proved best able to match 'high efficiency' in the economy with 'high equity' in the distribution of life chances (Sapir 2006). In other words, an ambitious, generous and active welfare state, with a strong social investment impetus, proved to be an asset rather than liability in the emerging knowledge economy, before the onslaught of the early twenty-first century Great Recession.

The current economic crisis will have profound repercussions for European welfare states. The years ahead will differ markedly from the epoch when the social investment ideas were first launched by Anthony Giddens, Gøsta Esping-Andersen et al., and Frank Vandenbroucke, and diffused by the OECD and the EU. Will the determined fiscal response in 2008 and 2009, based on an emergency reconversion to the economic teachings of John Maynard Keynes, be followed by a more general reappraisal of generous welfare states in the wake of the first crisis of twenty-first century capitalism? Will the social investment paradigm carry the day, or revert to marginality? Initially, the Member States of the EU have responded to the crisis by extending short-term working arrangements, training and activation, gender equality in labor markets, and later retirement, fairly consistently with social investment perspective. It remains, however, to be seen to what extent the pro-welfare consensus will be sustained once the calls for an 'exit strategy' of deficit and debt reduction, based on the mantra of balanced budgets and disinflation, grow louder. It seems highly likely that the massive increase in fiscal deficits and public debt to levels not seen since World War II will force policymakers to restrain welfare commitments in order sustain economic stability. After a two-decade loss of faith in public action, the final downfall of the neo-liberal efficient market and rational expectations hypotheses is no guarantee for the acceleration of welfare state renewal following the strictures of social investment policy analysis. But although the crisis is likely to put a strain on many welfare institutions, this could also engender positive consequences. For one, social policy has resurfaced at the centre of the political debate. People once again realize how important public institutions are to economic stability. Moreover, dire economic conditions will not make it politically opportune for policy makers to easily abandon welfare commitments. In this respect, the economic crisis may reinforce, I hope, rather than undermine, the portent of social investment welfare in the aftermath of the worst recession since the Great Depression.

REFERENCES

Agell, J., T. Lindh and H. Ohlsson (1997), 'Growth and the public sector: A critical review essay', *European Journal of Political Economy*, **13** (1), 33–52.

Akerlof, G. A. and R.J. Shiller (2009), *Animal Spirits: How Human Psychology Drives the Economy and Why It Matters for Global Capitalism*, Princeton: Princeton University Press.

Atkinson, A.B. (1999), *The Economic Consequences of Rolling Back the Welfare State*, Cambridge, MA: MIT Press.

Barr, N.A. (2001), *The Welfare State as Piggy Bank: Information, Risk, Uncertainty, and the Role of the State*, Oxford: Oxford University Press.

Blanchard, O. (2006), 'European unemployment: The evolution of facts and ideas', *Economic Policy*, **21** (45), 5–59.

Blanchard, O. and L. Summers (1987), 'Hysteresis in unemployment', *European Economic Review*, **31** (1–2), 288–95.

Blanchard, O.J. and J. Tirole (2007), *The Joint Design of Unemployment Insurance and Employment Protection. A First Pass*, CEPR Discussion paper DP6127, www.cepr.org/pubs/dps/DP6127.asp.asp.

Crouch, C. (1999), *Social Change in Western Europe*, Oxford: Oxford University Press.

Crozier, M., S.P. Huntington and J. Watanuki (1975), *The Crisis of Democracy: Report on the Governability of Democracies to the Trilateral Commission*, New York: New York University Press.

De Grauwe, P. (2008) 'Animal spirits and monetary policy', *Economic Theory*, published online: http://www.springerlink.com/content/k5884352p5113642/full-text.pdf.

Dolado, J., C. García-Serrano and J. Jimeno (2002), 'Drawing Lessons from the Boom of Temporary Jobs in Spain', *Economic Journal*, **112** (480), 270–95.

Esping-Andersen, G. (2009), *The Incomplete Revolution: Adapting to Women's New Roles*, Cambridge: Cambridge: Polity Press.

Esping-Andersen, G. (2006), 'Putting the Horse in Front of the Cart: Towards a social model for mid-century Europe', in S. Sasses and G. Esping-Andersen, *Towards a New Welfare State*, WRR lecture 2005, pp. 31–69.

Esping-Anderson, G. (2001), 'A Welfare State for the 21st Century', in Anthony Giddens (ed.) *The Global Third Way Debate*, Oxford: Policy Press/Blackwell.

Esping-Andersen, G. and D. Gallie, A. Hemerijck and J. Myles (2002), *Why We Need a New Welfare State*, Oxford: Oxford University Press.

European Commission (2008), *Renewed Social Agenda: Opportunities, Access and Solidarity in 21st Century Europe*, COM (2008), 412 final, Brussels: Commission of the European Communities.

European Commission (2006), *Implementing the Renewed Lisbon Strategy for Growth and Jobs: A Year of Delivery*, COM (2006), 816 final, Part I, Brussels: Commission of the European Communities.

Flora, P. (1986), *Growth to Limits: The Western European Welfare States since World War II*, Volumes 1 to 4. Berlin and New York: De Gruyter.

Giddens, Anthony (1998), *The Third Way: The Renewal of Social Democracy*, Cambridge: Polity Press.

Hall, P.A. (1989), *The Political Power of Economic Ideas: Keynesianism across Nations*, Princeton: Princeton University Press.

Hay, C. (2004), 'Common trajectories, variable paces, divergent outcomes? Models of European capitalism under conditions of complex economic interdependence', *Review of International Political Economy*, 11 (2), 231–62.

Heckman, J.J. (2000), 'Policies to foster human capital', *Research in Economics*, 54 (1), 3–56.

Heckman, J. and P. Carneiro. (2003), *Human Capital Policy*, NBER Working Paper no. 9495, http://www.nber.org/papers/w9495.

Heckman, J.J. and L. Lochner (2000), 'Rethinking myths about education and training: Understanding the sources of skill formation in a modern economy', in S. Danziger and J. Waldfogel (eds), *Securing the Future: Investing in Children from Birth to College*, Russell Sage Foundation: New York, pp. 47–83.

Hemerijck, A. (2012), *Changing Welfare States*, Oxford: Oxford University Press.

Hemerijck, A. (2002), 'The self- transformation of the European social model(s)', in Esping-Andersen, G. with D. Gallie, A. Hemerijck and J. Myles, *Why We Need a New Welfare State*, Oxford: Oxford University Press, pp. 173–244.

Hemerijck, A. (1997), *Social Policy as a Productive Factor*, The Hague and Brussels: Ministry of Social Affairs and Employment and European Commission.

Jenson, J. (2010), 'Diffusing Ideas for after Neoliberalism. The Social Investment Perspective in Europe and Latin America', *Global Social Policy*, 10 (1), 59–84.

Jenson, J. (2009), 'Lost in translation: The social investment perspective and gender equality', *Social Politics*, 16 (4), 446–83.

Keynes, J.M. (1973[1936]), *The General Theory of Employment, Interest and Money*, London: Macmillan for the Royal Economic Society.

Kok, W., C. Dell'Aringa, F.D. Lopez, A. Eckström, M.J. Rodrigues, A. Roux, and G. Schmid (2003), *Jobs, Jobs, Jobs: Creating More Employment in Europe: Report of the European Commission's Employment Taskforce*, Brussels: European Commission.

Lindert, P.H. (2004), *Growing Public: Social Spending and Economic Growth since the Eighteenth Century*, Cambridge: Cambridge University Press.

Lucas, R.E. (1988), 'On the mechanics of economic development', *Journal of Monetary Economics*, **22** (1), 3–42.

Marglin, S.A. and J.B. Schor (1990), *The Golden Age of Capitalism: Reinterpreting the Postwar Experience*, Oxford: Clarendon Press.

OECD (2008), *Growing Unequal*, Paris: OECD.

OECD (2007a), *Babies and Bosses*, Paris: OECD.

OECD (2007b), *Understanding the Social Outcomes of Learning*, Paris: OECD.

OECD (2006a), *OECD Employment Outlook. Boosting Jobs and Income*, Paris: OECD.

OECD (2006b), *Starting Strong*, Paris: OECD.

OECD (1997), *The OECD Jobs Strategy. Making Work Pay. Taxation, Benefits, Employment and Unemployment*, Paris: OECD.

OECD (1996), *Beyond 2000: The New Social Policy Agenda*, Paris: OECD.

OECD (1994), *The OECD Jobs Study. Facts, Analysis, Strategies*, Paris: OECD.

Pierson, P. (2002), 'Coping with permanent austerity: Welfare state restructuring in affluent democracies', *Revue Française de Sociologie*, **43** (2), 369–406.

Ruggie, J.G. (1994), 'Trade, Protectionism and the Future of Welfare Capitalism', *Journal of International Affairs*, **48** (1), 1–11.

Ruggie, J.G. (1982), 'International regimes, transactions, and change: Embedded liberalism in the postwar economic order', *International Organization*, **36** (2), 379–415.

Sabel, C. and J. Zeitlin (2003), 'Active welfare, experimental governance, pragmatic constitutionalism: The new transformation of Europe', draft paper prepared for the International Conference of the Hellenic Presidency of the European Union, Ionnina, Greece, 21–22 May 2003.

Sabel, C., A. Saxenian, R. Miettinen, P.H. Kristensen, and J. Hautamäki (2010), *Individualized Service Provision in the New Welfare State: Lessons from Special Education in Finland*, Draft Report Prepared for SITRA, Helsinki.

Sapir, A. (2006), 'Globalization and the Reform of European Social Models', *Journal of Common Market Studies*, **44** (2), 369–90.

Scharpf, F.W. (2003), 'The vitality of the nation state in 21st century Europe', in WRR, *De Vitaliteit van de Nationale Staat in het Europa van de 21ste Eeuw*, WRR lecture 2002, Groningen: Stenfert Kroese: 15–30.

Scharpf, F.W. (1991), *Crisis and Choice in European Social Democracy*. Ithaca/London: Cornell University Press.

Scharpf, F.W. and V.A. Schmidt (eds) (2000), *Welfare and Work in the Open Economy: From Vulnerability to Competitiveness* (Vol. 1), New York: Oxford University Press.

Schmid, G. (2008), *Full Employment in Europe: Managing Labour Market Transition and Risks*, Cheltenham: Edward Elgar.

4. Gender, family and the labour market in post-industrial societies: A new social compromise?

Teresa Jurado-Guerrero, María José González López and Manuela Naldini

INTRODUCTION

This chapter draws from Crouch's work on *Social Change in Western Europe* (1999), with regard to the coming of the post-industrial society and the possibilities for European social 'convergence'. Using a historical framework from the mid-1960s and mid-1990s, Crouch masterfully described the transformation of social institutions and social action. His starting point was the description of a 'mid-century social compromise' in which industrialism, capitalism, liberalism and citizenship achieved a distinctive balance in western Europe after World War II. He envisioned that transformations in gender relations were crucial for understanding the evolution of this 'social compromise'. In the period of the 'mid-century social compromise', employment and family were clearly separated spheres, which resulted in a segregation of roles between men (who were all in the labour market) and women (who were mainly in domestic and caring work), such that the male-breadwinner family was one of the social pillars of Fordist capitalism.

Today this 'compromise' has been severely modified. The male-breadwinner family model no longer forms the social basis of current European capitalist societies, since this family type represents only a minority of families with dependent children throughout the region. In northern and eastern Europe, as well as Portugal, dual-full-time earner families have become the norm, while in western, central and Mediterranean Europe, one-and-half earner together with dual-full-time earner families are the majority among young couples (Lewis 1992; OECD 2009). These dual-earner families may be considered part of the new social compromise of 'privatised Keynesianism' (Crouch 2008), but it is based on an unstable gender compromise. As we show, the western promise of equal opportunities for women has not been fulfilled, since women perform the greatest share of unpaid family work. This gender inequality has important consequences for the economy. First, it maintains obstacles to women's participation in employment and therefore wastes human capital. Second, it limits the demand for public and private care and housework services. Third, it deepens the demographic ageing crisis through relatively low female employment rates and through very low fertility levels in most European countries (Esping-Andersen 2009). Thus, the new family model adds destabilizing elements to an economy in the midst of a crisis.

Instead, a shift from dual-earner families to universal-carer families in which men become more like women and a great deal of family work is outsourced (e.g. Gornick and Meyer 2009) may provide more social stability by increasing use of a (highly qualified) female workforce and supporting the conciliation of employment and family work in ways other than simply reducing fertility. The aim of this chapter is to explore precisely the factors linked to the emergence of a new gender equality balance, and thus the conditions under which men in young adult couples living in post-industrial societies become equally engaged in housework. The indicator selected for 'gender equality' is the man's share of domestic activities. First, we explore the conditions under which men assume half or more hours of the total housework performed by the couple. We take into account whether the bargaining power of his partner (the woman), indicated by her relative income and her time spent in paid work, is still relevant when gender attitudes and the family structure are taken into account. Second, we explore how country differences in the prevalence of 'innovative men' (i.e. those doing half or more hours of housework) can be explained through female empowerment in the market, the family and the state. We argue that national contexts influence the gendered division of housework, independently of composition effects, through gender norms and institutions that influence bargaining power within couples. In order to achieve our research goals we develop a comprehensive multi-level and cross-national analysis, which we apply to 26 European countries using the 2004 European Social Survey.

WHAT DRIVES MEN'S NEW FAMILY ROLES IN EUROPEAN COUNTRIES?

This section uses existing literature to hypothesise about the main factors that favour the emergence of men's new roles in the household and, more specifically, their increased participation in domestic activities. Most influential theories propose that there are individual as well as institutional factors influencing gender roles. The theories that focus on individual factors to explain men's and women's participation in domestic activities date back to the early 1960s, for example, Becker's treatise on the family (1981), while more sophisticated theories were developed later based on social exchange and economic bargaining (Manser and Brown 1980; McElroy and Horney 1981; Lundberg and Pollack 1993). The latter considered that women might use economically-based bargaining power to get the partner to do housework. While in the traditional division of labour women had a weak 'threat point', as their human capital and participation in the labour force increased, they also attained a stronger 'voice' with which to assert their preferences. This renegotiation of gender roles and bargaining frequently involves conflict in the couple (Kluwer et al. 1997). Men's and women's time spent on housework has also been related to the employment hours of both partners by the so-called 'time availability hypothesis' (Blood and Wolfe 1960). Thus, men are supposed to do more housework when women are absent from home due to their long working hours. Another strand of theories focused on the individual emphasises the role of gender ideology and 'doing gender', whereby wives are supposed to perform housework in order to symbolically enact their femininity while husbands avoid it for reasons of symbolic masculinity (West and Zimmerman 1987; Connell 1987). Authors such as Brines (1994) and Bittman et al. (2003) showed that the more a husband relies on his wife for economic support, the less housework he does to compensate symbolically for this non-traditional economic relation (gender display effect).

The theories that focus on institutional factors mainly focus on the influence of politics, policies and laws or, more broadly defined, the welfare state on couples' gender relations. Recent integrative approaches have treated gender itself as a socially constructed stratification system (Risman 2004; Connell 1987). According to Risman (2004), gender has to be seen as an entity that affects very different aspects of society: at the individual level for the development of gendered selves; during interaction, since men and women face different cultural expectations; and at the institutional level, where explicit regulations on resource distribution and material goods are gender-specific.

Considering gender as a structure allows us to explain the gendered division of housework as the outcome of a complex set of factors that includes the distribution of resources, ideology and institutional contexts. Our aim in this study is to test factors which may precipitate changes towards a 'new social compromise', that is to say, a new scenario in which men and women share family and paid work responsibilities equally. We think that economic and bargaining theories are key to understanding men's housework participation. Nonetheless, economic explanations are not enough to make good predictions of time allocation. Men's behaviour is also influenced by gender ideology at both the couple and societal levels, as well as in bargaining and interaction processes with their female partners. We also believe that a couple's conflict over housework reflects one specific mechanism in the process of attaining a new gendered division of labour. Thus, we need to use a multi-dimensional model that takes into account individual, couple, and national contextual factors in order to account for the emergence of new gender roles.

In this study we re-test well-established hypotheses on couples' resources, women's relative resources, women's time availability and gender ideology. Additionally, at the individual and household level, we test a new hypothesis stating that a high degree of conflict within couples in the organisation of housework reflects an intense bargaining process. Therefore, we expect that higher degrees of conflict produce an increase in male participation in household work (*conflict hypothesis*). As argued before, micro variables are not isolated from the national context. Indeed, at the macro level we explore how country differences in the prevalence of innovative men can be explained through female empowerment in the market, the family, and the state.

In order to explain differences in the likelihood of innovative housework arrangements across European countries, we base our model on previous research. We re-test the gender empowerment hypothesis as measured by the Gender Empowerment Measure (Fuwa 2004) and by childcare services' coverage, which are considered work–family friendly policies (Fuwa and Cohen 2007). An indicator of the proportion of traditional gender attitudes in society is used to test the gender-ideology hypothesis (Breen and Cooke 2005) and the rate of cohabitation is used as an indicator of empowerment in the family, which we name the family *pluralisation hypothesis* (cf. Davis et al. 2007). We look for the extent to which composition effects may explain cross-national differences and we test a new macro variable, the proportion of professional occupations, as an approximation of the amount of housework that is externalised. We test whether European country differences are partly due to composition effects. This means that country differences may be related to the national diffusion of couples with favourable characteristics for male innovation in housework. Therefore, we expect that through the inclusion of relevant micro variables we will remove a significant part of country differences (*composition effects hypothesis*). We also test whether a more egalitarian division of housework is the consequence of the existence of a large service class (upper class in the Erikson-Goldthorpe class schema), mainly because such couples have a greater capacity to externalise housework (*social class context hypothesis*). Although these hypotheses are not independent of one another, the aim of this analysis is to explore their individual capacity to reduce cross-country variation not accounted for by the composition effects of individual and couple level factors.

RESEARCH METHODOLOGY: DATA, VARIABLES AND ANALYTICAL STRATEGY

Our analysis is based on the 2004 European Social Survey (ESS). This survey was designed as cross-sectional time series data (collection takes place every two years) that is representative of all individuals aged 15 and over who reside within private households (26 countries participated, as listed in Figure 4.1). In contrast to previous research, we restrict the sample to couples in which men are aged between 25 and 47 (N=11, 700) in order to decrease the heterogeneity of life-conditions of the group and

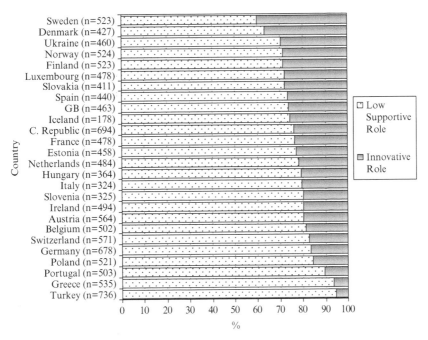

Note: 'n' indicates unweighted sample size.

Source: European Social Survey, 2004 (weighted data).

Figure 4.1 *Distribution of men aged 25–47 according to their share of housework in relation to female partner, 2004*

to ensure that the macro variables affect this group of people in a similar way, particularly concerning childcare services, employment in service-class jobs and non-traditional couples.

This analysis excludes family responsibilities such as care work. Domestic chores may cover a wide range of activities that must be differentiated in terms of their work-load, personal gratification, and gender identity implications. Research has shown that care activities must be considered separately from domestic work (Coltrane 2000; Gershuny 2000), owing to the fact that childcare and elderly care are also very different in their requirements and implications. Domestic work is captured in the survey by the following question: 'On a typical weekday, about how many hours, in total, do people in your household spend on housework for your home?' This is then followed by another question, which asks about the fraction of time that each partner spends on housework. Looking at both partners, we have created a new variable consisting of the fraction of domestic work undertaken by the male partner. This has been coded into two categories: those who are reluctant to cooperate (i.e. they either do much less or a bit less housework than their female partners), and those who are innovative (i.e. they do half or more of the housework). We call them 'innovative' because they are a minority group in most countries, as illustrated in Figure 4.1, where we have portrayed the dependent variable (low supportive versus innovative role). Because of the relative measure of housework, it must be noted that the innovative role of a man may be facilitated by factors that are independent of his actions, such as the reduction of the absolute time devoted to housework by the couple, which in turn is dependent on variables such as culture, demography, welfare state and technology. As may be seen, innovative men are more common in some countries than in others, with proportions ranging from 5 per cent in Turkey to 40 per cent in Sweden. However, the variation among countries may be smaller, if there is a bias towards 'politically' correct answers and if this bias varies cross-nationally.

The independent variables at the individual and couple level used to test our hypotheses were the combined couple's educational resources, which are meant to be a proxy for the couple's externalisation capacity. We decided not to use the variable for total household income, since we would have lost 13% of our cases due to missing information. We also consider women's contributions to household income, women's working hours, gender ideology (based on the statement 'a woman should be prepared to cut down on her paid work for the sake of her family'), and disagreement over organising housework. It should be noted that the last two variables do not capture men's gender ideology or conflict, but the respondents' answers: one half of the respondents were men and the other half were women, all of whom gave information about themselves and about their male or female partners.

In order to test the macro hypotheses, we introduced five contextual variables (see descriptive statistics and data sources in Table 4.1): the Gender Empowerment Measure (GEM), traditional gender ideology context (percentage of ESS respondents agreeing with the statement 'a woman should be prepared to cut down on her paid work for the sake of her family'), participation rates in day-care for children under three, non-traditional family patterns context (rate of consensual unions with respect to total unions), and the weight of the service class (aggregated from ESS). The service class refers to Erikson and Goldthorpe's class categories I (Higher service) and II (Lower Service), which include legislators, senior officials, managers, and professionals, excluding small entrepreneurs and own-account workers (Erikson and Goldthorpe 1992). They are based on ISCO-88 occupational categories.

A series of variables were introduced to control for confounders and the family cycle: age of male partner, age and number of children, absolute hours of housework, years living together as a couple, type of union, gender of respondent (to control for a well-established gender bias in housework hours estimation according to the respondent's gender), and couple's labour market situation.

This analysis relies on two-level logistic models that include 11 700 individuals (Level 1) grouped into 26 countries (Level 2). We examine the probability that a coupled man chooses to perform an innovative role in daily domestic activities in the household (coded 1), as opposed to providing some support or being reluctant to cooperate at all (coded 0). The log odds of binary choice were posited as a function of individual, couple and other demographic control variables at the household level (Level 1) and various central characteristics at the national level (Level 2). We use a random intercept model with which we aim to show that, after controlling for relevant micro level variables, the country context continues to influence the dependent variable. These country effects are then interpreted as institutional effects, since we control for the composition effects of relevant micro variables. At the next step, we introduce macro variables which try to operationalise (a part of) these institutional differences.

We have checked for country differences in micro level effects and found that all of them go in the same direction, differing only in their degree of significance and intensity in the sample of countries selected. With the statistical models, we test whether macro variables are good measures of our theoretical ideas. To this aim we use the standard deviation of Level-2 components (countries). If the country had no effect, the standard

Table 4.1   Weighted means and standard deviation of variables used in analysis (n=26): country variables

	SD	Countries
Gender Empowerment Measure (GEM)[1]		
0.298–0.614 (ref. cat.)	0.31	HU, PL, SI, TR, UA
0.622–0.660	0.06	CH, CZ, EE, GR, SK
0.692–0.788	0.33	AT, FR, UK, IE, IT, PT
0.794–0.875	0.26	BE, DE, DK, ES, IS, NL
0.887–0.910	0.03	FI, NO, SE
Missing data for Luxembourg	0.00	
Presence of traditional values[2]		
<25% (ref. cat.)	0.04	DK, FI, IS, NO, SE
25–44%	0.38	BE, FR, UK, GR, IE, IT, NL, SI, SK
45–59%	0.33	AT, CZ, DE, EE, ES, HU, LU, PL
>=60	0.25	CH, PT, TR, UA
Childcare coverage[3]		
<10% (ref. cat.)	0.50	AT, CH, CZ, DE, GR, HU, IT, PL, TR
10–20%	0.01	IE, LU, SK
21–30%	0.31	EE, ES, FR, UK, PT, SI
31–40%	0.07	BE, FI, NL, SE
>40%	0.02	DK, IS, NO
Missing data for Ukraine	0.08	
Presence of service class		
10–21% (ref. cat.)	0.25	GR, IT, PT, TR
22–34%	0.33	AT, CZ, DE, EE, LU, PL, SI, SK, UA
35–53%	0.41	BE, CH, DK, ES, FI, FR, UK, HU, IE, IS, NL, NO, SE
Cohabiting couples[4]		
0% (ref. cat.)	0.14	TR
1–5%	0.20	CZ, GR, IT, PL, SK
6–16%	0.43	AT, BE, CH, DE, ES, UK, HU, IE, LU, NL, PT, SI
17–25%	0.16	DK, EE, FI, FR, IS, NO, SE
Missing data for Ukraine	0.08	

Table 4.1   (continued)

Notes: Country abbreviations: AT=Austria, BE=Belgium, CH=Switzerland, CZ=Czech Republic, DE=Germany, DK=Denmark, EE= Estonia, ES=Spain, FI=Finland, FR=France, UK=United Kingdom, GR=Greece, HU=Hungary, IE=Ireland, IS= Iceland, IT=Italy, LU=Luxembourg, NL=the Netherlands, NO=Norway, PL=Poland, PT=Portugal, SE=Sweden, SI=Slovenia, SK= Slovakia, TR= Turkey, UA= Ukraine.

1   The GEM value is an index that reflects the gender distribution of seats in parliament; of legislators, senior officials and managers; of professional and technical workers; and the ratio of estimated female to male earned income (Human Development Report 2007, http://hdr.undp.org/en/reports/global/hdr2007-2008/).
2   Aggregated from ESS ('A woman should cut down paid work for the sake of family?').
3   These include different types of public and private institutions (centre-based care, family day care and pre-school), depending on the country (see Table PF13.1: Typology of Childcare in 'OECD Family Database'; http://www.oecd.org/els/social/family/database).
4   Consensual unions with respect to total couples. EUROSTAT 2008 (census data of 2001, http://epp.eurostat.ec.europa.eu/portal/page/portal/population/data/database) with the exception of France (data come from survey Étude de l'histoire familiale 1999, http://www.insee.fr/fr/ffc/docs_ffc/irsoc033.pdf), Iceland (Statistical Office data for 2001, http://www.statice.is/Statistics/Population/Family) and Sweden (data from the European Household Panel 2001, http://epp.eurostat.ec.europa.eu/cache/ITY_OFFPUB/KS-53-03-831/EN/KS-53-03-831-EN.PDF).

deviation measure (σ_u^2) would be 0. The technical idea is that, if the macro variables were perfect operationalisations of institutional context differences, then the standard deviation would be 0. Thus, we aimed to find macro variables that reduce σ_u^2 as much as possible. This means that if our macro variables are able to reduce σ_u^2, they contribute to explaining which institutional factors increase the likelihood of observing innovative men.

DISCUSSION OF RESULTS

What induces men to be innovative (i.e. to do the same amount of house-work or more than their partners) rather than having a low supportive role in different societal contexts? Individual choices have been modelled as nested within state-level influences. The results of the random intercept models are set out in Table 4.2, reporting fixed effects that can be interpreted as the regular output from a logit model. Table 4.2 also reports the estimated variance components or country differences ($\Sigma = \sigma_u^2 I$). Level 2 coefficients reflect random effects at the country level. A likelihood ratio test comparing the model to ordinary logistic regression is provided and turns out to be highly significant for these data. This means that we appropriately accounted for the data's multi-level structure.

We discuss only the results for the independent variables and omit

Table 4.2   Multi-level results predicting men's share of housework from micro-level and country-level variables using mixed-effects logistic regression (n=11 700 men of 26 countries)

	Model 1 (Null Model)	Model 2 (Couple)	Model 3 (Country GEM)	Model 4 (Country Values)	Model 5 (Country Childcare)	Model 6 (Country Cohabiting)	Model 7 (Country Professionals)
Level 1 (individual and couple):							
Household's hours domestic work *(0–2 h.)*							
3–4 hours		−0.28***	−0.28 ***	−0.28***	−0.28***	−0.28 ***	−0.28***
5+ hours		−0.10	−0.10	−0.10	−0.11	−0.10	−0.10
Missing		−0.35**	−0.35**	−0.35**	−0.34**	−0.33*	−0.35**
She tells about him *(he tells about him)*		−0.85***	−0.85***	−0.85***	−0.85***	−0.85***	−0.85***
Cohabiting *(married)*		0.09	0.08	0.08	0.08	0.07	0.08
Missing		0.07	0.07	0.06	0.07	0.04	0.06
Years living together *(+20 years)*							
9–19 years		−0.04	−0.04	−0.04	−0.04	−0.04	−0.04
6–8 years		0.12	0.12	0.12	0.12	0.13	0.12
5 or less years		0.15	0.16	0.16	0.16	0.17	0.16
Refusal/Don't know		0.37*	0.37*	0.37*	0.37*	0.39*	0.37*
Male age 35–47 *(25–34 years old)*		0.08	0.08	0.08	0.08	0.08	0.08
(Childless)							
Youngest child 0–3 years old		−0.08	−0.08	−0.08	−0.08	−0.08	−0.07
Youngest child 4–12		−0.05	−0.05	−0.06	−0.05	−0.06	−0.05
Youngest child 13+		−0.18	−0.17	−0.18	−0.18	−0.19*	−0.18

	(1)	(2)	(3)	(4)	(5)	(6)
Number of children	−0.10**	−0.10**	−0.10**	−0.10**	−0.10**	−0.10**
A woman should cut down paid work for the sake of the family?						
(Disagree/strongly disagree)						
Neither agree nor disagree	−0.21***	−0.21***	−0.22***	−0.21***	−0.21***	−0.21***
Agree strongly /Agree	−0.49***	−0.50***	−0.50***	−0.49***	−0.50***	−0.50***
Don't know	−0.01	−0.01	−0.01	−0.01	−0.01	−0.01
Couple disagree about housework						
(Never)						
Several times a month or less	−0.21***	−0.22***	−0.21***	−0.21***	−0.21***	−0.21***
Once a week or more	−0.50***	−0.50***	−0.49***	−0.50***	−0.50***	−0.49***
Missing	−0.01	−0.01	−0.01	−0.01	−0.01	−0.01
Relationship with labour market						
(Both employed)						
He employed & she not	−0.17*	−0.18**	−0.17*	−0.17*	−0.16*	−0.16*
She employed & he not	0.58***	0.58***	0.58***	0.58***	0.58***	0.58***
Both not employed	0.59***	0.58***	0.59***	0.59***	0.60***	0.60***
Other & Missing	−0.01	−0.03	−0.03	−0.02	−0.02	−0.02
Couple's Human Capital						
(Both with basic education)						
He/she basic and she/he secondary education	0.49***	0.47***	0.51***	0.50***	0.51***	0.51***
Both secondary education or he/she tertiary and she/he basic education	0.54***	0.52***	0.57***	0.56***	0.58***	0.56***

Table 4.2 (continued)

	Model 1 (Null Model)	Model 2 (Couple)	Model 3 (Country GEM)	Model 4 (Country Values)	Model 5 (Country Childcare)	Model 6 (Country Cohabiting)	Model 7 (Country Professionals)
Level 1 (individual and couple):							
He/she secondary and she/he tertiary education		0.63***	0.64***	0.62***	0.63***	0.58***	0.59***
Both tertiary education		0.76***	0.77***	0.75***	0.76***	0.71***	0.73***
Women's contribution to household income *(She has no earnings)*							
Her earnings are very small		0.04	0.04	0.03	0.04	0.02	0.02
Her earnings<1/2		0.37***	0.38 ***	0.36***	0.37***	0.36***	0.36***
Her earnings about 1/2		0.80***	0.80***	0.79***	0.79***	0.78***	0.78***
Her earnings>1/2		1.03***	1.03***	1.02***	1.03***	1.01***	1.01***
Her earnings very large		1.12***	1.13***	1.12***	1.13***	1.11***	1.11***
She earns all the household earnings		1.46***	1.46***	1.46***	1.46***	1.46***	1.45***
Missing		0.86***	0.87***	0.85***	0.86***	0.83***	0.84***
Women's working hours (She is not employed)							
She works <35 hours		0.27**	0.26**	0.27**	0.26**	0.25**	0.27**
She works 35–40 h		0.55***	0.55***	0.55***	0.54***	0.54***	0.54***
She works 41+h		0.81***	0.81***	0.81***	0.81***	0.80***	0.81***

Level 2

Gender Empowerment Measure (GEM)[1]

(0.298–0.614)
0.622–0.66	0.10
0.692–0.788	0.17
0.794–0.875	0.27
0.887–0.91	0.57**
Missing data (Luxembourg)	0.72*

Presence of traditional values[2]

(<25%)	
25–44%	−0.40*
45–59%	−0.24
>=60	−0.55**

Childcare coverage[3] (<10%)

11–20%	0.56**
21–30%	0.15
31–40%	0.41**
>40%	0.43*
No data (Ukraine)	0.66*

Presence of service class (<22%)

22–34%	0.67***
35–53%	0.79***

Table 4.2 (continued)

	Model 1 (Null Model)	Model 2 (Couple)	Model 3 (Country GEM)	Model 4 (Country Values)	Model 5 (Country Childcare)	Model 6 (Country Cohabiting)	Model 7 (Country Professionals)
Level 2							
Cohabiting couples[4] *(0%, Turkey)*							
1–5%						0.49	
6–16%						0.60	
18–25%						0.88	
No data (Ukraine)						1.08	
Intercept	−1.30 ***	−1.89 ***	−2.12 ***	−1.57 ***	−2.12 ***	−2.49 ***	−2.45 ***
Variance components:							
Level 2 (country)	**0.4903**	**0.3938**	**0.3413**	**0.3507**	**0.3220**	**0.3369**	**0.2966**
Standard errors	(0.0732)	(0.0627)	(0.05655)	(0.0577)	(0.0546)	(0.0557)	(0.0516)
Interclass variation:	0.129	0.107	0.094	0.096	0.089	0.090	0.082
Log likelihood =	**−5861.12**	**−5276.00**	**−5272.81**	**−5273.43**	**−5271.63**	**−5272.48**	**−5269.88**
Prob > chi2 =	0.0000	0.0000	0.0000	0.0000	0.0000	0.0000	0.0000

Notes: Reference category in parentheses. We used xtmelogit STATA function for multilevel mixed-effects logistic regression with unweighted data. The interclass variation estimated following assumption of the logistic model: $pi^2/3$.
* p<0.05, ** p<0.01, ***p<0.001.

comments on control variables for reasons of space and because their effects work in the expected way, as in previous studies. Our main independent variables are *gender ideology, economic resources* and *couple conflict*. We accounted for gender ideology by looking at whether one of the partners reports traditional attitudes. The results indicate that traditional attitudes reduce the likelihood of finding an innovative man. We also introduced this variable as an interaction with the respondent's sex in order to see whether his or her gender made a difference in the effect of traditional gender values. Since gender differences were not statistically significant, we preferred to keep the model simple. The existence of this effect, controlling for bargaining power and time constraints, confirms the explanatory power of the gender-ideology hypothesis.

Our models validated the *time constraints hypothesis*. The log of the odds that men perform an innovative role increases according to the increase in women's working hours. We also tested the role of *women's relative resources* on the likelihood that the man does as much or more housework than his partner, controlling for her working hours. The results confirm the relative-resources hypothesis, since the chances of a man being innovative increase in households where the woman's income contributes half or more of the household's income. The coefficients remain positive and significant even when women are the only income providers in the household. In other words, the results depict a clear linear effect. This is evidence against the 'display gender effect' found by Bittman et al. (2003), which is based on the observation of a curvilinear effect. We controlled for the fact that some women may be out of the labour market or searching for work (couple's relationship with labour market), which may obviously affect the couple's division of housework. Also, the couple's combined human capital was used as a proxy for the couple's economic resources and economic ability to externalise housework. Indeed, as couples' human capital increases, the likelihood of men performing an innovative role grows. This may be explained by, among other reasons, the fact that couples with high human capital normally have more resources with which to externalise domestic work, which reduces the total amount of housework to be done.

As argued above, disagreement and bargaining on the division of housework may be one of the mechanisms that induce a change in men's housework patterns. First, it must be emphasised that we find that 49 per cent of the respondents report disagreements with their partner about how to divide housework. Yet results indicate that, contrary to our *conflict hypothesis*, the presence of disagreement on the division of housework has a negative effect on the log odds of men performing an innovative role, net of gender ideology and economic variables. These results can be interpreted in light of the previously mentioned study by Kluwer et al. (1997). They found that conflict over housework occurs mainly in a destructive way, which means that conflict does not seem to promote a constructive bargaining process conducive to changing men's behaviour, but instead creates tension and leads to destructive interaction forms that impede conflict resolution. If this national research is representative of couples in other countries our data may suggest that, in many cases, conflict may lead to divorce rather than to a change in men's housework performance. But this is a question that needs to be studied more carefully with longitudinal and qualitative data.

We now move on to the analysis of Level 2, in which we tried to reduce cross-country standard deviation (σ_u^2). In other words, we explore the extent to which a model with macro-level variables is able to reduce cross-country variation (Models 3 to 7) compared with the model with micro variables only (Model 2). The main difficulty when testing the effect of aggregate variables is that problems of multi-collinearity may easily arise. There is a strong correlation between day-care for children under three and a traditional gender ideology context (coefficient of correlation: –0.47), a large service-class context and day-care coverage (–0.48), social class and a traditional values context (–0.52), and a non-traditional family context and day-care coverage (0.72). In order to avoid this problem, we tested macro effects by introducing explanatory variables independently and evaluating their respective power to reduce country variance compared to a model with compositional effects only (Model 2).

In this comparative framework, the first hypothesis to assess is whether most national gender differences in the household division of labour are due to pure compositional effects. In other words, if Italy had achieved the Swedish educational structure and female labour-market situation, would it have displayed levels of male cooperation in house-work similar to those in Swedish society? To what extent do we have compositional effects in this sample of 26 countries? We estimated a null model (Model 1) with the aim of assessing the amount of unexplained country variance in the absence of any explanatory variable. In the null model, this variance consisted of a standard deviation of 0.49 or an intra-class variation of 0.13 (Table 4.2). The inclusion of individual and couple level variables in Model 2 reduced intra-class variance to 0.11 and the unexplained standard deviation from 0.49 to 0.39 – that is, by 20 per cent. This confirms our *composition effects hypothesis*, since it is the aggregation of our micro level variables that reduces the unexplained variance at Level 2 to such a large extent. However, we are not able to reduce this variance to 0, which indicates that men's propensity to be innovative is not only determined by compositional effects (at least of the controlled variables), but also by national institutions and culture, to an important extent.

It is hypothesised that women in general would be more empowered to negotiate housework within the couple in countries with a high degree of gender equality in the public sphere (i.e., participation on equal terms in political, economic and decision-making processes) as well as with well-developed, family-friendly and employment-supportive services (indicated here by a large supply of day-care services for children). Consequently, men would be more inclined to perform an innovative role in housework. But the results indicate that this is only the case when countries reach a threshold at which GEM is relatively high: above 0.887. Finland, Norway, and Sweden are the only countries above that threshold (see Table 4.1). As far as childcare coverage is concerned, the results are mixed: childcare has a significant effect but it is not linear, since the male innovative role is more likely in countries with medium coverage compared to those with low coverage. This may be due to comparability problems concerning the data, as mentioned before, or to the fact that macro-level factors should be introduced as a configuration of different determinants in the future. The inclusion of these two macro-level variables reduced the unexplained standard deviation by 13 per cent and 18 per cent respectively, compared to the model with micro level variables only (Model 2 versus Model 3 and 5 in Table 4.1). We thus find some support for the *gender empowerment hypothesis*, as have other researchers.

We tested the *gender ideology hypothesis* in Model 4. The results indicate that the strong weight of traditional gender values at the country level significantly affects men's roles, thus confirming the hypothesis, although there is no linear pattern. This macro-level determinant reduces unexplained standard deviation by 11 per cent. We also addressed the *family pluralisation hypothesis* in Model 6, which states that in countries with a high proportion of cohabitation, women may perceive that they have options beyond marriage and, therefore, that they are more easily able to walk away from unwanted relationships. This in turn empowers them to negotiate on equal terms with their partners. Again, the results suggest that this applies only when countries reach a certain threshold. This variable reduces the unexplained standard deviation by 14 per cent.

Finally, we argue that the *diffusion of housework marketisation* is of utmost importance for studying the division of housework. Since we lack a direct indicator for it, we approximate it with a proxy. In a country with a high service-class presence (according to the EGP class typology), externalisation of housework may be more easily financed, in some places through the market and in others through tax-funded public services. This variable was highly significant and showed a clear linear pattern in which a larger service class increases the chances of men being innovative. Furthermore, this variable provides a standard deviation of 0.29, which significantly reduces the deviation explained by the composition effects of micro level variables in Model 2 by an additional 25 per cent. However, given that this measure is only an approximation, more research on this is needed in the future.

To summarise, there are individual, compositional and institutional features affecting the chances of men being innovative in housework. This study shows that three separate institutional features make it more likely to find innovative men: gender empowerment, family pluralisation and the development of a large service class.

CONCLUSION: GENDER ROLES AFTER THE 'MID-CENTURY SOCIAL COMPROMISE'

If in the 'mid-century social compromise' there was a rigid gender division of labour, current economic and family life uncertainties impose new gender roles. After this study three main conclusions arise. First we show that, in the European countries included in our analysis, women's relative income is of utmost importance for understanding why we find in some couples 'innovative men' (men doing half or more of the couple's total hours of domestic tasks). This effect is clearly linear, contrary to previous analyses, which found either no effect of relative earnings on men's housework hours or found a curvilinear effect (Bittman et al. 2003). Couples in which the woman provides all of the total household income are the most likely to live with an innovative man, compared to couples in which the man provides all of the total household income. These findings, together with the significant effects of women's time availability and men's unemployment on the likelihood of finding an innovative man, confirm the importance of the time-availability and relative-resources hypotheses in explaining the increase of dual-earner/dual-carer couples. Thus, women's and men's positions in the labour market clearly influence the roles they perform within the family.

Our cross-country comparison also shows that men's propensity to be innovative is due partly to differences at the societal level. Women's empowerment through institutions that facilitate their participation in politics and employment on relatively equal terms, the national prevalence of a non-traditional gender ideology, and a high prevalence of consensual unions are significant candidates for explaining cross-national differences. This confirms previous research and extends it to the 26 European countries of our study. The societal macro variable that reduces unexplained country variance the most is a post-industrial context with a high proportion of the service class, which we use as an indicator of the share of couples with the capacity to externalise housework.

The results of this work suggest a positive and negative scenario for further male participation in housework. The negative scenario is that men perform an 'innovative role' when housework is small in amount, partially externalised, and when there are few children at home. A positive interpretation stresses the importance of further empowering women in paid employment and of promoting gender egalitarian values in families and institutions. Therefore, it appears that women's full-time employment or men's working time reduction are *sine qua non* conditions for the transformation of gender roles after the 'mid-century social compromise'.

It should be noted that the results of this chapter correspond to data from the mid-2000s. The financial crisis of 2007 opens new questions about the transformation of gender roles. Governments will face more pressure to cut down on public services that help families reconcile paid work and care for children and the elderly, and many women will have less public and private resources to bargain the allocation of caring and domestic activities. The increase in male unemployment, however, may also induce husbands to participate in domestic activities. It has been documented that long-term unemployed men share more domestic work than other men in the labour market (Morris 2000). Men without paid work are also more engaged in domestic tasks when they rely on a female breadwinner, and men in general are more likely to participate in domestic work within couples where the woman works full-time (Pääkönen 2008). Further research needs to be done with recent data to fully evaluate the consequence of the global economic crisis on gender relations and, more particularly, of the indirect effect of institutional reforms on gender equity within couples.

REFERENCES

Becker, G. (1981), *A Treatise on the Family*, Cambridge: Harvard University Press.
Bittman, M., P. England, N. Folbre, L. Sayer and G. Matheson (2003), 'When does gender trump money? Bargaining and time household work', *American Journal of Sociology*, **109**, 186–214.
Blood, R.O. and D.M. Wolfe (1960), *Husbands and Wives*, Glence, IL: Free Press.
Breen, R. and L. Cooke (2005), 'The persistence of the gendered division of domestic labor', *European Sociological Review*, **21**, 43–57.
Brines, J. (1994), 'Economic dependency, gender, and the division of labor at home', *American Journal of Sociology*, **100**, 652–88.
Coltrane, S. (2000), 'Research on household labor: Modeling and measuring

the social embeddness of Routine Family Work', *Journal of Marriage and the Family*, **62**, 1208–33.

Connell, R.W. (1987), *Gender and Power: Society, the Person and Sexual Politics*, Cambridge: Policy Press.

Crouch, C. (1999), *Social Change in Western Europe*, Oxford: Oxford University Press.

Crouch, C. (2008), 'Privatised Keynesianism', *Political Quarterly*, **79**, 4, 476–87.

Davis, S., T. Greenstein and J. Marks (2007), 'Effects of union type on division of household labor. Do cohabiting men really perform more housework', *Journal of Family Issues*, **28**, 1246–72.

Erikson R. and J.H. Goldthorpe (1992), *The Constant Flux: A Study of Class Mobility in Industrial Societies*, Oxford: Clarendon Press.

Esping-Andersen, G. (2009), *The Incomplete Revolution. Adapting to Women's New Roles*, Cambridge: Polity Press.

Fuwa, M. (2004), 'Macro-level gender inequality and the division of household labor in 22 countries', *American Sociological Review*, **69**, 751–67.

Fuwa, M. and P. Cohen (2007), 'Housework and social policy', *Social Science Research*, **36**, 512–30.

Gershuny, J. (2000), *Changing Times: Work and Leisure in Post-industrial Society*, Oxford: Oxford University Press.

Gornick, J. and M.K. Meyer (2009), 'Institutions that support gender equality in parenthood and employment', in J. Gornick and M.K. Meyer (eds), *Gender Equality. Transforming Family Divisions of Labor. The Real Utopias Project*, London/New York: Verso, pp. 3–64.

Kluwer, E.S., J.A. Heesink and E. Van De Vliert (1997), 'The marital dynamics of conflict over the division of labor', *Journal of Marriage and the Family*, **59**, 635–53.

Lewis, J. (1992), 'Gender and the development of welfare regimes', *Journal of European Social Policy*, **2**, 3, 159–73.

Lundberg, S., and R. Pollack (1993), 'Separate sphere bargaining and the marriage market', *Journal of Political Economy*, **101**, 998–1010.

Manser, M. and M. Brown (1980), 'Marriage and household decision-making: A bargaining analysis', *International Economic Review*, **21**, 31–44.

McElroy, M.B. and M.J. Horney (1981), 'Nash-bargained household decisions: Toward a generalization of the theory of demand', *International Economic Review*, **22**, 333–49.

Morris, L. (2000), 'Domestic labour and employment status among married couples. A case study in Harlepool', in S. Himmelweit (ed.), *Inside the Household. From Labor to Care*, London: Macmillan, 65–79.

OECD (2009), *Family Database*, available at: www.oecd.org/els/social/family/database.

Pääkönen, H. (2009), 'Total work allocation in 4 European countries', *Social Indicators Research*, **93**, 1, 203–7.

Risman, B. (2004), 'Gender as a social structure. Theory wrestling with activism', *Gender & Society*, **18**, 429–50.

West, C. and D. Zimmerman (1987), 'Doing Gender', *Gender & Society*, **1**, 2, 125–51.

5. Academia's place in European capitalist systems and the Conservative reform movement

Simcha Jong

INTRODUCTION

Universities play a critical role in cultivating social-political elites, in educating members of various modern professions, and in forming society's technological knowledge base. Moreover, academic scholarship at universities shapes cultural debates as well as political, social, and esthetic categories. As a result, the way institutional systems of higher learning are set up has fundamental implications for the organization of capitalist systems, touching on many of the critical institutional outcomes scholarly debates in the political economy literature have been concerned with. For example, institutions of higher learning shape the competencies, and skills that workers across a wide range of sectors have at their disposal, provide support for innovation in critical sectors of the economy, and affect the organization of labor markets for professionals. Yet, scholars in the political economy literature have to date shown little interest in examining how the national frameworks governing these institutions affect the capitalist enterprise beyond their role in vocational training (Boyer and Hollingsworth 1997, Crouch and Streeck 1997, Hall and Soskice 2001).

The exclusive focus on traditional industrial organization and financial institutions in this literature seems out of place in today's knowledge-based economies. Firms increasingly rely for a comparative competitive advantage on universities, in particular in knowledge-intensive sectors such as information technology, life sciences, and clean energy. Universities' role in economic life entails both direct contributions to R&D as well as the education of knowledge workers. In addition, universities are gradually overtaking schools of vocational training as the institutions on which the competitive advantage of nations rests in the education realm. For example, 2009 OECD figures highlight that in 2007 56 per cent of OECD-country students finished secondary education and accessed education at tertiary type-B institutions (typically universities), up from 35 per cent in 1995. This increase further widened the gap between enrollment in academic and vocational training institutions. The percentage of students accessing tertiary type-A institutions with a vocational orientation remained flat at 12 per cent over the same period (OECD 2009).

Another potential reason universities have been left aside in 'varieties of capitalism' analyses of political economies is that placing universities center stage in these analyses would go against the dichotomy between so-called liberal- and coordinated-market economies in the traditional industrial relations literature. Universities across the industrialized world are 'public institutions' in the sense that these institutions rely on public funding to fulfill most of their key activities; only a small proportion of scholarship undertaken at universities, primarily scholarship in less capital intensive fields such as Business and Law, can be run without public support. Thus, incorporating universities in the political economy literature would result in important parts of the economy being coordinated with state actors playing a critical role. In fact, it is the United States, the archetype of a liberal market economy where federal and state governments have since the Second World War been most committed to offering federal and state support for universities in the form of funding allocations. This goes against much of what scholars such as Peter Hall and David Soskice (2001) have argued about the role of the state in liberal market economies.

Although state actors play a critical role in shaping scholarly life at universities, there are important variations in the organization of national university systems across capitalist societies. This chapter will examine how national systems of higher learning work together with other institutions in national political economies in producing social and economic outcomes. In particular, this chapter will focus on three dimensions along which the institutional set-up of universities in contemporary societies has an impact on the development of political economies. First, contemporary university systems are defined by the space permitted to academic scholars in their contributions to the national civic and political discourse. Second, contemporary university systems differ in terms of the interests academic scholarship at universities is supposed to serve (e.g. the economic interests of private enterprise versus broader socio-economic interests in fields such as health, energy or defense). Third, national university systems are distinguished by the governance structures used to organize the academic endeavor and the role of government in these structures.

The main empirical focus will be on the Conservative university reform movement of the 1980s and 1990s in the United Kingdom. This chapter will outline changes in the relationship of universities to the state and the economy in Britain over the past decades and will put these changes in the context of the broader neo-liberal shifts in the political economy of the United Kingdom over the course of the 1980s and 1990s. It will elaborate on how the Conservative university reform movement was in part an attempt to quell political dissent that was linked into a broader political agenda to weaken the position of civic institutions, and reassert the power of central government. Moreover, the chapter will discuss how the reorientation of academic curricula aided Conservatives' political efforts to empower private enterprising and introduce managerial methods of organizing activities across public and civic institutional spheres.

The reforms promoted by the Conservative governments of Margaret Thatcher and John Major are not only interesting for scholars of the British political economy as these reforms had an impact well beyond the United Kingdom. In fact, the Conservative university reform movement has probably introduced the most important institutional changes to institutions of higher learning since the rise of the American research university and the transformation of universities into institutions of mass education during the postwar decades. The institutional changes pushed through by this movement have guided university reforms in countries around the globe, with the notable exception of the United States, leading to a transformation of the relationship between universities and the national political economies of which they are a part. For example, this chapter will highlight how recent efforts by EU governments to create a common 'marketplace' for higher learning through the Bologna process have heavily relied on institutional governance models pioneered by the British Conservative university reform movement during the 1980s and 1990s.

BRITISH UNIVERSITIES DURING THE POSTWAR DECADES

The postwar British higher education system was a system geared towards reinforcing the country's traditional institutions of civic society and the state. Industrialization processes in the United Kingdom during the nineteenth and twentieth centuries took place in isolation from scholarly life at the nation's elite universities, Cambridge and Oxford, and graduates of these universities rarely moved into industry positions up until the 1970s. As a result, despite its supposedly favorable, liberal market conditions for entrepreneurship, the British economy had a presence that was certainly not more prominent than that of its continental European counterparts in the critical waves of entrepreneurial science-based innovation of the postwar era. In fact, most of the important new firms in crucial sectors driving innovation in industrialized economies such as the information technology, life sciences and, more recently, the clean energy sectors were based in American science and technology clusters such as Silicon Valley and Route 128.

The British university system was one of Europe's most elitist at the dawn of the Thatcher era. There were around 40 universities in the country, which enrolled about 10 percent of the population at university age (Trow 1998). Two universities, the universities of Cambridge and Oxford, stood at the pinnacle of the British system of higher learning and played a critical role in its development. These two universities formed the principal recruitment grounds for the higher ranks of the British civil service, the legal profession, the clergy of the Church of England, and the country's intellectual and cultural elites (Jong 2007). Moreover, to fulfill their role in elite formation for the nation's important civic and state institutions, Cambridge and Oxford enjoyed a state-mandated privileged position for most of their histories that provided these universities with a high degree of autonomy. The (traditional) curricula and academic practices at these universities formed institutional models for other English universities, leaving a mark on the way academic scholarship was conceived of in the United Kingdom at the end of the 1970s.

The privileged position of Cambridge and Oxford and, by extension, Britain's other universities was apparent in the realm of funding as well. Public funding for universities, which as in other Western political economies had expanded significantly over the postwar decades was primarily allocated in the form of five-year block grants administered by the University Grants Committee (UGC). The UGC's function primarily was that of a buffer between universities and the political realm of state and government (Anderson 2006). The UGC was controlled by academics and its block grants were exempted from any post-auditing during the first decades following the war (Berdhal 1990). Moreover, block grants were not earmarked with specifications for the use of funds for activities such as teaching, research, or individual academic subjects, allowing universities a large degree of discretion in designing academic curricula and setting spending priorities.

Another hallmark of the postwar British university system, in particular of the two elite institutions that stood at its pinnacle, was the detachment between the realms of academic enquiry and private enterprise (Jong 2007). The model of higher learning guiding academic scholarship at these two institutions was a traditional 'gentlemanly model' that was defined in opposition to a utilitarian worldview. This was the same model used at the public schools from which a large proportion of Cambridge and

Oxford students were recruited (Anderson 1992). Although, as in the United States, the state took on the role of principal patron of the sciences in Britain following the Second World War, support for the distinctive scholarly model Cambridge and Oxford represented remained strong.

Practical concerns continued to be seen as antithetical to the academic endeavor, even if the moral frames steering scholarship away from these concerns were contested at several points in history (Jong 2007). For example, Britain's diminishing international standing was blamed on the absence of 'experts' among British industrial and civil service elites during Britain's short 'technocratic moment' of the late 1950s and early 1960s (Beer 1982). These elites were still predominantly populated by Cambridge and Oxford graduates versed in 'gentlemanly' subjects such as English Literature and Classics rather than in applied subjects such as engineering (Leavis 1962, Ortolano 2009, Snow 1959). Although the debates surrounding Britain's 'technocratic moment' led to increased funding for universities, at Cambridge and Oxford this support primarily benefited scholarly groups that were already well established.

Thus, although scientific subjects had by the 1960s become an accepted part of the academic curriculum at Cambridge and Oxford, the pretence of the pursuit of commercial gain and involvement in practical applications based on this enquiry had not. Cambridge and Oxford graduates rarely moved into industry positions up until the 1970s and resistance to the incorporation of novel programs with a utilitarian bent in the curriculum remained strong (Anderson 1992, Jong 2007, Wiener 1981). For example, although plans for the establishment of a medical school at Cambridge dated back to the Second World War period, scholarly groups within the university successfully resisted the establishment of such a school until 1976 (Rook et al. 1991). Moreover, a Cambridge business school was only formed during the 1990s, more than half a century after the establishment of similar schools at many of America's top universities.

THATCHER'S ASSAULT ON CIVIC SOCIETY AND ITS IMPACT ON THE UNIVERSITIES

The Conservative reform movement led by Margaret Thatcher and her government in the university sector would lead to a rearrangement of the institutions that had defined the relationship between universities, the state, and the economy. This movement would reorient universities away from supporting civic society towards supporting private enterprise, and neutralize universities as a source of political dissent.

The incoming Tory government found itself in 1979 in a political environment that was increasingly hostile towards the country's academic establishment. England's university dons and the ideals of professional privilege they represented had gained a prominent place in the political discourse that swept the Thatcherites to power. Thus, universities would figure as prominent 'straw men' in the neo-liberal discourse of the Thatcher era. In this discourse Britain's universities were linked to the country's long period of industrial decline following the Second World War and seen as unable or unwilling to produce graduates with 'useful' skills. In fact, a range of popular contributions to the public discourse of the 1970s and 1980s singled out universities and the privileged position academic 'dons' had enjoyed in postwar Britain as exemplifying all that was wrong with Britain. Two particularly influential Thatcher-era critiques of the moral values Cambridge and Oxford (as well as England's elite public schools) were seen as representing, can be found in Martin Wiener's *English Culture and the Decline of the Industrial Spirit, 1850–1980* (1981), and Corelli Barnett's *The Collapse of British Power* (1972).

As it did in other social realms, the Thatcher government used the dire fiscal and economic situation of the early 1980s and the depressed national sentiment of the time as an opportunity to push through a radical reform agenda in the university realm. This agenda was critical to broader, ideological plans of the Tories for the British political economy in a number of respects.

First, the Conservative university reform movement of the 1980s was a movement aimed at quelling political dissent. Universities had made a progressive turn during the late1960s and 1970s and were seen as particularly hostile towards the blend of conservatism promoted by Margaret Thatcher and her followers within the Tory party. University reform proved an effective way of dealing with this source of political hostility. The Tories especially viewed professions in the social sciences and humanities as too vocal in their support for the status quo. It was Margaret Thatcher herself who quipped about sociology that 'there's no such thing as society – merely individuals and their families'. Social scientists and humanists would bear the brunt of funding cuts that became a hallmark of the Thatcher approach to higher education during the 1980s. During the 1980s Philosophy, for example, lost over 30 percent of its posts in British universities and 40 percent in the universities outside Oxford, Cambridge, and London (Shallock 1989).

Second, the university reform movement was linked into a broader political movement that sought to provide greater leeway for private enterprise and individuals in social realms traditionally occupied by civic institutions. The governments of Margaret Thatcher and John Major introduced a number of 'market reforms' into the higher education system lifting barriers that had previously existed for other institutions to enter the 'university market place'. One of the most important was introduced in the 1992 Further and Higher Education Act, which granted polytechnics, and some colleges, the right to brand themselves as universities and to award university degrees. This moreover entailed a 'nationalization' of the former polytechnics as these reforms brought the polytechnics, which had traditionally been under the control of local authorities, under the authority of the central government. The 1992 Further and Higher Education Act almost doubled the number of institutions with the power to award academic degrees, raising the number of universities in the United Kingdom from 47 to 88 (Anderson 2006). One of the rationales offered for these reforms by the Conservative reform movement was that introducing competition from the former polytechnics would put pressure on Britain's traditional universities to branch beyond their existing academic programs and develop programs conferring more 'useful' skills and knowledge.

Third, the Conservative university reform movement was linked into a broader Conservative political effort to curtail the power position of civic institutions in favor of that of the central government and private sector enterprise. This effort often conflicted with principles underlying the Conservatives' stated belief in 'free markets', as was arguably the case with the 'nationalization' of the former polytechnics under the 1992 Further and Higher Education Act as well as the Tories' insistence on having central government regulate pricing of university fees. However, this seeming conflict did not stand in the way of these policies being implemented and Conservatives' hostility towards civic institutions and decentralized government mostly trumped their affection for the 'free market' in enacting university reforms. Weakening the position of universities was achieved through measures that undermined universities' fiscal position and autonomy in governance.

Undermining universities' fiscal position took the form of the most sweeping postwar funding cuts for science and education. The Thatcher government cut university budgets around 14 percent over the three-year period 1981–84 (Berdhal 1990) and, from 1985 onwards, universities lost a further 2 percent per annum (Shallock 1989). As a result, four thousand academic posts were lost during the early 1980s. Moreover, over the entire period of Conservative government from 1977 until 1997 spending per student fell by over 40 percent (Anderson 2006).

Undermining the privileged position of universities did not only entail cutting funding support, it also entailed the assertion of government power over university governance. As with other civic institutions such as unions, professional associations, cooperative banks and building societies during the Thatcher era, so-called governance reforms were used to strengthen the leverage of government over universities. The institutional changes implemented by the Tory government in the higher education sector significantly curtailed university autonomy. These changes included, for example, the abolishment of the University Grants Committee in 1988, the independent body that had allocated most public funding to universities during the postwar decades. The UGC, whose membership was restricted to academics, was replaced by the Universities Funding Council (UFC), which was designed as a conduit for political directives and had a strong representation of members from the private sector. The UFC was replaced by the Higher Education Funding Council for England (HEFC) after the enactment of the Further and Higher Education Act of 1992. Academic autonomy was curtailed in other ways as well. Tenure was abolished for new members of academic staff in 1988; universities were subjected to extensive auditing and funding was earmarked, restricting the discretion universities had in using public funds.

Another lasting mark of the Conservative reform movement was the development of an elaborate system of centralized bureaucratic controls replacing the collegiate system of self-governance that had characterized significant parts of academic life in Britain until the early 1980s. In part, the Conservative reform movement introduced 'quality assurance' programs and other audit mechanisms to demonstrate that, despite major funding cuts, the quality of academic life at universities was not suffering (Trow 1998). However, governance reforms were also informed by a deep distrust of the willingness of academics to embrace and internalize the goals of the Conservative university reform movement. By all accounts this distrust was mutual. As mentioned before, British universities had not been a bastion of Conservative support during the period leading up to the ascent of the Tories during the 1970s. Once Margaret Thatcher and her allies had assumed their role in government, the rift between academia and the Conservative movement grew only wider. In 1964, 32 per cent of university academics voted Conservative, and in 1976 this figure was 29 per cent. However, by 1989 Conservative support had fallen to 18 per cent and reached a further low of 10 per cent in 2005. Over these same years, Labour support remained stable around 40 percent (Anderson 2006).

Thus, although the political discourse driving reforms was a liberal one, more often than not, central bureaucratic controls and government policy directives rather than the 'invisible hand' of the market were guiding the policies of the Conservative movement in higher education policy. This movement became ever more assertive in interfering in interactions between firms, universities, and students over the course of the 1980s and 1990s. For example, the Thatcher government took an assertive role in setting student quotas for university degree programs, increasing enrollments in science and engineering degree programs which it saw as better addressing the needs of business. The government was now able to restrict enrollments in some subjects and expand enrollments in others by using its newly gained leverage over universities through the Universities and Higher Education Funding Councils.

Apart from forming new funding councils, the Conservative reform movement spurred the formation of a series of new bodies charged with auditing universities. To monitor university teaching, the Higher Education Quality Council (HEQC) was established in 1993. The HEQC, which was succeeded by the Quality Assurance Agency (QAA) in 1997, was charged with auditing the academic standards and quality of higher education in the UK. Subject and academic reviews carried out across Britain's universities were primarily aimed at forcing compliance with centrally set quality benchmarks (Hodson and Thomas 2003). These benchmarks were primarily derived from recasting universities' teaching operations in managerial terms, dividing up these operations into sets of work processes, competencies, and operational outcomes that could be measured. The audits performed by the QAA inspectors developed into resource intensive exercises covering the performance of departments and universities against benchmarks in activities such as student marking, admission processes, student complaints, teaching, program approval, and review processes.

To monitor research, the government started the so-called Research Assessment Exercises (RAE) from 1986. These exercises were aimed at ensuring the quality of research at British universities and the outcomes of these assessments formed the basis for funding allocation decisions to individual university departments by the higher education funding councils. Like teaching audits, the research assessment exercises formed a major enterprise putting a significant additional bureaucratic burden on universities. For example, the 2598 submissions from 173 higher education institutions for the 2001 RAE represented the work of 50 000 researchers (RAE 2008). Because of the RAE's importance in ensuring government funding most universities had to invest in units within their organizations charged with managing submissions for the RAE, supporting the formulation of departmental RAE strategies, and ensuring university-wide compliance with performance benchmarks used in the RAE.

More generally, the extensive system of controls and financial incentives constructed around universities during the 1980s and 1990s led to a high level of bureaucratization of scholarly life within universities. To be more efficient in meeting constantly changing benchmarks set in the various assessments, universities developed into ever more 'managerial' organizations, a development that was embraced and encouraged by the

Conservative reform movement. Measures such as the abolishment of academic tenure were explicitly intended to give university principals more freedom in hiring and firing academics.

Universities became more centralized and administrators gained ever-stronger powers, even at the most collegial of universities. At the University of Cambridge, the highest administrative officer, the university Vice-Chancellor, had played a mostly symbolic role and had been subject to a one- or two-year term limit since 1412. To make the university more effective in shifting resources to meet changing requirements of the (semi-) public bodies it had become dependent on, the offices of the central administration were expanded, and the term limit for the university Vice-Chancellor was extended from two to seven years in 1989. Moreover, it was made possible to attract the university Vice-Chancellor from outside the university.

CONTINUITY AND CHANGE UNDER LABOUR

The rise to power of the Labour governments of Tony Blair and Gordon Brown following the Tories' electoral defeat in 1997 led to a new era for the British higher education sector. However, although Labour's higher education policies formed a departure from the Tory era in important respects, Labour never contested the radical changes of the Conservative reform movement that fundamentally altered the position of British universities in society during the 1980s and 1990s. In fact, Labour embraced the insistence of the Conservative university reform movement on the important role of government benchmarking and control in higher education and the limited role of traditional notions of scholarly autonomy in the academic enterprise.

Thus, the size of the system of bureaucratic controls guiding the higher education sector further increased during the Labour era. In many areas Labour expanded institutions formed by the Conservatives, such as in the case of the RAE, which enlarged its reach under Labour. In terms of costs, the size of the last research assessment exercise under Labour in 2008 was more than four times the size of the last research assessment exercise under the Conservatives in 1996 (RAE 2009). In other areas where Labour policy priorities diverged from those of the Tories, new audit agencies were created. For example, the Labour government created the Office for Fair Access through the Higher Education Act of 2004. This agency was formed to review university practices and policies in order to safeguard fair access to higher education for lower income and under-represented groups.

Labour also embraced the view promoted by the Conservative university reform movement that perhaps the principal rationale in providing public funding for universities is the support universities are to provide for business in training skilled professionals as well as in research and development. Labour policies towards science increasingly sought to encourage academic scientists to engage industry. For example, Labour proposed to take into account measures of individual scholars' social-economic 'impact' in rating these scholars in research assessment exercises. Moreover, the government made significant investments in public–private partnerships between universities and industry, for example, through the creation of the Technology Strategy Board in 2004. The Technology Strategy Board, with a budget of more than £1 billion, was charged with overseeing a range of these new public–private partnerships including the Collaborative Research and Development projects, the Knowledge Transfer Networks program, and the Knowledge Transfer Partnerships program. In addition, Labour used the leverage over university admissions that the government had gained under the Tories and further expanded university places in science and engineering subjects considered useful to the private sector, while at the same time restricting the growth of university places for students in the social sciences and humanities.

The changing conception of universities from guardians of the sciences and high culture during the postwar decades to institutions for higher learning, and on to institutions serving private sector enterprise is moreover reflected over the years in the government departments responsible for overseeing public funding to universities. To ensure its autonomy from policy interference, the principal funding body for the universities, the UGC, operated during the first decades following the war up until the late 1960s under the Treasury Department and not under the government department charged with Education. The UGC's successor institutions, the University Funding Council and the Higher Education Funding Councils were brought under the authority of the Department of Education and Science, which was succeeded by the Department of Education in 1993. Labour moved around the universities further, bringing these institutions under the authority of the Department for Education and Skills in 2001 and separating the authority over universities from that over other education institutions in 2007, moving universities under a new Department for Innovation, Universities and Skills. Finally, making the reorientation of universities towards private enterprise complete, this department was merged with the Department for Business, Enterprise and Regulatory Reform to create a new Department for Business, Innovation and Skills in 2009.

Apart from overlaps, there were also some important differences between the Conservative and Labour agendas for universities. Labour placed universities at the center of the new government's social mobility agenda, which had not been an issue particularly close to the hearts of the Tories. In a 1999 speech to Labour's annual conference, Tony Blair stated his goal to enroll in higher education 50 percent of young adults in the United Kingdom by 2010. Higher education participation in the United Kingdom had been historically low in comparison with other OECD countries and stood at 32 percent when Labour came to power in 1997 (Anderson 2006: 176). Although Labour did not hit its 50 per cent goal, the higher education initial participation rate (HEIPR) increased to 39.2 percent in 2000 and grew further to 45.0 percent in 2009 (Department of Business, Innovation and Skills 2010).

More generally, the relationship of the Labour governments with the universities was less adversarial than that of preceding governments, as these did not share the Tories' perennial yearning for fiscal savings in the education sector. In fact, as for other (semi-)public sectors, for universities the period under Labour was a prosperous one from a funding perspective. The British system of higher learning that New Labour inherited in 1997 was a system that had been financially squeezed out to achieve budget savings for two decades. Perennial cost cutting came to an end under the governments of Tony Blair and Gordon Brown. In fact, OECD figures show that over the period 2000–2006 per-student spending at higher education institutions grew more than in any other OECD country (OECD 2009).

Increases in higher education funding partly came from university fees paid by students and their parents, which were introduced by the Labour government in 1998. Tuition fees had been non-existent for undergraduate students in the United Kingdom and were introduced by Labour to fund its policy objectives for the higher education sector. Tuition fees for undergraduates were initially capped at £1000 per year but this cap was gradually increased to £3225 for 2009/2010.

Apart from introducing and gradually raising tuition fees, Labour increased public funding for universities as well. Block grants for research and teaching awarded to universities by the Higher Education Funding Council for England (HEFCE) saw significant increases. The HEFCE budget for 1997/1998 was £3.4 billion of which £2.4 billion was earmarked for teaching and £0.7 billion was earmarked for research (HEFCE 1997). By the end of Labour's tenure in government the HEFCE budget had more than doubled to £7.4 billion for 2010/2011 of which £4.7 billion was earmarked to support teaching and £1.6 billion to support research.

Labour's funding commitment to universities also extended to the scientific realm. In its first spending review in 1998 the Blair government provided funding for science with a 15 percent boost over three years (Clery 2007). Moreover, over the total tenure of the governments of Tony Blair and Gordon Brown, the science budget, which supports the nation's grant-giving research councils as well as subscriptions to the likes of the CERN particle physics laboratory and the European Southern Observatory, tripled from its 1997 level of £1.3 billion to just under £4 billion for the 2010/11 budget period (Clery 2007).

IMPACT OF REFORMS BEYOND BRITISH ACADEMIA

The British Conservative university reform movement achieved many of its aims and the impact of this movement has been felt well beyond the confines of British universities, reinforcing some of the changes brought about by the Thatcherites in the economic and industrial relations realms.

First, the Conservative reform movement was effective in toning down academia as a voice in the political discourse. The British academic establishment had a notable presence in this discourse during the postwar decades. The disputes between Friedrich von Hayek of the London School of Economics and John Maynard Keynes of the University of Cambridge shaped critical political debates during the aftermaths of the Great Depression as well as the Second World War in the United Kingdom and around the world. Moreover, academic scholars at the nation's elite institutions played an important role in the cultural politics of the late 1950s and early 1960s, providing an effective 'traditionalist' pushback against the technocratic movements of this era (Ortolano 2009). The postwar era was also a period during which the academic establishment was well represented in the highest ranks of government. For example, the postwar government of Clement Richard Attlee counted among its members several politicians with previous university careers including the Prime Minister himself and the Chancellor of the Exchequer (Treasury Secretary), who both had held academic positions at the London School of Economics.

However, by restricting the mandate of universities to research and teaching in areas deemed to serve government policy priorities, interventions of the Conservative reform movement effectively blocked much civic and political engagement by universities. Members of partisan think tanks as well as media pundits have mostly replaced the voices of academic scholars in the civic discourse, and the rift between the realms of politics and academia significantly has widened over the past decades. This has put Britain in a somewhat unique position among Western democracies. In the current David Cameron government there is no Tory cabinet member with previous experience as an academic scholar with the exception of the Secretary of State for Environment, Food and Rural Affairs who was a Research Fellow at the Centre for European Agricultural Studies of the University of Kent from 1989 until 1993. This rift forms a stark contrast with the situation in other Western democracies such as the United States (and most other major European democracies) where two of the last three presidents had careers as university professors and where the academic establishment has traditionally been well represented among cabinet level appointments. For example, upon taking office, Barack Obama filled some of his most important cabinet level posts by appointing university professors from the nation's top universities, such as the 1997 Nobel Prize winner in Physics Steven Chu and Professor of Economics Christina Romer, both of the University of California at Berkeley.

A second important result of the Conservative reform movement has been a strengthening of the ties between Britain's top universities and private enterprise. Over the course of the 1980s and 1990s, funding allocation decisions for both teaching and research by the research councils and higher education funding councils were increasingly coordinated with the business community, for example, by including managers from industry on the boards of the Higher Education Funding Councils. In addition, funding for research and teaching became in many cases contingent on forging ties with industrial partners and developing elaborate knowledge transfer plans. This opened up opportunities for industry to shape university curricula as a way to advance its business objectives and had an impact on the organization of scholarly life at the nation's top universities. For example, at Cambridge and Oxford up until the late 1970s, graduates who moved to industry positions were generally frowned upon, as were academic staff members with an interest in engaging in industry collaborations. However, the Conservative reform movement achieved a radical turnaround in attitudes. Cambridge and Oxford significantly expanded professional training programs from the 1970s onwards and both universities opened up business schools during the 1990s. In addition, collaborations with industry became widely accepted in academic research. An analysis of all publications by Cambridge scientists in academic journals demonstrates an almost twelve-fold increase in the number of publications with industrial partners over the period 1977–2007 from 18 to 213 publications per year.[1]

Third, perennial budget-cutting by the Conservative reform movement further weakened the position of British universities in new science-driven industries that have emerged since the 1980s, in which innovation is driven by advances in basic science. These industries, which include the bio-, information and clean technology industries were able to prosper around major American universities in clusters such as Silicon Valley and Route 128 during the 1980s and 1990s as a result of significant funding commitments to basic science of the American federal government but mostly failed to take off in the UK (Saxenian 1994, Jong 2006, Kenney 1986). The fiscal austerity measures of the Conservative reform movement further lowered British universities' science budgets which had already been low by OECD standards. As a result, with the exception of subfields such as genome sequencing, in which charities such as the Wellcome Trust and Cancer Research UK had taken up an important role, British universities faced increasing challenges during the 1980s and 1990s in competing in fundamental research fields driving innovation in novel industries.

Holding a more positive attitude towards the role of government in society, the successive Labour governments undertook efforts to improve conditions for fundamental scientific research in the United Kingdom and science at British universities enjoyed somewhat of a renaissance. However, although Labour undertook efforts during the late 1990s and 2000s to improve infrastructures for scientific research after years of financial cutbacks, these efforts were inadequate in closing the gap in R&D spending with other major political economies such as that of the United States. For 2009, funding appropriated by the American federal government for science and technology was $151.1 billion (≈£100.3 billion), which excludes $16 billion (≈£10.6 billion) appropriated for R&D in the 2009 stimulus package.[2] In contrast, the UK science budget was £4 billion for the 2010/2011 budget year (Department for Innovation, Universities and Skills 2007). Thus, based on these figures, even after the funding increases under Labour, American federal *per capita* spending on science and technology has remained at roughly five times the level of the UK science budget. This gap is likely to further increase in the near future as the return of the Tories to government in 2010 has witnessed a renewed embrace of Thatcherite budgetary policies in the academic realm.

Finally, the British Conservative university reform movement of the 1980s did not only leave a strong imprint on the British system of higher learning, but on systems of higher learning in other countries also. With the notable exception of the American system, which seems to have remained mostly immune to the ideas of this movement, governments across the industrialized world have embraced the new British bureaucratic agencies and governance structures as institutional models in their own higher education policies. The impact of the Conservative reform movement has been particularly felt across the European continent with governments moving away from their distinctive national academic funding and governance models in favor of British models.

For example, institutional governance mechanisms for the common 'marketplace' for higher learning created by European Union governments through the Bologna process that began in 1999 mirror those put in place in the UK. Across the European Union efforts are under way to abandon national academic degree cycles, traditions in awarding academic credit, and organizing university careers along the lines of British ones. For example, a critical aim of the Bologna process has been to create European-wide quality assurance mechanisms, mostly modeled on institutions pioneered by the British Conservative reform movement such as the UK Quality Assurance Agency for Higher Education and Research Assessment Exercises. For example, in 2005 European Ministers of Education adopted common 'Standards and Guidelines for Quality Assurance in the European Higher Education Area' similar to those in place in the UK that had been drafted by the European Network for Quality Assurance in Higher Education established in 2000 as a part of the Bologna process. Moreover, to implement these standards and guidelines across European countries, the European Quality Assurance Register for Higher Education was formed in 2007.

REASSESSING ACADEMIA'S PLACE IN MODERN POLITICAL ECONOMIES

The historical account of changes in the British system of higher learning over the past decades presented here has highlighted how universities are center stage in shaping the development of modern political economies. In particular, as these economies have become more 'knowledge intensive', it has become increasingly important to examine more in-depth how the institutional set-up of university systems determines how a nation's intellectual resources are deployed. This chapter on the development of the British system of higher learning following the ascent of the Tories to power in 1979 has sought to highlight how the institutional frameworks governing academia are linked into broader institutional shifts in political economies. Moreover, it has opened up avenues for future scholarship in the varieties of capitalism tradition to develop a more in-depth and systematic understanding of how these shifts across different national contexts affect critical social and economic outcomes that are used to measure the performance of modern political economies.

Complementing insights from the varieties of capitalism literature on the institutional set-up of labor and financial markets, this chapter has highlighted three dimensions along which the institutional set-up of national systems of higher education shape contemporary capitalist societies. First, like other civic institutions, autonomous scholarly communities at universities form a potential counterweight to the power of the central state and forces of free marketeering. The observations in this chapter show how British scholarly communities played such a role up until the dawn of the Thatcher era. Future varieties of capitalism analyses will be able to build on these observations and examine in more depth the relationship between the organization of national intellectual elites and the power of the central state as well as that of market actors.

Second, this chapter has shown how the set-up of academic institutions plays a role that complements the role of labor and financial institutions in the *governance* of economic life in capitalist systems. As the observations in this chapter about institutional shifts in the British system of higher learning underline, these shifts were integral to a broader shift in the British capitalist system towards a greater reliance on private, market-based governance models in the economy. The reorientation of the academic system towards more utilitarian goals was explicitly linked by the Conservative reform movement to the empowerment of private enterprise at the expense of coordinated models of governance in the British economy. Future scholarship in the varieties of capitalism literature should explore further the mechanisms through which systems of higher education play a role in such processes of institutional change that alter governance models guiding economic activity in contemporary societies.

Third, this chapter has outlined how the institutional set-up of national systems of higher learning potentially plays a role in supporting the competitive advantage of firms in certain industries. As universities have come to play an increasingly important role over the past decades in cultivating the expertise and skills firms require in gaining a competitive advantage in today's so-called knowledge-based societies, the world of academia has become critical in supporting the economic performance of firms in a range of high-tech sectors. Observations in this chapter about efforts to tighten links between the realms of academia and business, such as the formation of the British Technology Strategy Board and the incorporation of indicators of involvement in technology transfer as bureaucratic measures of academic performance, underline the efforts governments are undertaking to adapt capitalist systems to new modes of science-based innovation. Building on observations made in this study of the UK case, there is an opportunity for future studies in the varieties of capitalism tradition to carry out more expansive comparative studies on the effectiveness of different national academic support infrastructures for these new modes of innovation.

NOTES

1. ISI Web of Science publications by scientists of the University of Cambridge co-authored with scientists affiliated with firms listed as being a Limited Company (Ltd) or Incorporated (Inc).
2. Available at http://www.aaas.org/spp/rd/omnibus09.htm and http://www.aaas.org/spp/rd/stim09h.htm (accessed 26 June 2010).

BIBLIOGRAPHY

Anderson, R.D. (2006), *British Universities: Past and Present*, London: Hambledon Continuum.

Anderson, R.D. (1992), *Universities and Elites in Britain since 1800*, Basingstoke, Hampshire and London: Macmillan.

Barnett, C. (1972), *The Collapse of British Power*, New York: William Morrow & Co.

Beer, S.H. (1982), *Britain against Itself: The Political Contradictions of Collectivism*, London: W.W. Norton.

Berdahl, R. (1990), 'Academic freedom, autonomy and accountability in British universities', *Studies in Higher Education*, **15** (2), 169–80.

Boyer, R. and J.R. Hollingsworth (1997), *Contemporary Capitalism: The Embeddedness of Institutions*, Cambridge: Cambridge University Press.

Clery, D. (2007), 'Blair Departs After a Decade of Strong Support for Science', *Science* **316** (5827), 965–66.

Crouch, C. and W. Streeck (1997), *Political Economy of Modern Capitalism: Mapping Convergence and Diversity*, London: Sage.

Department of Business, Innovation and Skills (2010), *Participation Rates in Higher Education: Academic Years 2006/2007–2008/2009 (provisional)*, http://stats.berr.gov.uk/he/Participation_Rates_in_HE_2008–09.pdf (accessed 12 September 2010).

Department for Innovation, Universities and Skills (2007), The Allocations of the Science Budget 2008/09 to 2010/11, downloadable from http://www.bis.gov.uk/policies/science/science-funding (accessed 12 September 2010).

Hall, P.A. and D. Soskice (eds) (2001), *Varieties of Capitalism: The Institutional Foundations of Comparative Advantage*, Oxford: Oxford University Press.

HEFCE (2007), 'HEFCE announces £3.4 billion for teaching and research for 1997–98', HEFCE press release, 27 February 1997.

Hodson, P. and H. Thomas (2003), 'Quality assurance in Higher Education: Fit for the new millennium or simply year 2000 compliant?', *Higher Education* **45** (3), 375–87.

Jong, S. (2007), 'Scientific communities and the birth of new industries. How academic institutions supported the formation of new biotech industries in three regions', PhD dissertation, European University Institute, Florence, Italy.

Jong, S. (2006), 'How organizational structures in science shape spin-off firms; the biochemistry departments of Berkeley, Stanford and UCSF, and the birth of the biotech industry,' *Industrial and Corporate Change*, **15** (2), 251–83.

Kenney, M. (1986), *Biotechnology: The University Industrial Complex*, New Haven: Yale University Press.

Leavis, F.R. (1962), *Two Cultures? The Significance of C.P. Snow*, London: Chatto & Windus.

OECD (2009), *Education at a Glance 2009: OECD Indicators*, Paris: OECD.

Ortolano, G. (2009), *The Two Cultures Controversy: Science, Literature and Cultural Politics in Postwar Britain*, Cambridge: Cambridge University Press.

RAE (2009), 'Manager's report', available at http://www.rae.ac.uk/pubs/2009/manager/ (accessed 3 July 2010).

RAE (2008), 'History of the RAE', available at http://www.rae.ac.uk/aboutus/history.asp (accessed 3 July 2010).

Rook, A., M. Carlton and W. Graham Cannon (1991), *The History of Addenbrooke's Hospital*, Cambridge: University of Cambridge Press.

Saxenian, A. (1994), *Regional Advantage: Culture and Competition in Silicon Valley and Route 128*, Cambridge: Harvard University Press.

Shallock, M. (1989), 'Thatcherism and British Higher Education: Universities and the Enterprise Culture', *Change*, **21** (5), 30–39.

Snow, C.P. (1959), *The Two Cultures and The Scientific Revolution – The Rede Lecture 1959*, New York: Cambridge University Press.

Trow, M. (1998), 'Through the Revolution and out the Other Side,' *Oxford Review of Education*, **24** (1), 111–29.

Wiener, M. (1981), *English Culture and the Decline of the Industrial Spirit, 1850–1980*, Cambridge: Cambridge University Press.

6. Industrial relations *after* European state traditions?[1]

Guglielmo Meardi

INTRODUCTION

This chapter reviews and assesses theoretical approaches to the role of state traditions in comparative European industrial relations, in the light of increased internationalisation and specifically Europeanisation of work since the 1990s.

A first section will discuss the interaction between state and national research traditions in industrial relations, assessing Frege's (2007) work. It will be argued that Frege's account, by focusing on Germany–Anglo-American contrast, like the Varieties of Capitalism approach (Hall and Soskice 2001), underestimates differences among continental European countries. In particular, while the role of the state and of politics is more visible across the whole of continental Europe compared with the US (although not necessarily more important), its functioning varies country by country. In particular, the relation between state and society is conceived differently depending on the constitutional origins of the state itself, as is especially clear in the contrast between France and Germany. The roles of agriculture and of Catholicism also explain important intra-European differences in the link between state and industrial relations, in particular through the legacy of anarchosyndicalism.

The second section reviews different approaches to comparative industrial relations and focuses on Crouch's approach developed in *Industrial Relations and European State Traditions* (1993) as that best-suited for the understanding of the state. This work has distinctive strengths. First, unlike primarily economic approaches (e.g. Clegg 1976; Kassalow 1969) or primarily political approaches (e.g. Lipset 1983), it manages to combine political and economic variables, especially through attention to those European institutions that are at the same time economic and political. Second, in relation specifically to approaches developed in the Anglo-Saxon world, its historic sensitivity goes particularly far in avoiding ethnocentric standpoints, such as those betrayed by Dunlop (1958), but also by

Clegg (1976). Third, it includes a long-term historical perspective on the state and industrial relations.

The third part will provide a critical assessment of Crouch's work and of its reliance on 'state traditions' in relation to debates on globalisation and industrial relations theory (Giles 2000). This discussion will be rooted in the assessment of three important post-1992 transnational pressures relating to the internationalisation (and more specifically Europeanisation) of the three main industrial relations sides: capital, labour and the state. These three processes of internationalisation refer to the role of multi-national companies, the role of migration (and specifically intra-EU migration after the 2004 enlargement), and EU policies on employment (notably the European Employment Strategy and the promotion of the so-called 'soft acquis communautaire' to the new EU members). These developments challenge the claimed relevance of state traditions and call for a more nuanced categorisation of national models and of their dynamics, which was proposed by Crouch nearly 20 years ago.

The discussion is mostly theoretical but will also draw on an on-going analysis of change in industrial relations in the EU.[2]

NATIONAL RESEARCH TRADITIONS IN EUROPEAN INDUSTRIAL RELATIONS

In her account of employment relations research traditions, Frege (2007) has highlighted how different nations differ. In particular, she pointed at the different form of politicisation of industrial relations, which is deemed to have been stronger in Germany than in Anglophone countries. This, in turn, would have had theoretical and methodological implications, with a preference for political science and interpretative methods on the actors in Germany, contrasting with economic or psychology-inspired studies and quantitative methods in the US and, to a lesser extent, in the UK. The distinction drawn by Frege relates directly to the role of the state in shaping the understanding, not just the regulation, of industrial relations. There are clear differences between continental European and Anglophone environments in this respect. In comparison with the US, the longer history of European states, their interdependence due to unstable borders, the high density of population all contribute to the prominence of European concerns with social order and governance, which generally overshadow concerns with markets, efficiency and individual organisations. More recently, the emergence of the European Union as an actor and a level for industrial relations (Marginson and Sisson 2004) increases the reasons for distinguishing between Europe and America. Theoretically,

Frege's observation of German liking for Weber and Marx and other theoretical tradition differences from the US (Frege 2007, 39–40) relates to a more meta-theoretical aspect, that is, the contrast, however stylised, between a 'continental philosophy' preferring the role of critique (from idealism, to Marxism and post-modernism[3]) and an 'analytical' philosophy of Anglophone roots, opting for a more soberly sceptical empiricism. The methodological differences detected by Frege between German and Anglophone publications may then reflect deeper intellectual differences originating in different education systems, with the humanities being more central and more strictly related to state traditions in continental European countries (Frege 2007, 177–8; see also Jong in Chapter 5 of this volume).

Yet while Frege is accurate in detecting the differences between continental European and Anglophone traditions, and at second order differences between UK and US, she neglects differences among continental European countries by treating Germany as a 'typical example of Continental Europe' (Frege 2003, 243). Even if conceding the existence of 'substantial differences of industrial relations research within each region', Frege argues that 'differences within each region are weaker than the (inter-cultural) differences between the two regions' (ibid.). But while she then devotes a large space of her 2007 book to the actual differences between British and US industrial relations traditions, she never goes back to test the assumption of German typical representativeness of continental Europe, for which she provides only the evidence from 'personal communication with various European experts' (Frege 2003, 256). In fact, there are major differences across continental European countries. Frege (following Wagner et al. (1991)) detects in Weber the distinctive theoretical influence of continental European industrial relations, as opposed to US-typical functionalism. However, the most popular sociological introduction to industrial relations in France (Lallement 1996) discusses, as sociological foundations of industrial relations, Marx and Durkheim. The former has been largely 'mainstreamed' into British industrial relations (e.g. Hyman 1989; Blyton and Turnbull 2004; Darlington 2009), while the latter is the founder of functionalism, which was to shape industrial relations studies in the US; in contrast, Weber is omitted, but not through ignorance as Lallement has written a book on the founder of *verstehende Soziologie*. A more recent French industrial relations handbook (Bevort and Jobert 2008) imports the theoretical framework directly from the Anglophone world (the Webbs and Dunlop), combining it with those French authors (e.g. Reynaud) most influenced by functionalism (even if revising it deeply). Also methodologically, the qualitative–quantitative divide between Europe and the Anglophone world identified by Frege does not account for France appropriately, the most important empirical source being the workplace survey REPONSE, directly parallel to the British WERS in both method and interpretation (Amossé et al. 2008). The less central European countries have been even more open to Anglophone influences, also because of their weaker confidence in their own traditions. Dunlop's and the Oxford's school have been all translated into Italian, unlike into French or German,[4] and Central Eastern European countries have been even more open to Anglo-American influences. The European continent is indeed very diverse.

Without challenging the Frege's core argument on a difference between Anglophone and continental Europe, I will challenge her implicit point that differences among continental European countries matter less than those between UK and US. This will be done by refocusing exactly on the state traditions role that Frege refers to: if state traditions are crucial, it follows that (despite any German military and theoretical efforts) individual European countries have different traditions.

A first reason why there are differences among continental European countries is the role of political culture and language. Its relevance for employment and social policies has been described very effectively by Barbier (2008). In this respect it is apparent that the gap among European countries is greater than that between US and UK, owing to academic and linguistic proximities shared by the latter two. For instance, Barbier illustrates the differences between the French *question sociale* and the German *Arbeiterfrage*. As Hyman (2004: 273) put it, the reason for ethnocentrism in comparative industrial relations is that 'industrial relations scholars speak different languages', which is an issue in Europe more than between UK and US.

If the state is placed at the centre of the analysis, than the issue is not exactly between situations where the state has little relevance (the Anglophone countries and especially the US) and those where it is central. Indeed, welfare state coverage and labour market regulations differ massively between continental Europe and Anglophone countries. Yet it may be more a matter of different forms of state relevance rather than a dichotomy between state or non-state, or even a one-dimensional continuum between more and less state. Economic sociology has shown that the role of government in shaping economic and social relations in the US is, for instance, as crucial as elsewhere (Fligstein 2002). Even more, the size of the 'economic stimulus' packages and the nationalisation of banks in the US and UK following the financial crisis of 2007–08, and the return of industrial policy suggests that what matters is not simply the actual role of the state at a given moment, but rather its potential role. Once needed, British and American governments intervened massively into the economy, to compensate for the lack of planned intervention that characterises continental European countries. The size of the stimulus packages of 2008–09 was equal to 81 per cent of the GDP in the US, 82 per cent in the UK and as much as 267 per cent in Ireland – as against 22 per cent in Germany and 19 per cent in 'statist' France (IMF data). Rather than an alternative between intervention and non-intervention, we witness alternatives between different forms of intervention.

If we focus on the form of the state, rather than its 'dominance', it emerges that state traditions, if all are relevant across Europe, can be very different from each other. This can be easily exemplified by the Franco-German contrasts in constitutional traditions. The French *République* has an ontological priority over *le peuple* in France, as the French people itself, as citizenship, is constructed by the 'Republic' and the act of the Revolution. By contrast, the German state, while a philosophically grand concept, is ontologically secondary to *das Volk*. In other words, one is a *citoyen* and therefore French, while one is German and therefore a German citizen (Brubaker 1992), other European states (e.g. Italy or Poland) combining elements of both models. A major implication is the scepticism of the French state towards any particularism or group right, whether cultural or social, and its strong rejection of corporatism – which instead characterises much of the Germanic world. In most classic typologies of corporatism (Crouch 1993, 14), France is as far away from corporatism and from Germany as the UK and the US. Indeed, the concept itself of corporatism is hardly understood in the French context, *corporatisme* referring rather to actors' sectionalism (in this sense, French observers actually characterise France as corporatist). Much of the German, or German-inspired industrial relations reflection on associational governance, therefore, is alien to the French context, which prefers to focus on concepts such as conflict and participation. The political traditions are different between the two countries. According to Lipset's model, French and German labour movements occupy opposite cases (Lipset 1983). The French received early political rights, but late social rights, resulting in moderated socialist parties but radical unions; while exactly the opposite was the case in Germany. Also, the roles of agriculture and of the Catholic Church explain the importance of anarchosyndicalist traditions in countries such as France, Spain and Italy, but not UK, Netherlands or Germany. If, then, countries are so different, how can we study them together?

THE SHORTCOMINGS OF TYPOLOGIES

A reasonable way to overcome the interpretative difficulty of national variation is to raise the level of abstraction and detect 'types' according to the theory-based most important variables. However, existing typologies of industrial relations systems are strikingly out-of-date. The period of most intensive production of comparative industrial relations studies was around 1990 (e.g. Baglioni and Crouch 1990; Bamber and Lansbury 1987; Bean 1994; Crouch 1993; Ferner and Hyman 1992, 1994 and 1998; Van Ruysseveldt and Visser 1996). The following two decades, while still producing a large amount of research, ideas and findings, have not offered any integrated effort at understanding industrial relations comparatively. The most important works have appeared in the form of policy-oriented reports (e.g. the European Commission's *Industrial Relations in Europe Reports* and the European Industrial Relations Observatory) or contributions to specific, if important issues (e.g. Traxler et al. 2001; Hyman 2001; Frege and Kelly 2004; Marginson and Sisson 2004).

One limit of industrial relations typologies is the shortage of large-scale qualitative studies including a sufficiently high number of countries and dimensions. Most large-scale studies are quantitative and only focus on simple quantifiable dimensions of unionism: union density, collective bargaining coverage, strike volume, sometimes integrated by qualitative but still one-dimensional variables such as collective bargaining centralisation. Apart from the notorious limitations of data on these dimensions, these are actually the variables on which scepticism is most appropriate: being a union member and going on strike have completely different meanings in different contexts (Hyman 2001). On the other side, most qualitative studies – which could lead to more elaborated typologies – generally focus on very few countries, for evident reasons of feasibility. With rare commendable exceptions, they focus on a maximum of six countries, but more commonly two or three. Moreover, many studies have an Anglo-Saxon bias. Some only include Anglophone countries (e.g. the six ones in Fairbrother and Griffin 2002). Narrowing down the boundaries of the comparison to one ethnic area may be appropriate methodologically, but the implications of this are rarely considered and the generalisability of the findings is undermined. Other studies include non-Anglophone countries, but they do not treat them equally: they rely on them for secondary sources, mostly in English (risking a landslide effect of ethnocentric distortion) and they analyse them through a different lens, more 'cultural' and less 'rational'. Dunlop's classic study is an example (Dunlop 1958): the further you move away from the American rational system, the more politicised distortions you will find.

Some studies however manage to build theoretical comparisons across countries. An important example is Clegg's (1976) elegant theory: the main dimensions of union organisation and action depend on the main dimensions of collective bargaining, which, in turn, depend on the structure of the employers' side. The causal links in Clegg's theory have been widely criticised, and although in general it is true that employers' structure is associated with the form of collective bargaining more than union structure is (Traxler et al. 2001: 291), later developments have suggested that this is not always the case. Collective bargaining structure may also depend on other actors such as the state (France after 1982, and again after 1998) or the trade unions (Italy, in the 1970s), or on all three actors together (Italy, after 1992). But the main point here is another one, as noted by Frege and Kelly (2003: 11): 'Clegg's emphasis on collective bargaining seems too embedded in an Anglo-American understanding of industrial relations to be able to account for cross-national differences'. Moreover, the idea of unions being determined by (and 'under') collective bargaining reduces the scope for the study of trade unions as changing and active actors, as the study of union strategies does.

Moving away from Anglophone studies, similar considerations can be made about the French work by Martinet (1979), according to which seven countries coincide with *sept syndicalismes*, each different and unique, but with some broad 'groupings'. Martinet provides some graphic illustration of how different models of unionism can be contrasted: 'compared to these [British, US and German union officers] disciplined sergeants of the great labour army, the Latin militants – French, Italian, Spanish, Portuguese – often look like guerrilla fighters' (Martinet 1979). With a rhetoric effort, Martinet manages to put the Latin unions in a better light than the Anglo-Saxon ones, but the core of the distinction remains the same. Another typology with an 'ethnic' flavour is the one by Slomp (1996), distinguishing between 'British', 'Germanic', 'Latin' and 'Central European' unions, although allowing for a couple of non-ethnic exceptions (Greece, Finland and arguably Bulgaria).

Visser's (1996) analysis of industrial relations system is probably the most relevant today, and it has been updated in the *Industrial Relations in Europe Report* of 2008 with substantial quantitative data (European Commission 2008). Visser draws a direct link between industrial relations systems and trade unions, although not in a mono-causal way as Clegg. In the *Industrial Relations in Europe Report*, he draws useful links between industrial relations and production, welfare and employment regimes. The outcome is the detection of five geographic clusters in Europe: North (organised corporatism), Centre-west (social partnership), South (polarised/state centred), West (liberal pluralism) and Centre-east (fragmented/state centred).

By contrast, other authors have tried to move beyond the risk of national typologies. Hyman (2001) distinguishes clearly between ideal types and historical configurations, something the Varieties of Capitalisms approach, with its predilection for USA–Germany dichotomies, has been criticised for not doing (Crouch 2005). Three pure models of trade union-ism ('the eternal triangle') are identified: market, society and class, which can be differently combined in each country. As they are ideal types, these models are, in their pure form, unsustainable in the long term. Actually existing unionism is therefore based on compromises between two of these models, which are themselves unstable. These are exemplified by Britain (market and class), Germany (society and market), and Italy (class and society). The main contributions of Hyman's framework are the challenge to the most stereotyped versions of union models as based on one charac-ter only, the explanation of 'changes' and 'movements' within the triangle, and the provision of 'transnational' theoretical concepts that may be used for comparative purposes. On the other side, the extraordinary theoretical elegance of the triangular model is based on very high abstraction, which is of limited help for a detailed analysis of industrial relations.

Another, more systematic and descriptive, cross-national typology of unions is provided by Cella and Treu (2001). While drawing in part on Clegg, Cella and Treu's additional insight is the distinction among unions *within* countries and not only *between* countries, although such attention to detail remains basically limited to their own home country, Italy, given the impossibility of putting the two main Italian confederations (CGIL and CISL) within the same 'model'.

'Geographic' typologies are not altogether wrong, obviously, and Visser's effort is particularly convincing as a descriptive device. The problem is when the identification of 'clusters' is transformed, from a descriptive/analytical device, into an explanatory one, which is not what clusters can offer. The fact that two countries are, at a given moment in time, in the same position does not imply that they are moving in the same direction.

But doubts can also be raised on the 'methodological nationalism' of these typologies. The distinction between national frameworks is relevant for the many factors that have been historically constructed along (mainly) national lines, such as the political space or legal support. However, typologies often neglect to explicitly state what factors are 'national', to what extent and why. Indeed path-dependency is a reality in industrial relations (e.g. Traxler et al. 2001). Path-dependency theory, if it is trying to come to terms with the problem of how to explain change (e.g. Crouch and Farrell 2002), still has difficulties in allowing for external influences. Indeed, external influences may be treated as external shocks, but this is of little help when they are frequent and their impact is changeable, as will be discussed in the next section.

The same fact of using the prescription-flavoured term 'models' exaggerates the internal coherence and continuity of union types, as if they had their own comprehensive logic (an essence) instead of a number of competing dynamics. This is all the more true for the approaches that also speak of 'systems', but to an extent remains true even for the most dialectic and dynamic approaches like Hyman's (who defines unions as 'contested organisations'). The effect is the exaggeration, and often distortion, of differences between countries. In what sense are British trade unions politically more 'moderate' than Italian ones (Lipset 1983), after an increasing number of British unions is led by leftists deserving the nickname of 'awkward squad' while Italian CISL and UIL collaborate with a right-wing government such as Berlusconi's? Ten years of teaching comparative industrial relations has taught me that typologies, rather than being useful introductory concepts, act as easy stereotypes and barriers to in-depth thinking on actual industrial relations dynamics.

National typologies overestimate homogeneity within countries. Within a country different sectors may display very different industrial relations structures (Bechter et al. 2012). And, within a country, different 'types' of trade unions may coexist. CISL and CGIL, FO and CGT, LO and TCO, Solidarity and OPZZ are not just competing organisations within the same model – they represent radically different meanings of trade unionism. As unions are largely opposition bodies, it is actually normal for them to aspire to different models than those of their own countries. For instance, the distinction between CISL and CGIL is not just political: CISL built its own identity around the priority of collective bargaining in a way strongly influenced by American models, and its horizontal structures are pale additions in comparison to CGIL's strong *Camere del Lavoro*. Similarly, CGT-FO stresses the importance of bargaining and promotes a form of a political 'bread-and-butter' unionism that does not correspond to the 'Latin' image (although it also includes a significant Trotskyist minority). Differences in terms of 'union models' could not be larger in the case of the two main competing Polish unions: horizontally-structured, social-movement oriented Solidarity versus industrially-organised, social partnership oriented OPZZ.

One important aspect where national model can be internally diversified is gender. This has been neglected by classic typologies, which have been drawn around male workers' profiles but assumed to be working in the same way for female workers. Yet, for instance, German employee representation institutions work very differently for men and women, and the high degree of associational strength of the former cannot be extended to the latter (Hassel 2007). The neglect of gender is, in a way, paradoxical for approaches that stress national differences, because gender relations are strongly embedded in national cultures and regimes (see Jurado Guerrero et al., Chapter 4 in this volume), which in turn interacts with industrial relations and welfare (O'Reilly and Spee 1998); yet the consideration of gender would have probably modified the dominant national stereotypes and has therefore been sidelined.

Some important studies of European trade unionism in the last decade have departed from national-level institutionalism. A French study of 'everyday' unionism in France, Germany, Britain and Italy (Dufour and Hege 2002) directly questioned the representation of different national unions based on different institutions. Seen from the shopfloor, unions reveal to Dufour and Hege striking cross-national similarity in processes and dilemmas. For instance, the distinction between dual channels of representation (unions and works councils), which is generally seen as crucially important in shaping industrial relations, emerges as a very complicated affair, with major confusions of roles between the two. As a result, the meaning of popular labels such as 'co-determination' for Germany is questioned: 'nobody [among German representatives] would even think of analysing representative action from the perspective of co-determination rights' (66). The general lesson is that 'actors inscribe their strategies in logics that go beyond the 'rationality' of institutions' (75). National frameworks do not determine unions: local representation has its own social dynamics that do not remain within the existing rules and structures and cannot be deducted from its institutions (186). Similar implications derive from studies of union 'revitalisation', which assume a capacity by the actors to contest and transform the situations they are in (Frege and Kelly 2004; Heery 2008). Union revitalisation also opens a new space for transnational learning: 'it is time to move beyond union jingoism: labour everywhere needs to learn and import lessons from abroad' (Baccaro et al. 2003: 130).

An additional, apparently more accidental limitation is that existing typologies are still unable to classify unions in post-communist countries, abandoned in an undifferentiated residual group of (post) state-socialist unionism. The most recent account (European Commission 2008), interestingly, leaves a number of major question marks on the 'Centre-east' cluster. Statist or liberal economy? Segmented or residual welfare? Yet a less static analysis would point to the fact that in central eastern Europe the 'statist' and 'segmented welfare' dimensions are largely residual legacies from the past, which are gradually declining to leave space for much more flexible employment regimes (Meardi 2012).

Crouch's work stands out in the literature. His *Industrial Relations and European State Traditions* (Crouch 1993), as a single-authored work based on extensive in-depth knowledge and contextualisation, marked a clear departure from previous comparative studies. It avoided the two main limitations we have identified: ethnocentrism and the over-use of the idea of 'models' as coherent, permanent, uncontaminated and internally homogeneous types (e.g. much of the earlier literature on 'corporatism'). Crouch's book covers the largest number of European countries and the longest period. Such scope allows for the inclusion of more variables, from the 'strength' of labour to the role of the 'exposed' sector, and therefore avoids simplifications, for instance, providing a more nuanced understanding of 'corporatism'. The distinction between models of industrial relations is purely theoretical and does not pretend to portray all historical situations that are then investigated.

An original argument made by Crouch relates to the role of political traditions. This can be summarised by three main propositions: pre-industrial corporatist traditions foster strong, political unionism; Catholicism fosters divided, political unionism; and liberal traditions foster weak, fragmented unionism. These propositions only partially overlap with the theoretical distinctions of industrial relations models, but within the historical complexity of Europe the association is still quite strong. Crouch's approach also allows for change, notably in the UK, which is seen as moving (against American evolutionary approaches like Dunlop's) from pluralism to (shy) corporatist attempts and eventually contestation, to then oscillate within a flexible employment regime (Crouch 2003, 2010).

THREE TRANSNATIONAL TESTS FOR STATE TRADITIONS

However, there are reasons for departing from Crouch's work of 1993 in some respects. First, the process of internationalisation has accelerated (Gumbrell-McCormick 2008), leading to the debates on so-called globalisation. From a globalisation perspectives, implying that 'the international is no less "social" than other levels' (Giles 2000, 180), Giles criticises the dominant view of unions as rooted in a specific national societies and cultures. For instance,

> unionism, despite its many national variations, is an international phenomenon *par excellence*: national trade union movements were not constructed out of whole cloth, but were each shaped, from their very origins, through the transnational diffusion of ideas, practices and organisational forms. (187)

Indeed, trends in wage development, class structure and industrial relations are not encapsulated in national settings (Hasse and Leiulfsrud 2002). Giles's point may suffer from an insufficiently clear definition of 'globalisation', but the overall meaning seems plain: in order to challenge the normative and determinist versions of the globalisation discourse, what is required is a serious engagement with the 'international'. By contrast, a withdrawal into the 'national' (such as in the Varieties of Capitalism approach) involves self-exclusion from the international level. Such criticism, as Giles himself acknowledges (177), converges in the critique of methodological nationalism with Locke's (1992) argument on the emergence of sub-national models, something that has increasingly attracted Crouch analysis (Crouch et al. 2001; Burroni, Chapter 10 in this volume). If there are such similarities across nations on one side, and differences within nations on the other, the primacy of national systems is to be questioned. Cross-border influences, imitation, and linkages, as they are emerging for instance in border regions within the European Union, call for a revision of national modelling, which otherwise can reproduce stereotypes, make cross-border dialogue more difficult and even turn into self-fulfilling prophecies.

Within Europe, in particular, international integration has made major leaps forward after *Industrial Relations and European State Traditions* was written: EMU, European Employment Strategy, increases in foreign direct investment and migration, and eastwards enlargement (Crouch only considered Western Europe). These have affected all three main actors of industrial relations: capital, labour and the state. If capital and labour are no longer tied to national boundaries, the regulatory power of the state is undermined; moreover, the development of intergovernmental and supranational institutions and policies limits the discretion of national states themselves. In this section, I will review the evidence on the internationalisation of all three actors in the EU.

Capital

The freedom of movement of capital and the rise of multinational corporations has been the main reason for concern for the future of national-level social regulations in the last two decades. Crouch himself expressed concern with multinationals' power to bypass national democratic regulations (Crouch 2004). These concerns relate to the capacity of multinationals to engage in 'regime shopping' and force a 'race to the bottom' in labour standards. Indeed, there have been several prominent cases of multinationals relocating their operations in order to avoid union power, starting from the Hoover case of relocation from Dijon in France to Cambuslang in Scotland in 1993. These cases multiplied after the 2004 EU enlargement eastwards increased the variation of employment conditions and regulations among EU member states. Companies such as Bosch and Siemens forced western workforces into concession bargaining under relocation threats, and companies like Hyundai, when deciding the location of its planned European investment, engaged in a sort of 'beauty contest' among the new member states of 2004, inducing national governments to compete on the grounds of concessions to employers.

Yet there are still doubts about the actual extent of such increase of the power of capital over national states. Data on relocations, for instance, are patchy and the interpretation is not straightforward. Most official estimates indicate that jobs are very rarely transferred abroad (Watt et al. 2008). Data from the European Restructuring Monitor (ERM) suggest that between 2005 and 2008 (before the shock of the recession destabilised all labour markets) 5.3 percent of job losses across the EU were due to international relocations, much less than those due to bankruptcy or internal restructuring. ERM data are not statistically representative and they may well be an over-representation of the reality owing to the higher reporting, and media impact, of redundancies related to relocations. The relocations recorded by the ERM in this period accounted for 108 000 job losses, which is not a macroscopic figure but it is sufficient to raise public interest and to act as a deterrent to states and workers (and indeed are dramatic events for those affected).

In terms of overall investment flows, some studies found evidence of 'regime shopping' in the significant correlation between US companies' investment flows and industrial relations: US multinationals, economic conditions and human capital being equal, seem to prefer countries with no statutory works councils and no legal extension of collective bargaining (Cooke 2001). However, more recent studies on the same US investment flows have challenged such finding within the EU context (Brandl et al. 2010). Studies such as the one by Cooke control for national market size, arguing that many multinationals choose to locate their operations for market access reasons; therefore, as most countries in Europe with weak industrial relations are small (most of the new EU member states) while some of the more regulated ones are large (Germany, France, Italy), large investment flows into small countries, such as Hungary or Slovakia, must be due to specific competitiveness reasons, such as favourable industrial relations settings. Brandl et al. disagree because the EU, having removed all tariff and non-tariff barriers to trade, is a 'macro-market' where national boundaries are redundant: in manufacturing, companies are free to locate their operations in Slovakia and serve the German market from there. If the control for market size is removed, the correlation between industrial relations and foreign direct investment disappears, and 'regime shopping' appears as largely a false alarm.

Qualitative research on this topic confirms the complexity of defining what a relocation is and why it happens (Meardi et al. 2009). It also shows that it is the 'threat' of relocations, rather than its actual occurrence, which permeate employment relations climates in European companies as well as in national debates. A review of multinationals and collective bargaining, however, shows that overall MNCs tend to respect the structure of collective bargaining in the EU, and that there have been cases of union mobilisation and regulatory adaptations to resist the disruptions that multinational capital can cause (Marginson and Meardi 2009). In only two, particularly economically dependent countries (Estonia and Latvia) multinationals seem to be covered by collective bargaining less than national companies. It is, in a way, a matter of employers 'barking' rather than 'biting' (Raess and Burgoon 2006). Barks often have real effects (concession bargaining and employer-friendly legal reforms), but the effects themselves depend on national reactions, not simply on the barks alone: states, therefore, still have a big role to play.

Labour

Until recently, labour mobility was neglected and it was assumed that labour was by definition 'local' in contrast with capital becoming 'global'. In the old EU, less than 2 per cent of EU nationals worked in a different country from their own. While it is true that the mobility potential of capital exceeds that of labour, recent years have challenged the relevance of such an assumption. The EU enlargement of 2004–07 has produced a massive movement of labour to affecting the balance of power in employment relations in the receiving countries but especially in the sending ones (Meardi 2012). Moreover, this movement is largely different from traditional 'migration', as it is mostly circular and transnational. Workers have proved to be able to engage in some activities that characterised multinational companies: regime shopping, coercive comparisons forcing employer concessions, relocation threats. The concern with employee retention has amplified in central eastern Europe among employers but also governments. Some have developed incentives for their workers to return and policies to prevent brain drain, if rather inconclusively. More importantly, countries such as Poland and Latvia have had to consider emigration constraints and the risk of losing core public sector employees when contemplating devaluation and public sector pay cuts.

Migration also affects receiving countries. Migrants provide important tests for national industrial relations for two reasons. First, 'outsider' status makes foreigners privileged revelatory observers of national arrangements, as argued by classic sociologists (Simmel 1908). For instance, the way diversity management is implemented and is faced by trade unions in different European companies is revealing of the nature of national systems (Wrench 2004, Marino 2012). In this respect, there are also some elements of international convergence, such as the increased attention for diversity management in France (Wieviorka 2008), parallel to its declining popularity in the UK.

Secondly, for a long time migrants have had a crucial role in 'contaminating' national labour movements: even the emergence of the Industrial Relations Commission in the US Congress in 1912, and therefore of industrial relations as a field of research, was prompted by concern about migrant labour. In particular, migrants have been innovators in the labour movement, and they are increasingly so, for instance in the US (Milkman 2006). Given the increased movement of labour within the enlarged EU, there is even more potential for such contaminating effects (Pries 2003; Hardy and Fitzgerald 2010; Meardi 2012). But there are also visible destabilising effects on national institutions stemming from the movement of workers. A particularly critical case is that of movement of services within the EU, which has led to conflicts in the construction and transport sectors and to rulings of the European Court of Justice (Laval, Viking, Rüffert and Luxembourg cases) that jeopardise national regulations, such as collective bargaining and the right to strike (Woolfson 2007; Dølvik and Visser 2009).

The flows of migrant labour have not obliterated state policies, however. Migration flows interact with national policies, whether conscious or not, as the UK and Ireland decision to open their labour markets to accession countries proves, in contrast with the choices of the corporatist systems of Austria and Germany. The form of integration of migrants is still largely affected by national policies and by national state traditions (Birsl et al. 2003). For instance, two UK sectors with the same recent massive influx of new foreign workers have experienced divergent trends depending on government policy: in manufacturing, migration, combined with reduced commitment to state vocational training, has caused an increase in wage inequality, with low-skilled workers suffering most. In the health sector, however, new public investment by the Labour government, together with the introduction of the national minimum wage, has produced wage increases across the whole spectrum of employment (Somerville and Sumption 2009). It is also possible for local actors to counteract the disruptive effects, as in cases of cross-border trade union collaboration, or campaigns for the regulations of the most vulnerable sectors such as temporary work agencies. In the EU, in particular, the European labour mobilisation against the so-called Bolkenstein directive liberalising service provision has achieved some success (Gajewska 2009; Erne, Chapter 7 in this volume).

State

The relevance of the national state is directly questioned by the emergence of supranational regulations and institutions, and nowhere is this more visible than in the EU, where an emerging 'multi-level governance' system has been detected (Marginson and Sisson 2004). There are notorious limits, however, to supranational institutions in industrial relations. EU integration has been mostly 'negative' and 'market-making' than 'positive' and 'market-correcting' (Streeck 1995). A striking example is provided by the very humble transfer of social regulations to the new member states after 2004 (Meardi 2012). EU-level social dialogue is still very far from producing anything reminiscent of collective bargaining. Still, there are some positive evaluations of the top–bottom impact of European social policies for national industrial relations (Kowalsky 2000; Weltz 2008). Moreover, social actors, such as trade unions, also react to negative integration and may foster some bottom-up Europeanisation (Erne 2008).

An important test of the capacity of the EU to affect employment relations is provided by the European Employment Strategy, initiated in 1997, and especially its focus on 'flexicurity' as a strategy for solving European employment problems. Although the European Commission accepts that there may be different 'pathways' to flexicurity, fitting to different national cases (European Expert Group on Flexicurity 2007), the overall aim of its promotion relies on one single objective for all European countries, that is, a combination of employment flexibility, active labour market policies and generous, but conditional, unemployment insurance, all inspired by the Danish experience. The flexicurity idea has been the object of criticism (e.g. Keune and Jepsen 2007; Funk 2008; Burroni and Keune 2010) and after 2008, given its evident inappropriateness to deal with a recession, it has been sidelined and in part redefined as working-time flexibility (European Council 2009). Yet it has been consistently promoted over several years, in particular through the inspiration of the European Council guidelines and recommendations for National Action Plans and National Reform Plans required by the European Employment Strategy. It constitutes, therefore, an interesting test for the capacity of supranational institutions to force national traditions into convergence.

Qualitative studies have detected that, actually, there are still major barriers to the implementation of convergence among member states through the policy mechanism of the European Employment Strategy, that is, the Open Method of Co-ordination. While the Open Method of Co-ordination has the potential to overcome some limits of EU-level policy-making (Zeitlin and Pochet 2005), there are limits to how much countries can learn from each other (Casey and Gold 2005).

The evolution of the indicators the EU uses for measuring flexicurity offer some information about the extent of convergence produced among EU countries. The OECD Employment Protection Legislation index (OECD employment database, our elaboration) shows a clear converging downward trend towards more flexibility across the 14 EU countries affected by the European Employment Strategy since 1997 (excluding Luxembourg because of size and the new member states that joined either in 2004 or 2007). In these countries, the average EPL indicator (which ranges from 0 to 5) declined from 2.25 to 2.05 between 1997 and 2008, and the variance among them declined from 0.79 to 0.53. The most flexible countries, such as UK and Ireland, experienced a slight increase in rigidity, and the rigid ones, such as Italy, Greece and Belgium, a major increase in flexibility. However, this cannot be easily interpreted as a direct effect of EU policies: in fact, the trend had started much earlier than the EES, at least from 1985 (when the EPL average was 2.78 and variance was 1.07), that is, well before the EU started proselytising on flexicurity. It is probably related more to the overall political climate and trade union weakening that started in the 1980s, than to what happens in Brussels.

The EU effect on convergence since 1997 seems clearer on the security axis of flexicurity. For expenditure on Active Labour Market Programs (ALMP) as a share of the GDP (OECD employment database, our elaboration), variance among the EU15 (minus Luxembourg) declined sharply from 0.32 to 0.11 between 1997 and 2007, while it had been increasing in the previous period (from 0.23 in 1987). The importance of this convergence is ambiguous, though. In absolute terms average ALMP expenditure actually declined from 0.95 per cent to 0.76 per cent between 1997 and 2007, rather than increasing, as it should have done according to the EES, and as it had done before the EES (the average was 0.80 per cent in 1987). But expenditure on labour market programs is obviously closely related to unemployment levels, which were increasing before 1997 and declining afterwards. After controlling for unemployment, the intensity of ALMP expenditure (calculated as share of the GDP spent/unemployment rate) has actually increased between 1997 and 2007 (from 11.46 to 13.69), while it had declined in the previous decade (13.57 in 1987).[5] This suggests that there has been, therefore, an effect of Brussels policies on convergence as well as on direction of change – but not to the point of radical change given that expenditure intensity in 2007 is the same as it was in 1987.

Data are not equally updated with regard to the third, and crucial, dimension of the flexicurity triangle, that is, the replacement rate of unemployment benefits: the OECD database covers only to 2003. Using the OECD summary measure of replacement levels as indicator (OECD Database of Benefits and Wages), replacement rates have remained virtually constant between 1997 and 2003 (average for the EU15 minus Luxembourg having moved from 33.2 per cent to 34.5 per cent). Four important countries (Spain, UK, Greece and most significantly Denmark) went in the opposite direction from flexicurity and reduced their replacement rates. This has all but interrupted the historic trend towards improvement of social security: the EU14 average replacement level was 30.8 per cent in 1987. As with EPL, variance declined between 1997 and 2007, but it had also declined between 1987 and 1997, in a longer-term process of convergence.

This ambiguous effect of European policies on flexicurity has also affected how we look at types of labour market and industrial relations models. The European Commission's *Employment in Europe Report* of 2006 (European Commission 2006, 103–7) contained, within a long analysis of flexicurity, a cluster analysis of EU countries that portrayed five clear models along the two flexibility and security axes: an 'Anglo-Saxon' system (high flexibility, low security); a continental system (medium flexibility and security); a Mediterrenean system (low flexibility, rather low security); an Eastern European system (high flexibility and low security); and a Scandinavian system (flexicurity). These clusters appear to be very neat and to confirm industrial relations typologies: they are very close to the already mentioned five industrial relations regimes identified in the *Industrial Relations Report* two years later (European Commission 2008). Yet, this is a static picture that does not account for change. The effect of change is particularly neat for Italy, which is a country considered as particularly affected by the EU in its socio-economic institutions and even 'rescued by Europe' (Ferrera and Gualmini 2004). Italy, in the *Employment in Europe Report* cluster, does not appear in its traditional 'Mediterranean group', but in the 'Eastern European' one. In fact, it is a clear case of distorted, or selective, effects of EU pressures: while flexibility has increased massively in the last few years (with the labour market reforms of 1997 and 2003), security has clearly declined. As a result, far from catching up with Denmark, Italy has fallen to Eastern European levels. Important developments also affect other EU countries, for instance, Germany with the Hartz reforms, which however have responded to endogenous pressures rather than European ones, deserving the definition of 'typically German reform' (Hassel and Schiller 2010).

In substance, EU pressures exist and are important but are still strongly mediated and 'bent' by national institutions and traditions. EU countries differ in their 'cultures of compliance' (Falkner et al. 2004) with EU policies, making the end results rather different from the proclaimed intentions. Moreover, there is possible national contestation of EU policies, from populism (such as for the Euro-sceptic governments of UK, Poland and Slovakia) to cross-border actions to mediate the effects of EU policies, such as collective bargaining co-ordination in the Germanic group of countries – co-ordination that grows on a longer history.

CONCLUSION

The evidence since 1992 in Europe is that state arrangements have changed more radically than expected by most institutional approaches, such as that of the Varieties of Capitalism; but also, that state traditions are still visible, despite internationalisation and internal differentiation. And they become more contested, in the sense of being compared more frequently, and therefore, paradoxically, more important. Actors (especially multinational companies, but to some extent also migrant workers) are increasingly aware of national differences and can either exploit them or use them within national debates. The role of political culture and language in particular is still very important (Barbier 2008), and there are limits to what states can learn from each other within the EU Open Method of Co-ordination.

Can we still talk of national models and of national typologies, as most comparative industrial relations literature has done for half a century? Instead of the term model, which presupposes stability, coherence and even harmony, I suggest the term 'style'. A 'style' calls for co-ordination and harmonisation, but does not require it *a priori*, and it does not exclude constant adaptation, change and innovation: to bring the metaphor to its extremes, there are 'casual' styles, and styles evolve with fashion. While the concept of 'style' may sound inappropriate for a supposedly 'hard' field of social sciences like industrial relations, it is noteworthy that Crouch (1993: 296) used the term in his account of industrial relations diversity arguing that, while it 'may seem a trivial variable' and 'an epiphenomenon if there ever was one', actually 'it is not to be written off in this way' and represents well the established (but changeable) ways in which organisations face (changing) situations.

NOTES

1. Fragments of the sections 'National research traditions. . .' and 'State' have appeared in G. Meardi (2011), 'Flexicurity Meets State Traditions: The Differential National Effects of European Employment Policies', *International Journal of Comparative Labour Law and Industrial Relations*, **27**.
2. Research programme 'Why Industrial Relations Matters: An Integrated Approach to Comparative European Industrial Relations', funded by the Economic and Social Research Council, 2010–12.

3. A paradoxical counter-trend in this respect is the original re-interpretation and re-appropriation (also due to partial translations) of Foucault by British sociologists of work, which has had a major influence on labour process and critical management debates in Britain, while Foucault is completely ignored by all forms of labour studies in his native country.

4. In this regard the French are the most reluctant to import Anglophone works: even the Webbs' *Industrial Relations* had to wait for at least a very partial French translation until 2008, while the German one appeared in 1898, one year after the original, and the Italian one in 1912.

5. If we remove the outlier Sweden (which in 1987 had near-full employment and therefore extremely high intensity of labour market expenditure), the trend is linear and the turning point of 1997 disappears. Without Sweden, the average intensity of expenditure on ALMP was 8.36 in 1987, 10.71 in 1997 and 13.3 in 2007.

REFERENCES

Amossé, T., C. Bloch-London and L. Wolff (eds) (2008), *Les relations sociales en enterprise*, Paris: La Découverte.

Baccaro, L., K. Hamann and L. Turner (2003), 'The politics of labour movement revitalisation: The need for a revitalized perspective', *European Journal of Industrial Relations*, **9** (1), 119–33.

Baglioni, G. and C. Crouch (eds) (1990), *European Industrial Relations: The Challenge of Flexibility*, London: Sage.

Bamber, G. and R. Lansbury (eds) (1987), *International and Comparative Industrial Relations: A Study of Developed Market Economies*, London: Allen and Unwin.

Barbier, J. (2008), *La langue marche de l'Europe sociale*, Paris: Presses Universitaires de France.

Bean, R. (1994), *Comparative Industrial Relations*, London: Thomson.

Bechter, B., B. Brandl and G. Meardi (2012), 'Sectors or Countries? Typologies and Levels of Analysis in Comparative Industrial Relations', *European Journal of Industrial Relations*, forthcoming.

Bevort, A. and A. Jobert (2008), *Sociologie du travail: Les relations profession-nelles*, Paris: Armand Colin.

Birsl, U., R. Bitzan, C. Solé, S. Parella, A. Alarcón, J. Schmidt and S. French (2003), *Migration und Interkulturalität in Grossbritannien, Deutschland und Spanien*, Opladen: Leske + Budrich.

Blyton, P. and P. Turnbull (2004), *The Dynamics of Employee Relations*, Basingstoke: Palgrave Macmillan.

Brandl, B., S. Strohmer and F. Traxler (2010), 'US Foreign Direct Investment, Macro Markets and Labour Relations: The case of enlarged Europe', *Industrial Relations Journal*, **41** (6), 622–38.

Brubaker, R. (1992), *Citizenship and Nationhood in France and Germany*, Cambridge: Harvard University Press.

Burroni, L. and M. Keune (2010), 'Flexicurity: A conceptual critique', *European Journal of Industrial Relations*, **17** (1) 75–91.

Casey, B. and M. Gold (2005), 'Peer review of labour market policies in the European Union: What can countries really learn from one another?', *Journal of European Public Policy*, **12** (1), 23–43.

Cella, G. and T. Treu (2001), 'National trade union movements', in R. Blanpain and C. Engels (eds) *Comparative Labour Law and Industrial Relations*, Boston: Kluwer, pp. 445–82.

Clegg, H. (1976), *Trade Unionism under Collective Bargaining: A Theory Based on Comparisons of Six Countries*, Oxford: Blackwell.

Cooke, W. (2001), 'The effects of labour costs and workplace constraints on Foreign Direct Investment among highly industrialised countries', *International Journal of Human Resource Management*, **12** (5), 697–716.

Crouch, C. (1993), *Industrial Relations and European State Traditions*, Oxford: Oxford University Press.

Crouch, C. (2004), *Post-democracy*, Oxford: Polity.

Crouch, C. (2005), *Capitalist Diversity and Change: Recombinant Governance and Institutional Entrepreneurs*, Oxford: Oxford University Press.

Crouch, C. (2010), 'British Industrial Relations: Between Security and Flexibility', in T. Colling and M. Terry (eds) *Industrial Relations: Theory and Practice*, Chichester: Wiley, pp. 29–53.

Crouch, C. and H. Farrell (2002), 'Breaking the path of institutional development? Alternatives to the new determinism', Florence: EUI WP SPS 02/4.

Crouch, C., P. Le Galès, C. Trigilia and H. Voelzkow (eds) (2001) *Local Production Systems in Europe. Rise or Demise?*, Oxford, Oxford University Press.

Darlington, R. (ed.) (2004), *What's the Point of Industrial Relations?*, Manchester: BUIRA.

Dølvik, J.E. and J. Visser (2009), 'Free movement, equal treatment and workers' rights: Can the European Union solve its trilemma of fundamental principles?', *Industrial Relations Journal*, **40**, 491–509.

Dufour, C. and A. Hege (2002), *L'Europe syndicale au quotidien*, Brussels: Lang.

Dunlop, J. (1958), *Industrial Relations Systems*, New York: Holt.

Erne, R. (2008), *European Unions. Labor Quest for a Transnational Democracy*, Ithaca: ILR Press.

European Commission (2006), *Employment in Europe 2006*, Luxembourg: Office for Official Publications of the European Communities.

European Commission (2008), *Industrial Relations in Europe Report*, Luxembourg: Office for Official Publications of the European Communities.

European Council (2009), *Council Conclusions on Flexicurity in Times of Crisis*, Luxembourg.

European Expert Group on Flexicurity (2007), *Flexicurity Pathways: Turning Hurdles into Stepping Stones*, Brussels: European Commission.

Fairbrother, P. and G. Griffin (2002), *Changing Prospects for Trade Unionism: Comparisons between Six Countries*, London: Continuum.

Falkner, G., O. Treib, M. Hartlapp and S. Leiber (2004), *Complying With Europe: EU Harmonization and Soft Law in the Member States*, Cambridge: Cambridge University Press.

Ferner, A. and R. Hyman (1994), *New Frontiers in European Industrial Relations*, Oxford: Blackwell.

Ferner, A. and R. Hyman (1998), *Changing Industrial Relations in Europe*, Oxford: Blackwell.

Ferner, A. and R. Hyman (eds) (1992), *Industrial Relations in the New Europe*, Oxford: Blackwell.

Ferrera, M. and E. Gualmini (2004) *Rescued by Europe? Social and Labour Market*

Reforms from Maastricht to Berlusconi, Amsterdam: Amsterdam University Press.

Fligstein, N. (2002), *The Architecture of Markets: An Economic Sociology of Twenty-First-Century Capitalist Societies*, Princeton: Princeton University Press.

Frege, C. (2003), 'Industrial relations in Continental Europe', in P. Ackers and A. Wilkinson (eds) *Understanding Work and Employment*, Oxford: Oxford University Press, pp. 242–62.

Frege, C. (2007), *Employment Research and State Traditions: A Comparative History of Britain, Germany, and the United States*, Oxford: Oxford University Press.

Frege, C. and J. Kelly (2003), 'Union revitalization strategies in comparative perspective', *European Journal of Industrial Relations*, **9** (1), 7–24.

Frege, C. and J. Kelly (eds) (2004), *Varieties of Unionism: Struggles for Union Revitalization in a Globalizing Economy*, Oxford: Oxford University Press.

Funk, L. (2008), 'European Flexicurity Policies: A critical assessment', *International Journal of Comparative Labour Law and Industrial Relations*, **24**, 349–84.

Gajewska, K. (2009), *Transnational Labour Solidarity*, London: Routledge.

Giles, A. (2000), 'Globalisation and Industrial Relations Theory', *Journal of Industrial Relations*, **42** (2), 173–94.

Gumbrell-McCormick, R. (2008), 'International actors and international regulations', in P. Blyton, N. Bacon, J. Fiorito and E. Heery (eds), *The SAGE Handbook of Industrial Relations*, London: Sage, pp. 325–45.

Hall, P. and D. Soskice (eds) (2001), *Varieties of Capitalism. Institutional Foundations of Comparative Advantage*, Oxford: Oxford University Press.

Hardy, J. and I. Fitzgerald (2010), 'Negotiating 'Solidarity' and Internationalism: The Response of Polish Trade Unions to Migration', *Industrial Relations Journal*, **41** (4), 367–81.

Hasse, R. and H. Leiulfsrud (2002), 'From disorganized capitalism to transnational fine tuning?', *British Journal of Sociology*, **53** (1), 107–26.

Hassel, A. (2007), 'The curse of institutional security', *Industrielle Beziehungen*, **14** (2), 176–91.

Hassel, A. and C. Schiller (2010), *Der Fall Hartz IV. Wie es zur Agenda 2010 kam und wie es weiter geht*, Frankfurt: Campus.

Heery, E. (2008), 'System and change in industrial relations analysis', in P. Blyton, N. Bacon, J. Fiorito and E. Heery (eds) *The SAGE Handbook of Industrial Relations*, London: Sage, pp. 69–91.

Hyman, R. (1989), *The Political Economy of Industrial Relations*, Basingstoke: Macmillan.

Hyman, R. (2001), *Understanding European Trade Unionism*, London: Sage.

Hyman, R. (2004), 'Is Industrial Relations theory always ethnocentric?', in B. Kaufman (ed.), *Theoretical Perspectives on Work and the Employment Relationship*, IRRA, pp. 265–92.

Kassalow, E.M. (1969), *Trade Unions and Industrial Relations. An International Comparison*, New York: Random House.

Keune, M. and M. Jepsen (2007), *Not Balanced and Hardly New: The European Commission's Quest for Flexicurity*, Brussels: ETUI Working Paper 1/2007.

Kowalsky, W. (2000), *Focus on European Social Policy*, Brussels: ETUI.

Lallement, M. (1996), *Sociologie des relations professionnelles*, Paris: La Découverte.

Lipset, M. (1983), 'Radicalism or reformism: The sources of working-class politics', *American Political Science Review*, **77**, 1–18.

Locke, R. (1992), 'The demise of the national union in Italy: Lessons for comparative industrial relations theory', *Industrial and Labor Relations Review*, **45** (2), 229–49.

Marginson, P. and G. Meardi (2009), *Multinational Companies and Collective Bargaining*, Dublin: European Industrial Relations Observatory.

Marginson, P. and K. Sisson (2004), *European Integration and Industrial Relations*, Basingstoke: Palgrave Macmillan.

Marino, S. (2012), 'Trade Union Inlcusion of Migrant and Ethnic Minority Workers: An Italy–Netherlands Comparison', *European Journal of Industrial Relations*, forthcoming.

Martinet, G. (1979), *Sept syndicalismes*, Paris: Seuil.

Meardi, G. (2012), *Social Failures of EU Enlargement. A Case of Workers Voting with Their Feet*, London: Routledge.

Meardi, G., P. Marginson, M. Fichter, M. Frybes, M. Stanojević and A. Tóth (2009), 'The complexity of relocation and the diversity of trade union responses: Efficiency-oriented Foreign Direct Investment in Central Europe', *European Journal of Industrial Relations*, **15** (1), 27–47.

Milkman, R. (2006), *L.A. Story: Immigrant Workers and the Future of the U.S. Labor Movement*, New York: Russell Sage.

O' Reilly, J. and C. Spee (1998), 'The future of regulation of work and welfare: Time for a revised social and gender contract?', *European Journal of Industrial Relations*, **4** (3), 259–81.

Pries, L. (2003), 'Labour migration, social incorporation and transmigration in the old and new Europe. The case of Germany in a comparative perspective', *Transfer*, **9** (3), 432–51.

Raess, D. and B. Burgoon (2006), 'The dogs that sometimes bark: globalization and works council bargaining in Germany', *European Journal of Industrial Relations*, **12** (3), 287–309.

Simmel, G. (1908), *Soziologie. Untersuchungen über die Formen der Vergesellschaftung*, Lepizig: Duncker und Humboldt.

Slomp, H. (1996), *Between Bargaining and Politics: An Introduction to European Labor Relations*, Westport: Praeger.

Somerville, W. and N. Sumption (2009), *Immigration and the Labour Market: Theory, Evidence and Policy*, London: Equality and Human Rights Commission.

Streeck, W. (1995), 'Neo-voluntarism: A new European policy regime', *European Law Journal*, **1** (1), 31–59.

Traxler, F., S. Blaschke and B. Kittel (2001), *National Labor Relations in Internationalised Markets*, Oxford: Oxford University Press.

Van Ruysseveldt, J. and J. Visser (eds) (1996), *Industrial Relations in Europe: Traditions and Transitions*, London: Sage.

Visser, J. (1996), 'Traditions and Transitions', in J. Van De Ruysseveldt and J. Visser (eds) *Industrial Relations in Europe*, London: Sage, pp. 1–41.

Wagner, P., B. Wittrock and R. Whitley (eds) (1991), *Discourses on Society: The Shaping of Social Science Disciplines*, Dodrecht: Kluwer.

Watt, A., M. Keune and B. Galgóczi (eds) (2008) *Jobs on the Move. An Analytical Approach to Relocation and its Impact on Employment*. Brussels: Peter Lang.

Weltz, C. (2008), *The European Social Dialogue under Articles 138 and 139 of the EC Treaty*, Amsterdam: Kluwer Law International.
Wieviorka, M. (2008), *La diversité*, Paris: Robert Laffont.
Woolfson, C. (2007), 'Labour standards and labour migration in the new Europe: Post-communist legacies and perspectives', *European Journal of Industrial Relations*, **13** (2), 199–218.
Wrench, J. (2004), 'Trade union responses to immigrants and ethnic inequality in Denmark and the UK', *European Journal of Industrial Relations*, **10** (1), 7–30.
Zeitlin, J. and P. Pochet (eds) (2005), *The Open Method of Co-ordination in Action*: *The European Employment and Social Inclusion Strategies*, Brussels: Peter Lang.

7.   European unions after the crisis[1]

Roland Erne

INTRODUCTION

Times of crisis allow the doubtful privilege of witnessing interesting times. The current global economic and financial crisis has brought so much hardship to so many people across the globe that nobody can be happy about its occurrence. Even so, the current crisis of global financial capitalism is also enlightening, as it reveals concealed socio-economic and political dynamics. The crisis not only causes pain, but also questions the legitimacy of free market capitalism and the dominant socio-economic and political order. Following Karl Polanyi's ([1944] 2001) study of past waves of untempered global market capitalism, we should expect a rise of protective counter-movements that aim to subordinate the economy to society.

In its first section, this chapter shows that the idea of a self-regulating market has once again been discredited. Yet, it remains to be seen what measures society will be taking to protect itself against future fallouts of the global markets. Whereas there is a growing consensus that the economy needs to be governed by tighter regulations, this does not necessarily mean that people around the globe will engage 'in a common effort to subordinate the economy to democratic politics and rebuild the economy on the basis of international cooperation' (Block 2001: xxxvii). Nevertheless, the chapter concludes that any fatalism about the prospects of a democratic counter-movement against the marketisation of society is misplaced. Without doubt, the initial political reaction to the crisis – namely the huge bailouts for private banks and the subsequent cutbacks in public services – do not augur well for the future of labour and egalitarian democracy. Conversely, the more socio-economic decisions are taken by tangible political and corporate elites rather than abstract market forces, the more difficult it is to mystify the underlying business interests. Arguably, this also makes it easier for social movements to mobilise discontent and to politicise the economy.

RETHINKING ECONOMY AND SOCIETY AFTER THE CRISIS

Days after the collapse of the global finance corporation Lehman Brothers a *Guardian* journalist asked a panel of experts and public intellectuals if the past week of turmoil has changed the world (Butselaar 2008). The heterodox US economist Joseph Stiglitz responded with the confidence of someone who is at long last winning the academic argument against his orthodox peers.

> In some ways, from an intellectual perspective, this is as important as the Great Depression. The Depression taught us that markets are not self-correcting, at least not in the relevant time frame. This is a failure of microeconomics equivalent to the macroeconomic failures of the 1930s. The financial markets have not done what they are supposed to do, which is to manage risk and allocate capital well. The result is that there are no free-marketers left. Both the left and the right are arguing that there is a role for government to maintain the economy on an even level. (Stiglitz 2008)

By contrast, the Canadian author and global justice activist Naomi Klein very much doubted that the global financial meltdown as such will lead to fundamental policy shifts away from the corporate pro-business paradigms that dominated economic policy-making since the late 1970s.

> Nobody should believe the overblown claims that 'free market' ideology is now dead. During boom times it is profitable to preach laissez-faire, because an absentee government allows speculative bubbles to inflate. When those bubbles burst, the ideology becomes a hindrance, and it goes dormant while the government rides to the rescue. But rest assured: the ideology will come roaring back when the bailouts are done. The massive debt the public is accumulating to bail out the speculators will then become part of a global budget crisis that will be the rationalisation for deep cuts to social programmes, and for a renewed push to privatise what is left of the public sector. (Klein 2008)

Two years after the collapse of Lehman Brothers, Klein's doubts are proven to have been more than appropriate. The intellectual victories of heterodox economists over free-marketers in September 2008 did not prevent 'the great American robbery' (Stiglitz 2010a: 109) and the other bank bailouts that followed suit across the world. Moreover, the critical advice that the subsequent austerity measures will prolong the crisis and therefore cause unnecessary sufferings has been ignored (Krugman 2010).

Paradoxically, the financial meltdown showed that even the imminent ruin of a financial corporation can become an effective political tool for business interests. Obviously, corporations have an advantage not only because they tend to spend more money on political lobbying than other organisations. In capitalist democracies politicians structurally depend on the holders of capital, as shown by Claus Offe and Helmut Wiesenthal (1985). As any single investment decision – or corporate bankruptcy, as we might add in the light of recent events – has an impact on the economic growth of a territory, politicians must consider the views of capitalists whether they are organised or not. This simplifies the task of business interest representation enormously. Business associations do not face the difficult collective action problems that trade unions and other citizens' organisations face. Whereas investment strikes by capital holders do not require collective action, the withdrawal of labour requires organisation and the willingness of workers to act together despite the availability of individual exit options (Erne 2011). In this context, governments are not only implementing further privatisations of public services and welfare cuts. Governments, central banks, and supranational organisations, like the European Commission, the European Central Bank, the Organisation for Economic Cooperation and Development, and the International Monetary Fund, are even advocating outright wage cuts and working time extensions that go beyond both the current working day and retirement age (Erne 2012). Although neo-liberal theory is discredited, the political project that aims 'to re-establish the conditions for capital accumulation and to restore the power of economic elites' (Harvey 2005: 19) is still with us.

It seems that governments across the world have degenerated into a mere 'service provider for financial capital' (Bode and Pink 2010). Almost everywhere, democratic procedures have been bent to allow bank bailouts. Even in Switzerland, which is frequently portrayed as the most direct democracy of the world, the 6 billion francs bailout of UBS was adopted by an emergency ordinance of the executive that shielded the deal from being a subject of parliamentary and popular scrutiny (Bundesrat 2008, Boos 2008). Although the parliament subsequently supported the executive's action implicitly, namely by not calling it to account, the adoption of the UBS emergency decree 'in order to counter existing or imminent threats of serious disruption to public order or internal or external security' (Article 185-3 Swiss Constitution) effectively twisted the constitutional right of 50 000 citizens to request parliamentary acts and emergency legislation to be submitted to a vote of the people (Article 141 Swiss Constitution). Arguably, 'theories and concepts of public law change under the impact of political events' as Carl Schmitt ([1922] 1985: 16), the infamous German lawyer and apologist of the fascist *Führerstaat*, had argued.

Almost everywhere, advocates of deregulation, failed regulators, or investment bankers – thus, the people that have been responsible for the mess in the first pace – were put in charge of repair. Unsurprisingly, the solutions adopted to remedy the mess are based on the same principles that caused it in the first place. Toxic assets were simply shifted from banks to the government, even if that does not make them less toxic. Whereas the social welfare state meant protecting individuals against the failures of the market, the current crisis gave rise to a new 'corporate' welfare regime in which the state assumes the role as bearer of risk of last resort. When private financial firms were at the brink of collapse, their financial risks of gigantic proportions were simply shifted to the public. Observing how the costs had to be covered by public spending and wage cuts, while bank bonuses were to be kept, Stiglitz had to revisit his (above-mentioned) opinion of 2008: 'the Hooverites – the advocates of the pre-Keynesian policies according to which downturns were met with austerity – are having their revenge. In many quarters, the Keynesians, having enjoyed their moment of glory just a year ago, seem to be in retreat' (Stiglitz 2010b).

Given the ensuing legacy of public debt that 'will compromise economic and social programmes for years to come', the bank bailouts of the Bush and Obama administrations will almost surely 'rank among the most costly mistakes of any democratic government at any time' (Stiglitz 2010a: 110). But is Joseph Stiglitz correct when he describes the bank bailouts as a 'mistake'? Yet, such 'mistake', involving state support for private banks that breaks all rules of neo-liberal economic theory, indirectly demonstrates that John Maynard Keynes and his followers are wrong to believe

> that the power of vested interest is vastly exaggerated compared with the gradual encroachment of ideas. Not, indeed, immediately, but after a certain interval; for in the field of economic and political philosophy there are not many who are influenced by new theories after they are twenty-five or thirty years of age, so that the ideas which civil servants and politicians and even agitators apply to current events are not likely to be the newest. But, soon or late, it is ideas, not vested interests, which are dangerous for good or evil. (Keynes [1936] 2008)

Considering the rapid disposal of Keynesian paradigms only a year after the financial meltdown (Sachs 2010), it seems nevertheless accurate to emphasise the dominant role of interest politics and subsidiary role of ideas in socio-economic policy-making (Crouch 2010). Arguably, Keynesianism, that is a theory that encompassed the sectional interests of both capital and labour, 'could only have become the basis of policy under the conditions of social balance' (Skidelsky 2010). This leads to the key question of the next sections: what are the possibilities for counter-movements against global financial capitalism after the meltdown?; will society be able to resist this new wave of marketisation, as we could assume following Polanyi's study of past waves of marketisation and the counter-movements it triggered?; or should we share instead the 'uncompromising pessimism' (Burawoy 2010: 311) that seem to have affected many labour and industrial relations scholars (Baccaro et al. 2010)?

REASONS FOR UNCOMPROMISING PESSIMISM

Since the collapse of Lehman Brothers in September 2008, numerous scholars have attempted to explain the origins of the current global economic and financial crisis. Whereas bibliographic searches in the world's journal databases at the time of writing produced amazingly scarce results, reflecting the long lead time of publishing in assumingly 'high-impact' journals (Erne 2007), the list of books that deal with the issue is impressive. Books about the crisis lead bestseller listings in many countries that were hit by the financial meltdown. There is a broad consensus that the neo-liberal deregulation policies of the last three decades led to the current situation. Accordingly, the reintroduction of tighter regulations for the financial sector is part of almost every post-crisis reform programme. However, not only Marxists (Burawoy 2010, Harvey 2010, Foster and Magdoff 2009), but also scholars that stand in the tradition of gradual social reform doubt that regulatory reforms – that is 'the most practical set of remedies on offer' (Gamble 2009: 155) – will allow a return to social democracy and full employment (Crouch 2009a).

Colin Crouch (2009a) highlighted that the growth of the US and UK economies during the past neo-liberal area did not rely on a triumph of the free market, but rather on the dubious success of an unacknowledged policy regime which he called 'privatised Keynesianism'. It is generally acknowledged that the neo-liberal labour market reforms and the efforts of business to escape national regulations secured higher profit shares for capitalists. Accordingly, the shift to economic globalisation and neo-liberalism has frequently been analysed as a business response to the declining rate of profit that Marx predicted (Skidelsky 2010, Glyn 2006). But it is not so often acknowledged that neo-liberal wage moderation pressures would have prevented growth and continued capital accumulation, if unsecured consumer credit had not sustained the necessary aggregate consumer demand. Accordingly, the term 'privatised Keynesianism' refers to the fact that economic growth in the US, the UK, and other neo-liberal economies has been sustained by private deficit spending, which in turn depended on house price inflation and stock exchange bubbles.

In the export-led East Asian and European economies, notably in Germany and China, consumer borrowing remained at a lower rate.

Yet these economies also benefited from the privatised deficit spending within the neo-liberal economies. It would not have been possible for so-called 'coordinated market economies' (Hancké 2010) to pursue export-led growth policies, if global aggregate consumer demand had not been supported by the asset price bubbles that occurred in liberal market economies. Likewise, the profits generated by the trade surpluses of core Eurozone countries, along with the surpluses of other world regions notably in East Asia, further fuelled these asset prise bubbles in so far as they were actually financing the privatised Keynesianism in the US, UK and the peripheral Eurozone countries.

This shows how problematic varieties of capitalism typologies are, when they overstate the centrality of national institutions and disregard the interdependences of the capitalist world system, as acknowledged by institutionalist scholars who had emphasised the importance of different state traditions in the past (Crouch 2009b: 92; Meardi, Chapter 6 in this volume). Surely, national economies play different roles in the global economy. Yet it is more accurate to distinguish them based on their location in the core or the periphery of an integrated capitalist world system, as shown, for instance, by Stefanie Hürtgen's analysis of European labour politics across transnational supply chains (2008). This conclusion is also supported by Becker and Jäger's (2009) study of the surprisingly diverging responses to the crisis in Western and Eastern Europe. Whereas UK policy-makers facilitated a devaluation of the Pound, the Central and East European central banks resisted currency devaluations; arguably, to support the Western banks that have taken control over the local banking systems, even if this 'Eurozation' policy is hurting domestic industry in the East (Becker and Jäger 2009).

The interdependence of coordinated and liberal market economies not only questions varieties of capitalism typologies, it also entails important political implications for any counter-movement against finance capitalism. If capitalism is a world system, isn't it reasonable to suggest that national responses to its crisis will not be sufficient? It has been argued that any counter-movement to global capitalism 'must begin at the global level for it is only at that level that it is possible to contest the destruction of nature, let alone tackle the global machinations of financial capital' (Burawoy 2010: 311). Even if some sort of a global counter-movement to contain capitalism's rapacious tendencies may be necessary for human survival, Michael Burawoy fears that would not be very likely to happen:

> Optimism today has to be countered by an uncompromising pessimism, not an alarmism but a careful and detailed analysis of the way capitalism combines

the commodification of nature, money and labor, and thereby destroys the very ground upon which a 'counter-movement' could be built. (Ibid: 312)

However, even if the challenges that we are facing are indeed global, this does not necessarily validate the claim that a counter-movement to global capitalism has to begin at the global level. The just-in-time logistics of global corporations is heavily dependent on a smooth management of its transnational production chains. Within a postfordist production network, even a local strike can make a huge impact (Moody 1997). This was shown by the strike of only 1900 workers at the Honda Auto Parts Manufacturing Co. in Foshan in June 2010 that brought Honda's operations across China to a standstill. Moreover, after the striking Honda workers obtained substantial wage increases, the protest movement spilled over and triggered not only an amazing strike wave in favour of higher pay and better working conditions, but also demands for a democratic labour movement in the People's Republic (Dongfang 2010). Nevertheless, Burawoy correctly highlights that even if excessive marketisation triggered counter-movements in the past, this does not guarantee the rise of a successful and progressive counter-movement in the future. Whereas the Chinese rulers seem to have learnt the Polanyian lesson that market society requires state regulation, it is noteworthy that this does not preclude authoritarian solutions; incidentally, the great crash of 1929 led not only to the New Deal and social democratic mid-century class compromises, but also to the rise of fascism and a consolidation of Stalin's Soviet Union.

TOWARDS POST-DEMOCRACY?

While there are few signs for a relapse into direct autocratic authoritarianism, the failures of the market society may also favour anti-democratic impulses. Whereas Polanyi insisted that democratic market regulation and control can 'achieve freedom not only for the few, but for all' ([1944] 2001: 265), societies may also be protected from disruptive market forces by sacrificing democracy. Colin Crouch argued even in his first book, *The Student Revolt*, published in 1970, that there is no inherent link between democracy and capitalism.

> Political systems do not exist in a vacuum. They exist in the context of, and are sustained by, social institutions, and it is not possible for a society to maintain just any structure of politics or to ensure to its citizens a system of rights and freedoms simply by wishing it were so (. . .). It is therefore entirely possible that the structure of economic powers in our society and the increasing

interdependence of our political, economic, educational and social institutions should lead us to a position where our rhetoric of pluralist democracy shall cease to bear any but the most tangential relation to reality. (Crouch 1970: 240)

It follows that the future of democracy depends not only on democratic beliefs but crucially also on a balance of power between the countervailing social interests, notably between the organisations of capital and labour. Only in this case can the outcome of the policy-making process reflect the best arguments, rather than mere power relations between social classes.

While democracy was instrumental in removing feudal obstacles to social change in the nineteenth century, today the active use of civic, political and social citizenship rights is often perceived to be a problem. Capitalists accepted the social democratic mid-twentieth-century class compromise as long as it was 'the best deal that liberal capitalism could expect in a world veering towards the political extremes' (Skideslsky 2010: 326). Yet, capitalists were never really enthusiastic about sharing power with countervailing interests. It is therefore not surprising that business associations actively supported the trend towards neo-liberal politics in the late 1970s, associated with Margaret Thatcher in the United Kingdom and Ronald Reagan in the USA (Harvey 2005). After the deregulation of financial markets brought the world economy at the brink of collapse, there is a growing consensus – even within the business class – that markets ought to be re-regulated. Re-regulation, however, does not require democracy, as emphasised by the technocratic regulatory capitalism of the European Union or the authoritarian 'capitalism with Asian values' of Singapore's long-time leader Lew Quan Yew that Deng Xiaoping praised as the model China should follow (Žižek 2009: 131).

In contrast, trade unions have been playing a very important role in the promotion of democratic rights in both the political arena and the workplace in the past (Harcourt and Wood 2004). More recently, Stevis and Boswell (2007) saw unions contributing to the democratising of global governance. Indeed, the analysis of a variety of European-level union activity challenges the assertion that no realistic prospect exists for remedying the European Union's democratic deficit, that is, its domination by corporate interests and lack of a cohesive European people (Erne 2008). But even before the global crisis, several analysts detected a diminishing, hollowing, or even partial displacement of democracy in the Western world (Skocpol 2003; Mair 2006; Crouch 2004). Arguably, the rise of technocratic governance and the declining of autonomy of the democratic nation state in a globalising economy hamper the prospects of egalitarian democracy. Are there any prospects in unions and their political allies pushing for an alternative to the continued dominance of global financial capitalism and the demise of social and political citizenship that is associated with it? Is it possible to reconcile democracy and interest politics, if politics – despite the global financial meltdown – still seems to be dominated by a self-confident global shareholding and business executive class?

In the wake of the current economic and financial crisis, Crouch gave a very pessimistic answer to these questions: whereas democratic politics would continue to play a role in some areas, the democratic state would be vacating its 'former heartland of basic economic strategy'. Instead, economic policy would be shaped by 'the great corporations, particularly those in the financial sector' (Crouch 2009a: 398), due to the decline of the manual working class and the failure of new social movements to constitute a new class that can claim to stand for the general interest of society. Even if the contemporary orthodoxy that social class no longer exists can be contested with sociological analysis, the increasing difficulty of subordinate groups to unite as a class entails major consequences for interest politics and democracy alike (Crouch 2004: 53). Consequently, economic policy would become a private matter of technocratic agencies and multinational corporations, even if corporations may, at times, be held accountable by public appeals to corporate social responsibility (Crouch 2009a).

REASONS FOR CAUTIOUS OPTIMISM?

Without doubt, the current crisis is putting unions under huge pressure. Nevertheless, it is also possible that the global shareholding and business executive class emerges weakened from it. The banks' successful raids on public coffers across the world certainly demonstrated the 'strategic role' that global finance occupies in the world economy (Crouch 2010: 356). But crude demonstrations of power can also undermine the legitimacy of rulers. Successful regimes do not depend on coercion but much more crucially on their capacity to integrate subordinate groups (Cox 1983; van Apeldoorn et al. 2009). Even if economic policies are not determined by ideas, claims that an action is consistent with the public interest are nevertheless influential in political debates. Socio-economic interest groups rely on a convincing intellectual defence of their preferences.

Given the declining ideological strength of neo-liberal theory after the financial crisis, a shift from *laissez-faire* to a regulation and corporation-based defence of business interests is to be expected (Crouch 2009a). It should, however, also be noted that this implies a symbolic rather than practical shift. The pursuit of the neo-liberal agenda always required a strong state; for instance, a state that is capable of restricting trade union action (Block 2007). In liberal market economies with weak and fragmented government structures, such as in Canada (Thompson and Taras 2004), neo-liberalism was nearly as successful by comparison to the US and the UK, where free-marketers could count on the support of strong governments (Harvey 2005). It follows that the recent shift from free market rhetoric to the rhetoric of regulatory capitalism does not mean a substantial shift in the preferences of capitalists. Nevertheless the shifting intellectual defence of capitalists' preferences defence does matter because technocratic regulatory governance explicitly contradicts democratic norms that play a central role in the integration of subordinate classes and thus the legitimisation of the current political order.

According to Majone (1994) regulatory governance is meant to relieve the political process of the assumingly negative consequences of democratic electoral pressures on the quality of regulation. Supporters of regulatory policy-making have even argued that the Chilean experience could serve as an example for the European Union. After all, Pinochet effectively excluded clientelistic influences on economic policies (Drago 1998). In other words, advocates of regulatory governance aim to reduce popular influences by the exclusion of elected politicians from the policy-making process. Policy-making would be better if it was left to independent agencies: for example, to independent central banks in relation to monetary policy, or independent competition authorities in relation to competition policy. It goes without saying that the exclusion of democratic interest intermediation from the policy-making process of regulatory agencies is at variance with both pluralist and neo-corporatist theories of democracy and interest politics. To some extent, the theory of regulatory governance comes closest to the unitarist republican paradigm, without its democratic rhetoric however (Erne 2011). But like republican democratic theory, regulatory governance faces a major problem: how can one be sure that regulatory agencies do not serve the interest that was able to capture a dominant position in the decision-making process?

Regulatory agencies tend to be shaped by powerful political actors and ideologies, as shown, for instance, by the exclusion of social interests from the frames of references that govern the monetary policy of the European Central Bank or the competition policy of the European Commission. Regulatory governance structure 'often masks ideological choices which are not debated and subject to public scrutiny beyond the immediate interests related to the regulatory management area' (Weiler et al. 1995: 33). In this vein, regulatory governance might be more properly understood if it is conceptualised as a form of private interest government (Erne 2011). If compared with the relative ease by which exploitation in the labour market can be obscured (Burawoy 1979), however, it is nevertheless more difficult to mystify the underlying business interests of regulatory governance.

For this very reason, the increasing visibility and role of corporations and regulatory agencies in economic policy-making, which Crouch (2009a) predicted in the wake of the global crisis, might actually facilitate protective counter-movements. In fact, it is easier to politicise decisions of corporations or regulatory agencies than to politicise abstract market forces, precisely because regulatory governance is based on concrete decisions made by tangible elites. By contrast, in the market place the mutual 'relations of the producers, within which the social character of their labour affirms itself, take the form of a social relation between the products' (Marx [1887] 1999, ch. 1.4). Accordingly, the making of the Single European market as such did not trigger transnational unionisms, whereas the restructuring plans of multinational corporations and the recent attacks on national labour regulation by the European Commission and the European Court of Justice politicised the race to the bottom in wages and working conditions and triggered several cases of European collective action by labour.

My own analysis of emerging transnational trade union networks across Europe (Erne 2008) showed that organised labour can re-politicise technocratic policy-making, even in policy areas that are insulated from partisan politics, such as EU competition policy. Even ostensibly technocratic institutions are permeable to cross-border activist pressures. This led me to the argument that the gradual replacement of democracy by technocratic modes of governance is not irreversible. More studies have corroborated this argument since (Gajewska 2009, Meardi 2012). Whereas the making the European single market and the monetary union has not yet led to an effective coordination of unions' wage policies, the increasingly supranational decision-making processes in multinational firms and international organisations and the free movement of workers and services in the enlarged EU has become in several cases significant crystallisation points for transnational union resistance.

CONCLUSION

The question was raised whether the various cases of transnational union resistance would give sufficient ground for cautious optimism (Phelan et al. 2009; Mitchell 2009; Martin 2009). Would a counter-movement against the ongoing wave of marketisation of society not require a universal uprising of the masses (Burawoy 2010)? Not necessarily. First, it would be wrong to perceive radical and pragmatic action repertoires as mutually exclusive (Pereira 2009; Mouriaux 2010). Transformative counter-movements will only be able to mobilise people if they are able to propel concrete improvements as well as a 'reasoned utopia' (Bourdieu 1998) that can serve as an alternative to the economic fatalism of the market society. But what could the essence of such an alternative vision of economy-society relations be? Put in simple Polanyian terms, counter-movements should insist that the economic system ceases to lay down the law to society. The primacy of society over that system ought to be restored. For Polanyi, labour, land and money are fictitious commodities, because they were not originally produced for the market. Accordingly, he argued that the disestablishment of the commodity fiction, that is, the democratic control of labour, land, and money markets, would not be an unrealistic fantasy but lie 'in all directions of the social compass' ([1944] 2001, 258f).

Second, counter-movements can also exploit the contradictions between market society and political democracy. Neither the EU nor its member states are autocratic dictatorships. Therefore, the contradiction between the declared democratic norms and the technocratic practice of socio-economic governance provides social actors with opportunities to politicise the economy not only at the level of constitutional politics, but also at lower levels of everyday policy-making. The advocates of regulatory governance perceive policy-making as an apolitical process in quest of 'best practice' and take objective criteria for decision-making quality for granted. But if citizens have divergent interests, not least as a result of their position in the production process, this assumption turns out to be very problematic; what is a good regulation for one citizen may be a bad one for another. For this reason, the democratisation of economic policy at both the national and the supranational levels requires above all collective action which politicises everyday policy-making. There is a need for the conflict resolution mechanism offered by democratic procedures only if social actors articulate conflicting interests. As long as policy-making can be seen as a technical process, due to the absence of social and political contestation, there is no need for democratic procedures.

So far, in today's Europe, trade unions are struggling to cope with the drastic results of the global financial, economic, and political crisis for their members. They have differed in their approaches, some militant ones organising general strikes, others complying more or less reluctantly with unprecedented attacks on their members' wages and working conditions. These are early days, but one thing is clear: the time now seems set for one of increasing conflict. Although some European unions accepted the post-crisis austerity measures proposed by governments more or less reluctantly, the integration of subordinate classes into the dominant socio-economic regime by social packs between the peak associations of capital and labour and the government seems to be increasingly difficult (Rehfeldt 2009, van Apeldoorn et al. 2009). While workers have accepted the logic of national 'competitive corporatism' – that is, a smaller slice of the national income when the GDP was growing (Erne 2008) – it is arguably much more difficult to convince workers to accept a smaller slice of a shrinking cake. Given the fading prospects for growth, it is likely that there will be an intensification of the distributional conflict between wages and profits in the years to come. This may, once again, lead to an unexpected 'resurgence of class conflict' (Crouch and Pizzorno 1978), which could reignite the engines of political conflict and ideological division that gave Europe its social and democratic impetus in the past (Anderson 2009).

NOTE

1. An earlier version of this chapter has been published in Italian: R. Erne (2011). 'I sindacati europei dopo la crisi globale' in Quaderni Rassegna Sindacale – Lavori XII (1) 157–76.

REFERENCES

Anderson, P. (2009), *The New Old World*, London: Verso.
Baccaro, L., R. Boyer, C. Crouch, M. Regini, P. Marginson, R. Hyman, R. Gumbrell-McCormick and R. Milkman (2009), 'Discussion Forum I: Labour and the global financial crisis', *Socio-Economic Review*, **8**, 341–76.
Becker, J. and J. Jäger (2009), 'Die EU und die große Krise', *Prokla. Zeitschrift für Kritische Sozialwissenschaft*, **39** (4), 541–58.
Block, F. (2001), 'Introduction', in K. Polanyi, *The Great Transformation*, Boston: Beacon Press, i–xxxviii.
Block, F. (2007), 'Understanding the diverging trajectories of the United States and Western Europe: A Neo-Polanyian Analysis', *Politics and Society*, **35** (1), 3–33.
Bode, T. and K. Pink (2010), 'Die Finanzkrise als Demokratiekrise', *Blätter für deutsche und internationale Politik*, **55** (6), 45–55.
Boos, S. (2008), 'Notrecht: Geld im Ausnahmezustand', *Die Wochenzeitung*, 23 October.
Bourdieu, P. (1998), 'A Reasoned utopia and economic fatalism', *New Left Review*, **227**.
Bundesrat (2008), 'Verordnung über die Rekapitalisierung der UBS AG vom 15. Oktober, SR 611.055 ', available at: http://www.admin.ch/ch/d/as/2008/4741. pdf.
Burawoy, M. (1979), *Manufacturing Consent*, Chicago: University of Chicago Press.
Burawoy, M. (2010), 'From Polanyi to Pollyanna: The false optimism of global labor studies', *Global Labour Journal*, **1** (2), 301–13.

Butselaar, E. (2008), 'Banking crisis: Expert views: After a week of turmoil, has the world changed?', *The Guardian*, 20 September.

Cox, R.W. (1983), 'Gramsci, hegemony and international relations: An essay in method', *Millennium - Journal of International Studies*, **12**, 162–75.

Crouch, C. (1970), *The Student Revolt*, London: Bodley Head.

Crouch, C. (2004), *Post-Democracy*, Cambridge: Polity.

Crouch, C. (2009a), 'Privatised Keynesianism: An unacknowledged policy regime', *British Journal of Politics & International Relations,* **11** (3), 382–99.

Crouch, C. (2009b), 'Typologies of capitalism', in B. Hancké (ed.) *Debating Varieties of Capitalism*, Oxford: Oxford University Press, pp. 75–94.

Crouch, C. (2010), 'The financial crisis a new chance for labour movements? Not yet', *Socio-Economic Review*, **8**, 353–6.

Crouch, C. and A. Pizzorno (eds) (1978), *The Resurgence of Class Conflict in Western Europe since 1968. Vol. 2, Comparative Analysis*, New York: Holmes and Meier Publishers.

Dongfang, H. (2010), 'China's workers are stirring', *International Herald Tribune*, 17 June.

Drago, M.E. (1998), *The Institutional Base of Chile's Economic 'Miracle': Institutions, Government Discretionary Authority, and Economic Performance under Two Policy Regimes,* Florence: PhD thesis: European University Institute.

Erne, R. (2007), 'On the use and abuse of bibliometric performance indicators: A critique of Hix's "global ranking of political science departments"', *European Political Science*, **6** (3), 306–14.

Erne, R. (2008), *European Unions. Labour's Quest for a Transnational Democracy*, Ithaca, NY: Cornell University Press.

Erne, R. (2011), 'Interest Associations', in D. Caramani (ed.) *Comparative Politics*, 2nd edition, Oxford: Oxford University Press, pp. 259–74.

Erne, R. (2012), 'European Industrial Relations after the Crisis. A Postscript', in S. Smismans (ed.), *The European Union and Industrial Relations. New Procedures, New Context,* Manchester: Manchester University Press, forthcoming.

Foster, J.B. and F. Magdoff (2009), *The Great Financial Crisis: Causes and Consequences*, New York: Monthly Review Press.

Gajewska, K. (2009), *Transnational Labour Solidarity. Mechanisms of Commitment to Cooperation within the European Trade Union Movement,* Abingdon, Oxon: Routledge.

Gamble, A. (2009), *The Spectre at the Feast: Capitalist Crisis and the Politics of Recession*, Basingstoke: Palgrave Macmillan.

Glyn, A. (2006), *Capitalism Unleashed*, Oxford: Oxford University Press.

Hancké, B. (eds) (2010), *Debating Varieties of Capitalism*, Oxford: Oxford University Press.

Harcourt, M and G.E. Wood (ed.) (2004), *Trade Unions and Democracy: Strategies and Perspectives,* Manchester University Press, 2004.

Harvey, D. (2005), *A Brief History of Neoliberalism*, Oxford: Oxford University Press.

Harvey, D. (2010), *The Enigma of Capital and the Crisis of Capitalism*, London: Profile Books.

Hürtgen, S. (2008), *Trasnationales Co-Management. Betriebliche Politik in der globalen Konkurenz,* Münster: Westfälisches Dampfboot.

Keynes, J.M. ([1936] 2008]) *The General Theory of Employment, Interest and Money,* Thousand Oaks, CA: BN Publishing.

Klein, N. (2008), 'Banking crisis: Expert views: After a week of turmoil, has the world changed?', *The Guardian*, 20 September.

Krugman, P. (2010), 'The pain caucus', *The New York Times*, 31 May.

Mair, P. (2006), 'Ruling the void: The hollowing of western democracy', *New Left Review,* **42**, 25–51.

Majone, G. (1994), 'The Rise of the Regulatory State in Europe', *West European Politics*, **17** (3), 77–101.

Martin, S.B. (2009), 'Review of 'European Unions'', *Perspectives on Politics,* **7** (4), 1003–4.

Marx, K. ([1887] 1999), *Capital*, Volume One, available at: http://www.marxists.org/archive/marx/works/1867-c1/index.htm

Meardi, G. (2012), 'Union immobility? Trade unions and the freedoms of movement in the enlarged EU', *British Journal of Industrial Relations*, **50** (1), forthcoming.

Mitchell, K.E. (2009), 'Review of 'European Unions'', *Industrial & Labor Relations Review*, **62** (3), 437–9.

Moody, K. (1997), *Workers in a Lean World: Unions in the International Economy*, New York: Verso.

Mouriaux, R. (2010), 'Le mouvement syndicale et la crise', *Contretemps*, **5**, 63–75.

Offe, C. and H. Wiesenthal (1985), 'Two logics of collective action: Theoretical notes on social class and organizational form', in C. Offe, *Disorganized Capitalism*, Cambridge: Polity, pp. 175–220.

Pereira, I. (2009), *Peut-on être radical et pragmatique?*, Paris: Éditions textuel.

Phelan, C., A. Martin, B. Hancké, L. Baccaro, and R. Erne (2009), 'Labour History symposium: Roland Erne, European unions', *Labor History*, **50** (2), 187–216.

Polanyi, K. ([1944] 2001), *The Great Transformation*, Boston: Beacon Press.

Rehfeldt, U. (2009), 'La concertation au sommet toujours d'actualité face à la crise? Théorie du néocorporatime et analyse comparée des relations profession-nelles en Europe', *Chronique International de l'IRES*, **121**, 40–49.

Sachs, J. (2010), 'It is time to plan for the world after Keynes', *Financial Times*, 8 June.

Schmitt, C. ([1922] 1985), *Political Theology. Four Chapters on the Concept of Sovereignty,* Cambridge, Mass.: MIT Press.

Skidelsky, R. (2010), 'The crisis of capitalism: Keynes versus Marx', *Indian Journal of Industrial Relations*, **45** (3), 321–35.

Skocpol, T. (2003), *Diminished Democracy: From Membership to Management in American Civic Life*, Norman: University of Oklahoma Press.

Stevis, D. and T. Boswell (2007), *Globalization and Labor: Democratizing Global Governance*, Lanham, MD: Rowman and Littlefield.

Stiglitz, J. (2008), 'Banking crisis: Expert views: After a week of turmoil, has the world changed?', *The Guardian*, 20 September.

Stiglitz, J. (2010a), *Freefall: Free Markets and the Sinking of the Global Economy,* London: Allen Lane.

Stiglitz, J. (2010b), 'The non-existent hand: Book review of "Keynes: The Return of the Master" by Robert Skidelsky', *London Review of Books*, **32** (8), 17–18.

Thompson, M. and D.G. Taras (2004), 'Employment relations in Canada', in G. Bamber, R.D. Lansbury and N. Wailes (eds), *International and Comparative Employment Relations*, London: Sage, 91–118.

Van Apeldoorn, B., J. Drahokoupil and L. Horn (eds) (2009), *Contradictions and*

Limits of Neoliberal European Governance: From Lisbon to Lisbon, Basingstoke: Palgrave Macmillan.

Weiler, J.H.H., U. Haltern, and F.C. Mayer. (1995), 'European democracy and its critique', *West European Politics*, **18** (4), 4–39.

Žižek, S. (2009), *First as Tragedy, then as Farce*, London: Verso.

8. States in transition, research about the state in flux

Patrick Le Galès

The question of the state remains central in social sciences. Theda Skocpol's famous 'Bringing the state back in' (in Evans et al. 1985) has been remarkably successful; there is no need to do it again. There is no need either to claim 'new' debates of the state as such. However, the interest for the state is modified by two intellectual dynamics: first, more and more research deals with the making and evolution of the state in less linear ways in different parts of the world (Vu 2010). In particular, the conditions of creation of states, their dynamics, and examples of state failures all bring in explanations and characterization of states which are more and more divergent from the standard European nation state seen through the experience of France, the UK or Germany. Recent literature from American historians and political scientists emphasize the particular story and characteristics of the US state. In a provocative paper 'ironies of state building', King and Lieberman in particular use insights from the making of states in Eastern Europe to characterize the American state (2011). In other words, the accumulation of cases about state creation and transformations and the development of innovative comparative projects reveal a messier but also a stimulating world of social science concerning the state (Zurn and Leipfried 2005).

For instance, the dichotomy strong states/weak states (Badie and Birnbaum 1982) has been more or less abandoned in favour of more nuanced typologies or a serious rethinking about key variables of statehoodness. More systematic comparative research about states in Asia, Latin America and Africa have emphasized the role of colonial inheritance, dynamics of religious influences, competition between parties and interest groups, that is, the role of internal actors in competition to shape forms of state simultaneously influenced by norms and forces from outside. An innovative literature is for instance focusing on state failures, on the difficulties of the failures of states to tax, to provide goods and services to the population, or to protect the population. States, or elites of the state, may also be active in order to steal, oppress or develop violence against their own population (Rothberg 2004).

Secondly, the debate in the 1990s was very much shaped by the opposition between those emphasizing the eternal strength of the state and those making a living out of prophesizing its demise in relation to globalization trends. Books and articles speak volumes in this respect: 'the dismantling state', 'the virtual state', 'the retreating state' (Strange 1996), 'the hollowing out of the state' (Rhodes 1994), 'the destatization process' (Jessop 2002), 'the splintered state' (Dupuy and Thoenig 1985), 'the organizational state'; some even have a question mark – 'the state, obsolete or obstinate?' (Hoffman 1995). Comparative political economy scholars in the vein of neo-institutionalism seemed to give a less central role to the state as a key variable as was made clear in either Crouch and Streeck 'Political economy of modern capitalism' (1997) or Hall and Soskice's major 'Varieties of capitalisms' (2001).

This question of the disappearance of the state is not central anymore. The debate about the state is now clearly framed in terms of the analysis of the 'restructuring of the state', to use Wright and Cassese's title of an agenda-setting book on the state (1997). Actors within the state are active agents of the globalization processes. Some sections of the state are gaining ground and developing new forms of authority. The economic crisis since 2007/2008 has also been a powerful reminder of the role of the state at times of crisis. However, the analysis of the restructuring of the state is fraught with many conceptual difficulties: where to start? What is the correct length of time to consider? What variables should be emphasized? What are the dynamics of change? This chapter is a small contribution to this vast research domain, focusing on definition issues before underlining two dynamics of state restructuring.

LOOKING FOR A WORKING DEFINITION OR SEARCHING FOR THE GRAAL?

Needless to say, the fact that attempting to clarify the debate about the state to analyse its transformation is an intimidating task. It is clear, for instance, that some of the more distinctive contributions to the state debate have been initiated by scholars pursuing long-term intellectual interests in the understanding of the state. For instance, Michael Mann, the British sociologist from UCLA, is currently writing the third volume of his exceptional trilogy about the state, 'Sources of social power'. The last volume will deal with globalization. In Florence, the patriarch of Italian social science, Alessandro Pizzorno, has assembled a team to work on the dynamics of democracy and the state. Quentin Skinner, the leading figure of the Cambridge School, is working on the genealogy of the state analysed through his particular methodology based upon ideas and discourses. Wolfgang Streeck, the director of the Max Planck Institute of Cologne, is preparing a book on the fiscal crisis of the state. From a different intellectual horizon, Mitchell Dean in Sidney is developing his analysis of the state based upon ideas of governmentality and rationality derived from the work of Michel Foucault. Bob Jessop in Lancaster offers the most precise critique of the role of the state to adapt and support globalized capitalism. Steven Skorownek at Yale, a leading figure of neo-institutionalism and the 'American political development group', works on the long-term institutionalization of the American state. Stephen Leibfried in Bremen, a leading scholar on the welfare state, is in charge of a massive 15-year research project on the transformation of the state, Transtate. The anthropologist James Scott at Yale analyses the state from the point of view of the resistance towards it and state failures. Rational choice scholars from M. Levi to A. Greif rewrite the story of the making of states by taking into account their individual preferences. And Charles Tilly died prematurely while working on yet another essential book, 'Cities and states in world history'. At the very least, this impressive line-up reveals the salience of the subject.

A second issue is the diversity of research dealing with the state going in all sorts of direction. The now classic 'fiscal military model' of state formation epitomized in particular in Tilly's work has been contested from various social science corners, including comparative historical sociology (Vu 2010, Jessop 2006). To mention a few examples there is now a substantial gender literature about the state (Adams 2005). STS scholars (Sociology of Science and Technologies) inspired by the work of B. Latour, J. Law or M. Callon but also M. Foucault and N. Elias have in particular emphasized the construction of states in relation to the emergence of different kinds of knowledge, technologies, representations, materialities, networks, produced for instance by engineers or doctors (Baldwin 2005, Carroll 2006). Porter's (1995) or Desrosiere's (1993) classic books on quantification and the production of figures have been crucial landmarks in the understanding of the state, echoing Weber's rationalization process or James Scott's powerful argument about the modern state making society legible (1999). 'The state can be understood simultaneously as an idea, a system, and a country, as a complex of meanings, practices, and materialities. The state idea has become a powerful discursive formation, a cognitive structure, and assemblage of institutions: the state system has become a vast organizational apparatus that is practiced with varying degree of coherence (and indeed incoherence) from the heads of executive agencies to the most mundane aspect of everyday life: and the state country is constituted through the materialities of land, built environment, and bodies/people, transformed by the co-productive agencies of science and government and rendered in the new forms of techno-territory, infrastructural jurisdiction and bio-population' (Carroll 2009: 592).

Research about the state has been seriously critically revised under the influence of cultural studies scholars and post-positivist research (Marinetto 2007). In particular they have contributed to the deconstruction of the state as a being, as a stable institution. By contrast they stress the fact that the state is a contingent form, always in question, always changing in relation to discourse, a radical constructivist point of view. In their 2010 book, *The State as Cultural Practice*, Bevir and Rhodes suggest an alternative to positivism by defining the state in terms of meanings in action, that is, 'the state appears as a differentiated cultural practice composed of all kinds of contigent and shifting beliefs and actions, where these beliefs and actions can be explained through an historical understanding' (8).

In parallel, constructivist sociologists have emphasized the historicity and contingency of processes leading to state formation in order to avoid either the reification of the state or to take the europeano-centric conception of the state for granted. Migdal (2009) suggests for instance to differentiate at least between three waves of state formation in the twentieth century beyond classic European models: the post-First World War wave, the decolonization wave, the end of the soviet empire wave. At each period, different forms of capitalism, national ideologies, norms of nation states and power relations between states may explain the emergence of different processes of state making. More comparative and historical work suggests considering a wider range of state emergence and trajectories. This irreducible contingency of the state is central in comparative historical sociology of the state emphasizing bottom-up processes, the fluidity of state-making trajectories, and the diversity of historical experiences. Leguil-Bayart, in his work on African states, stresses hybridization processes related to diverse colonial experiences. His group of researchers emphasize intersection points between overlapping levels and overlapping historical periods. Hibou's volume on the privatization of the state (1999) is also anti-functionalist as she shows non-linear trajectories of states' de-differentiation, transfers of functions to agencies or families (patrimonalization), focusing on different forms of interactions between states and societies in different parts of the world.

In other words, the state is complex and so is the analysis of the state. Reviewing various developments of the sociology of the state, Migdal concludes: 'Studying the state involves probing a multilayered, multipurposed entity, whose parts frequently work at cross purposes. And this complex state operates in a similarly complex multitiered environment, which deeply affects the state, and, in turn is affected by the state . . . All this complexity has turned the experience of researching the state into an eclectic enterprise. It demands a full toolkit – an amalgation of culturalist, structuralist, and rationalist tools and of historical, case and quantitative methods' (2009: 192). It might be slightly overwhelming though in terms of method. One radical solution following the same line of argument is to get rid of any definition in order to avoid any essentialism. Skinner's method of 'Ideas in context' leads to that conclusion. In a recent paper on the genealogy of the modern state, a follow up to his classic books, he makes the following point about the word state: 'I consequently focus as much as possible on how this particular word came to figure in successive debates about the nature of public power . . . to investigate the genealogy of the state is to discover that there has never been any agreed concept to which the word state has answered' (2009: 325–26). This is a fascinating intellectual journey but radical constructivism does not help comparative research. The argument has a logic. However, moderate constructivism seems a more fruitful perspective from which to analyse contemporary changes.

Although neo-Marxist analysis of the state has never disappeared, the current economic crisis shows at length the relevance on many Marxist insights about the state.[1] Marx was the first thinker to have shown that the self-regulated market, the putatively free and effective play of market forces, required the state. On Marxist and neo-Marxist accounts, the state played an essential role, namely in connection with primitive accumulation of capital and ideology, the latter a reflection of the dominant force in society. This argument has been applied in various empirical studies; for example, Logan and Molotch's classic 1987 sociological study of urban growth coalitions and how urban real estate markets operate in the United States, which empirically clarifies the social role of the state in growth coalitions: the state first intervenes as guarantor of social order, namely through ideology and by regulating the various social interests (a classic neo-Marxist argument), as social order is an essential condition for real estate investment; it later intervenes in the accumulation phase, making below-market-price land or subsidies available to real estate developers. Those developments are also used in relation to the globalization of capitalism. Jessop (2002, 2006) and Brenner (2004) provide an ambitious theoretical framework and analyse the transformation of the state under current conditions of capitalism. They argue that although the importance of the national state-controlled scale of political power has been in decline, states are still very active and control many resources. They develop a political economy of scale to analyse the rescaling of the state, or rather, *statehood* based upon an analysis of the struggle to reorganize both statehood and capitalism following the destabilization of the nation state primacy in organizing both society and capitalism. They contrast the postwar fordist Keynesian state with the more competitiveness-driven approaches to contemporary state that Jessop named the Schumpeterian Workfare state. They develop a sophisticated (what they call) strategic relational approach to the state to stress that the state is a strategic site of structuration of globalization.

In contrast to anti-essentialist views, generations of lawyers have defined the state in terms of an independent territory, an institutional apparatus of government and the source of the law (Loughlin 2009). But beyond this, there is a real ambiguity about what should be analysed. As Jessop put it: 'Is the state best defined by its legal form, coercive capacities, institutional composition and boundaries, internal operations and modes of calculation, declared aims, functions for the broader society, or sovereign place in the international system? Is it a thing, a subject, a social relations or a construct that helps to orient political actions? Is stateness a variable and, if so, what are its central dimensions? What is the relationship between the state and law, the state and politics, the state and civil society, the public and the private, state power and micropower relations? Is the state best studied in isolation: only as part of the political system: or, indeed, in terms of a more general social theory? Do states have institutional, decisional, or operational autonomy and, if so, what are its sources and limits?' (2006: 111–12). As is made explicit in that quote, a lot of the confusion about the state, and the analysis of the contemporary restructuring process, derives from the variables but also the period chosen to understand change.

To answer these questions, one may start by following the classic Weberian route. Although there is a debate about several definitions of the state, the most well-known Weberian definition of the state in terms of political institutions attempt to monopolize violence. As is well known, the institutional dimension of the state is a key dimension for Weber (1978). In the macro historical comparative sociology tradition, Badie and Birnbaum (1982) or Lachmann (2010) in particular have emphasized the differentiation and autonomization of elites, different from social or economic elites, professionals claiming a monopoly of being in charge of governing and developing specialised institutions. In that tradition of research, the key variable of the state is the construction of an autonomous political space and the differentiation of elites. Of course, in this perspective, there are different types of states but the analysis of the contemporary restructuring of the state does not make much sense. What is central is the long-term construction of states which are central in structuring societies. For Badie and Birnbaum, tensions between states and various forms of capitalism are irrelevant, and the whole development of the welfare state and public policies are third-rate questions.

In a similar Weberian vein, Du Gay and Scott (2010) argue that much confusion about the state derives from the choice of periods. They shed doubts about the literature dealing with the restructuring of the state because most of it tends to identify a high point of the state in the 1960s (a golden age according to the Transtate programme in Bremen), and to reify some post-golden age period. They argue that this dichotomy does not make much sense because both comparative macro sociologist of state formation, or scholars of the so called Cambridge School (Skinner Pollock, Greuss) have shown at length the gradual process of state formation, slowly taking a modern form over several centuries. In other words, they argue, the relevance of short term radical change is likely to be weak. They also stress the fact that confusion is increased by the most recent developments of the state (welfare state in the twentieth century). In other words, they criticize the choice made by many scholars to analyse the state first and foremost in terms of government, of the actions and activities of the state instead of the state as being. By contrast, they argue in favour of a parsimonious, quasi-essentialist definition of the state. The state is an independent coercive apparatus also defined by the centrality of the rule of law as argued by Poggi (1983). Defined in these terms, the state is about 'being' and the activities play no roles. These authors suggest rehabilitating Aron's concept 'regime' to talk about the rest, including government. Beyond the fact that the relations between regime and state are not – yet – clearly defined in this account, this definition suggests that the development of government policies over the last 200 years was a minor point in comparison with the making of the state itself. It also suggests that these developments are independent from the noble structure of the state and had no effect whatsoever on the state itself. Nevertheless, Du Gay and Scott make a strong point: it is useful to distinguish the state from the government in order, in particular, not to assume that changes concerning governments automatically signal state changes.

Following this route also leads to the analysis of the apparatus of the state, the organization of the state. Many empirical projects, sometimes initiated by public administration scholars, have attempted to document the restructuring of the state bureaucracy, that is, the demise of hierarchical large administrations and ministries, of external services of the state and the rise of agencies – known as the agencification of the state (Benamouzig 2005; Thatcher 2007; Pollitt 2004), of auditing organizations (Hood 1998, Flinders 2008). In most European countries, states reforming themselves has become a central political question. What Bezes has smartly called 'Le souci de soi de l'Etat', is a good indicator of serious changes that even parsimonious Weberians would find hard to put aside.

All in all, in the Weberian tradition, there is widespread consensus around a definition of the state understood in terms of relative monopoly and concentration of coercion. It is defined as a complex of interdependent institutions, relatively differentiated and legitimate, autonomous, based upon a defined territory and recognized as a state by other states. The state is also characterized by its administrative capacity to steer, to govern a society, to establish constraining rules, property rights, to guarantee exchanges, to tax and concentrate resources, to organize economic development and to protect its citizens (Mann 1984, Tilly 2008, Levi 2002). The state takes different shapes according to periods, to countries; it is not a given rigid form.

INFRASTRUCTURAL POWER AND THE POLICY STATE

One line of the debate about the state suggests studying the state with parsimony, concentrating on its basic institutions and functions, on its formation and the classic criteria of elite differentiation. However, it may also be fruitful to think about the state by looking at what it does, the activities, the interactions, the capacity to structure and steer society, as government. In other words, the development of public policies over one century may not just be a strange appendix to the 'pure' state which may be easily cut off. What happens in the policy realm, in relation to politics, may have structural consequences for states, secession or bankruptcy for instance.

A useful point of departure is Mann's classic distinction between what he calls the despotic power of the state, that is, 'the range of actions which the elite is empowered to undertake without routine, institutionalized negotiation with civil society groups' and the infrastructural power, that is, 'the capacity of the state actually to penetrate civil society, and to implement logistically political decisions throughout the realms' (1984: 193). Combining these two analytically distinctive dimensions allow Mann to show, in his wonderful two volumes on the state, the weakening of the first dimension and the strengthening of the second in relation to the rise and rise of public policies in Europe over the twentieth century.

Following Lowi's classic insight on policies structuring politics, many public policy scholars, neo-institutionalists in particular, have tried to show how the implementation of policies, and their results, were crucial elements of the structuring of political conflicts, and of the legitimacy of the state (Duran 2009).

Three very different research strategies are therefore at play in analysing the restructuring of the state. One concentrates on the classic question of elites and institutions, on the being of the state, in order to show the long-term resistance and robustness of the state. Another, in contrast, stresses ever-changing configurations. A last assumes that the long-term entropy of the state has had long-term consequences also on the being of the state. Analysing the 'government' dimension of the state, the policy state to borrow the phrase coined by Skorownek, may be central to understanding the institutional dimension of the state, sometimes its survival. Policy successes and policy failures are not without consequence on the legitimacy of the state. In a number of cases, from the US to Greece, Spain or Belgium, the sustainability of the state in its current form is at stake (Jacobs and King 2009).

In Western Europe and in the US, empirical research points to different, sometimes contradictory directions, hence the research agenda defined in terms of the restructuring of the state (Wright and Cassese 1997). A large body of research has tried to identify the failures of the state to govern. The contemporary debate about the state, very much influenced both by comparative political economy research and by the governance question, tends to focus on the question of capacity. In the late 1990s Crouch and Streeck joined an increasing number of scholars who pointed towards the decreasing ability of the state to govern society. The argument is well known: globalization trends, however contradictory they might be, may give a role to the state to force the adaptation of society but they also make society more difficult to govern because of the rise of exit strategy, firms and economic flux in particular. The hidden secret of state was therefore one of a growing inability to govern society, to tax, to implement decisions, questions well identified by governance scholars (Mayntz 1993).

They developed a new research agenda based upon classic questions associated to governance and government alike: not just who governs but how governments and various actors involved in governance processes operate. This is not a new idea. Foucault in particular made the point about the importance of governmental activities to understand change of governmentality and the theme was central for Miller and Rose when they started their long-term research project on governmentatility (2008). However, to raise this issue is to underline the fact that the governance research agenda is historically related to the 1970s research about public policy failures, well represented by the work of Pressman and Wildavsky (1973). One then wondered whether complex societies were becoming ungovernable or if, at the very least, governments and states' elites were less and less able to govern society through the administration, taxes and laws. Ever since, this debate has led to a dynamic governance research domain organized around the following questions: Can government govern, steer or row (Peters 1997) Do governments always govern? What do they govern, and how? What is not governed? Can we identify dysfunctions of governments over time? Can groups or sectors escape from governments (Mayntz 1993)? What does it mean to govern complex societies (Pierre and Peters 2005)? Political economy scholars, emphasizing the role of the globalization of capitalism, have even more developed the idea of the powerless state in economic terms (classic work from Strange for instance), or at the very least the state heavily constrained by financial markets, the strategy of large firms or globalized exchanges. In a recent ongoing contribution to this debate, Streeck in particular has precisely underlined the fiscal crisis of the state. If inheritance is a classic theme in public policy (Rose and Davies 1994), Streeck shows, before the crisis, the structural development of public deficits in most developed countries followed by rising debt and dramatically reduced capacity to govern (2010). Needless to say, the argument has not lost its force with the coming of the financial crisis.

By contrast, many scholars have also pointed out, at the same time, that state operations, public policies have been expanding in new spheres (Levy 2006, Jacobs and King 2009). States have become more intrusive or have developed new policies in matters of education, gender, discrimination, environment, but also security, defence or surveillance. New bureaucracies are developing in the field of auditing and control to change the behaviour of individuals through mechanisms of sanctions and rewards (Le Galès and Scott 2010). In terms of relations between states and markets, neo-Marxist, Polanyian and neo-institutionalists have for a long time stressed the fact that markets were sustained by state activities, policies, ideology and finances. As Levy rightly documents, the rise of market-making activities and policies has become a notable feature of state elites more influenced by neo-liberal ideas. Both the Thatcher and the New Labour governments were characterized not only by privatization and the introduction of market mechanisms in the public sector but also centralization, and a stronger and more authoritarian state (Gamble 1993, Faucher-King and Le Galès 2010). In the US, a whole series of research is emphasizing the same apparently contradictory pattern (Jacobs and King 2009).

The financial and economic crisis since 2008 illustrates more than ever this apparent paradox of weakened states in relation to banks, hedge funds, or large firms escaping taxes and reinforced states to bail out the financial sector and transfer the private debt to the public sector. Despite the structural weakening of financial state capacity, some attempts have been made to recover the infrastructural power of the state, to use Mann's turn of phrase. Again, innovations in public policies and activities of the state are probably very revealing of state restructuring.

RECOVERING STATE CAPACITY TO GOVERN? TWO DYNAMICS

Instead of focusing on the impact on the crisis as such, as it is still early days, the last section of the chapter deals with one aspect of state restructuring, that is, the making of two very different modes of governance in the making, one could say the left hand and the right hand of the state.[2] This also echoes some of the ideas that Peters (2008) has expressed on the future of governing, that is, the simultaneous development of new public management and centralizing tendencies together with forms of negotiated governance.

Firstly, one distinctive transformation of modes of governance is related to the rise and rise of those policy instruments requiring the mobilization of various actors and groups for the construction of the collective good, and the implementation of public policies. Agreements, charters, contracts, reveal a different conceptualization of the state aiming at mobilizing different actors and their resources. This mode of intervention has become generalized in a context strongly critical of bureaucracy – of its cumbersome yet abstract nature, and of the way it reduces accountability (Salamon 2002). The interventionist state is therefore supposed to be giving way to a state that is a prime mover or coordinator, non-interventionist and principally mobilizing, integrating and bringing into coherence. This echoes a view of a democracy of protest, of collective actors. In the US and in the EU all organizations want to become political actors. But what is an actor? Who knows (Meyer 2000)? This profound uncertainty both constrains and facilitates mobilization within groups and organizations to attain the status of actor and to gain recognition as such by others, thus marking a strong dependence on outside models of legitimation. More generally, the actors mobilize to gain recognition as an actor. Internal mobilization towards this status meets outside injunctions and produces a dynamic system driven by all sorts of models and norms.

In many cities, for instance, governance is not just organized by coalitions such as urban regimes (Stone 1989). Protest can limit the implementation of projects decided by urban growth coalitions (Logan and Molotch 1987). Overcoming implementation failure often requires a long process of consultation, of enrolment of different groups, of local construction of the general interest, of deliberation, of contracts, partnerships or charters to stabilize the relationship between various actors, including state actors among others, to define common goals and instruments to reach them, hence making more likely the desired outcomes of a mode of governance. Instruments have also a life of their own, and once in place sometimes significantly contribute to the outcome (Lascoumes and Le Galès 2007, Bezes 2009, Jacquot 2010).

In many countries, in different sectors, the systematic introduction of those mobilizing policy instruments is giving rise to modes of governance characterized by negotiation between various group, the 'enchanted land of governance', leading to the normative view of a deliberative democracy, free of conflicts, market inequalities and power relations.

A second development, which has attracted less interest, except in the UK, points to the rise of policy instruments based upon norms, standards, performance indicators, management instruments and the rise of a new bureaucracy in particular to 'govern at a distance', including networks and agencies. This leads to profound changes of behaviours and allows a remarkable comeback of state elite to govern and to constrain various groups in society. The New Labour experiment in the UK is probably one of the most remarkable example of this new governance in the making (and its failures) (Moran 2003; Hood 2007; Bevir 2005; Faucher-King and Le Galès 2010).

For the Blair and Brown teams, the invention that is 'New Labour' served to demonstrate the distance they had put between themselves and previous Labour governments and the unions. They promised to regenerate the declining public sector and provide better services, challenge the excesses of competition, and offer protection for employees and workers. They committed themselves to principles of management and responsibility, democratization of public agencies, performance indicators, and a valorization of associations and the 'third sector'. Several authors have shown the debt the New Labour project owes to ideas about communitarianism, social inclusion and even to the rise of neo-institutionalism. Bevir, taking an interpretative standpoint, in particular argues that New Labour was a kind of social democratic approach to questions and issues brought to the fore by the New Right. New Labour developed discourse of partnership, joined-up governance, inspired by new institutionalism. Many policy instruments developed in that framework makes sense in that line of thinking in contrast to market rationality advocated by the right and based upon micro-economics.

However, this is only one part of the story, another part of the New Labour project is the continuity of the market-making society promoted by Mrs Thatcher and the new right and legitimized by the massive use of economics, rational choice and micro-economics in particular, determining

policy instrumentation, that is, choice of instruments characterizing New
Labour governance.

The Thatcher governments centralized and reformed the state, and
destroyed traditional social structures (including at the heart of the British
establishment, in the organization of the City, and in the legal and medical
professions), social solidarities, and institutions. They encouraged actors
to behave like egoistic, rational individuals. Establishing rewards and
penalties makes it possible to pilot changes in individual and organizational behaviour. According to Max Weber, the 'bureaucratic revolution'
changes individuals 'from without' by transforming the conditions to
which they must adapt (Le Galès and Scott 2010). Bureaucracy is a force
for social change, for the destruction of traditional social systems and the
creation of new systems, with all that that entails in terms of violence and
resistance. Bureaucratic rationalization is wholly compatible with modernization of the economy. It makes behaviour more predictable and helps
create social order organized on the basis of calculation and efficiency. The
bureaucratic revolution initiated by Margaret Thatcher was at the heart of
New Labour's strategy for modernizing Britain. New Labour wanted to
put consumers of public services at the centre of public services and, to the
maximum possible extent, limit the influence of producers – in particular,
the public sector unions, which were regarded as one of the most conservative forces in the country. Transformation of the mode of governing – that
is, incessant, sometimes contradictory reform of the public sector – was
the badge of the Blair governments. It took the form of autonomy for the
basic units of public management (schools, hospitals, social services), but
flanked by a battery of statistical measures, indicators, and objectives for
results or improvements in performance.

The New Labour team elected in 1997 was largely won over to the
rather vague theses of 'new public management' inspired by public choice
economics. These resulted in the application of the principles of rational
choice and classical micro-economics to public management, sometimes
by transferring the recipes of private management to public management.
Blair and Brown clearly understood that a redefinition of the rules of
political action (in the direction of the regulatory state) went hand in hand
with an increase in controls. While part of the traditional bureaucracy
was dismantled and subjected to market mechanisms, the core executive
gained in independence. The new government did not intend to reconsider
the framework of public management left by the Conservatives. The inheritance was adopted, mobilized, and consolidated by New Labour, whose
action can be characterized as follows: indicators for good public management extending beyond performance were developed for the precise
piloting of public action; according to the social model of neo-classical

economists, individuals respond to stimulation; the delivery of public policy combined public and private partners in flexible ways; priority was given to delivery and the definition of objectives; power was centralized in order to initiate reforms, monitor delivery, and make government action coherent; the inspiration for reforms no longer derived from the senior civil service, but from think tanks, experts, consultants, academics, and foreign experience (essentially the United States).

New Labour systematized a way of steering government on the basis of performance objectives, league tables, and strict financial control. These developments revealed their credence in the magical powers of synthetic indicators to bring about rapid changes. Moreover, this was one of the characteristics of New Labour management: radical reforms were conducted through a proliferation of indicators and a rapid redefinition of targets and programmes. In their eyes, the social world was malleable, reactive, and dynamic. Under pressure, it reacts forthwith to commands for mobilization from the masters of the moment.

One cannot but be surprised by the extraordinary ambition of piloting society through such indicators and the discrepancy as regards service provision to the population. Thus, as early as 1998, the government announced the creation of 300 performance objectives for all departments. Each of them might make for newspaper headlines! These objectives were bound up with the resources allocated by the Treasury; each of its objectives was then divided up into dozens or hundreds of specific indicators by area. In view of the importance of the rhetoric of modernization, New Labour made it a point of pride to mobilize every 'modern' technique, not just the latest managerial fashions, but also the systematic production of aggregate indictors thanks to increasingly sophisticated new technologies. They promoted the development of e-government with enthusiasm. Following the example of the managerial software used in large firms to know the activity of different units in real time, they generalized the activity of reporting from agency or unit heads to the lowest level.

In line with Polanyi's argument on fear and hunger, systems of rewards and sanctions were gradually put in place. In universities, schools, hospitals, and local governments the development of ranking based upon aggregated indicators was associated to a constraining system of rewards (such as 'earned autonomy' in terms of budget) and sanctions. The disciplining effect over time, over several years, was remarkable as individuals and organizations alike learned the rules of the game, anticipated the effects, and learned to cheat with the rules (Hood 2007) and the rules became progressively naturalized. The routinization of league tables legitimated penalties – that is, closure of a school, a department, a hospital. The same approach prevailed in numerous areas of public action:

primary and secondary education, higher education, the environment, social services, and so on. The logic of the audit and inspection progressively led to more standardization, with the 'managerial' dimension getting the upper hand over the more political dimension of administration; the pressure on workforces was increasingly strong. Strategic priorities, the needs of local populations, and political choices were set aside, in favour of competition to obtain the maximum score, which counted as political and professional success. Thus, the culture of the audit, which derived from firms, was gradually transferred to all areas of British public life and affected political parties, associations, and charitable organizations alike (Power 1999). While the government decentralized public service provision, and encouraged the participation of the voluntary sector in managing public services, it combined this decentralization with new quid pro quos. All sectors were henceforth subject to an assessment of their performance and procedures. The illusion of the total 'inspectability' of society betrayed the influence of the utilitarianism of the philosopher Jeremy Bentham. But the proliferation of audits eroded trust in the professional ethic and sense of public service. Social control of this kind contradicts the idea that everyone acts in good faith and destroys trust in the competence of social actors.

The audit has become natural in British society. Control is now present at all levels of social and political life. It transfers the management of uncertainty, especially economic uncertainty, from political authorities to individuals. The constant invocation of individual responsibility, which is the quid pro quo of the logic of multiplying the choices offered to the citizen-consumer, aids the internalization of controls and the adoption of individualistic strategies that rupture existing solidarities or loyalties. Summoned to take responsibility for the costs of their choices, individuals cannot be the counter-powers formerly represented by groups. When the audit does not yield satisfactory results, it is rarely the audit itself that is called into question, but instead the skills of the auditors. The whole of society is affected: political parties, agencies, schools, associations.

Indicators of performance are great policy instruments for government because they can change the indicators relatively easily. On the basis of the British case, even constant modification of instruments can be seen as significant in that this obliges the actors to adapt all the time, 'running along behind' instruments that are constantly changing in the name of efficiency and rationality. This instrumentalization of the instrumentation considerably increases the degree of control by central élites and marginalizes the issue of aims and objectives even further – or at the very least, euphemizes them. From this angle, public policy instruments may be seen as revealing the behaviours of actors, with the actors becoming more visible and more predictable through the workings of instruments (an essential factor from the point of view of the state's élites).

CONCLUSION

This chapter argues that among many different routes followed to understand one of the great puzzles of social science in the contemporary period, that is, what is going on with states, tracking public policy and state activities was a promising avenue in capturing some of the paradoxes of state restructuring. Despite all the limits and weaknesses rightly stressed by the political economy literature, state elites are developing (at least) two different strategies to recover capacity to govern their societies, or infrastructural power, according to Mann's turn of phrase, that is, negotiated governance and centralization through indicators, rewards and sanctions. It is also argued that both may coexist in different sectors with little attempt to overcome contradictions. This does not come as any surprise, public policy is rarely a rational exercise. It is therefore hoped that by developing more precisely the idea of a policy state, one may develop a different conception of the contemporary European state.

NOTES

1. This section derives from Le Galès and Scott (2010).
2. Part of this argument is developed more in Faucher-King and Le Galès (2010), Le Galès and Scott (2009) and Le Galès (2010).

REFERENCES

Adams, J. (2005), *The Familial State: Ruling Families and Merchant Capitalism in Early Modern Europe*, Ithaca NY: Cornell University Press.
Badie, B. and P. Birnbaum (1982), *Sociologie de l'Etat*, Paris: Hachette.
Baldwin, P. (2005), 'Beyond weak and strong: Rethinking the state in comparative policy history', *Journal of Policy History*, **17** (1), 12–33.
Benamouzig, D. (2005), 'Administrer un monde incertain: les nouvelles bureaucraties techniques: le cas des agences sanitaires en France', *Sociologie du Travail*, **47** (3), 301–22.
Bevir, M. (2005), *New Labour: A Critique*, London: Routledge.
Bevir, M. and R. Rhodes (2010), *The State as Cultural Practice*, Oxford: Oxford University Press.
Bezes, P. (2009), *Réinventer l'État: Les réformes de l'administration française, 1962–2008*, Paris: PUF.

Brenner, N. (2004), *New State Spaces*, Oxford: Oxford University Press.

Carroll, P. (2006), *Science, Culture, and Modern State Formation.* Berkeley: University of California Press.

Carroll, P. (2009), 'Articulating theories of states and state formation', *Journal of Historical Sociology*, **22** (4), 553–603.

Crouch, C. and W. Streeck (eds) (1997), *Political Economy of Modern Capitalism*, London: Sage.

Dean, M. (2010), *Governmentality: power and rule in modern society* (2nd edition), London: Sage.

Desrosière, A. (1993), *La Politique des grands nombres. Histoire de la raison statistique*, Paris: La Découverte.

Du Gay P. and A. Scott (2010), 'State Transformation or Regime Shift? Addressing Some Confusions in the Theory and Sociology of the State', *Sociologica*, 2.

Dupuy, F. and J.C. Thoenig (1985), *L'Administration en miettes*, Paris: Fayard.

Duran, P. (2009), 'Légitimité, droit et action publique', *Année Sociologique*, **59** (2), 323–44.

Evans, P., Rueschemeyer, D. and T. Skocpol (eds) (1985), *Bringing the state back in*, Cambridge, Cambridge University Press.

Faucher-King, F. and P. Le Galès (2010), *The New Labour Experiment*, Standford: Standford University Press.

Flinders, M. (2008), *Delegated Governance in the British State: Walking Without Order*, Oxford: Oxford University Press.

Gamble, A. (1993), *The Free Market and the Strong State*, Basingstoke: Palgrave.

Hall, P. and D. Soskice (eds) (2001), *Varieties of Capitalism*, Oxford: Oxford University Press.

Hibou, B. (ed.) (1999), *La privatisation de l'Etat*, Paris: Karthala.

Hoffman, J. (1995), *Beyond the State*, Oxford: Blackwell.

Hood, C. (1998), *The Art of the State: Culture, Rhetoric and Public Management*, Oxford: Oxford University Press.

Hood, C. (2007), 'Public Service Management by Numbers: Why Does it Vary? Where Has it Come From? What Are the Gaps and the Puzzles?', *Public Money and Management* **27** (2), 95–102.

Jacobs, L. and D. King (eds) (2009), *The Unsustainable American State*, Oxford: Oxford University Press.

Jacquot, S. (2010), 'The Paradox of Gender Mainstreaming. The Unanticipated Effects of New Modes of Governance in the Gender Equality Domain', *West European Politics*, **33** (1), 118–35.

Jessop, B. (2002), *The Future of the Capitalist State*, Cambridge: Cambridge University Press.

Jessop, B. (2006), 'State and state-building', in R. Rhodes, S. Binder, B. Rockman (eds), *The Oxford Handbook of Political Institutions*, Oxford: Oxford University Press.

King, D. and R. Lieberman (2011), 'L'Etat aux Etats-Unis: pour en finir avec le mythe de l'Etat faible', *Revue Française de Sociologie*, **52** (3), 481–508.

Lachmann, R. (2010), *State and Power*, Cambridge: Policy Press.

Lascoumes, P. and P. Le Galès (2007), 'From the Nature of Instruments to the Sociology of Public Policy Instrumentation', *Governance*, 'Understanding Public Policy throught its Instruments', **20** (1), 1–21.

Le Galès, P. and A. Scott (2010), 'A British bureaucratic revolution ? Autonomy without control or "Freer actors more rules"', English Annual selection, *Revue Française de Sociologie*, vol. 51–1, 119–46.

Le Galès P. (2010), 'Policy instruments and governance', in Mark Bevir (ed.), *Handbook of Governance*, London: Sage

Leipfried, S. and M. Zurn (eds) (2007), *Transforming the Golden-Age Nation State?*, Palgrave Macmillan.

Levi, M. (2002), 'The state of the study of the state', in I. Katznelson and H. Milner (eds), *The State of the Discipline*, New York: Norton/APSA.

Levy, J. (ed.) (2006), *The State after Statism: New State Activities in the Age of Liberalization*, Harvard University Press.

Logan, J. and H. Molotch (1987), *Urban Fortunes. The Political Economy of Place*, Berkeley, University of California Press.

Loughlin, M. (2009) 'In defence of *Staatslehre*', *Der staat* 4 (1), 1–28.

Mann, M. (1984), 'The autonomous power of the state: Its origins, mechanisms and results, *Archives Européennes de Sociologie*, **25**, 185–213.

Mann, M. (1993), *The Sources of Social Power*, vol. 2, Cambridge: Cambridge University Press.

Mann, M. (1997), 'Has globalisation ended the rise and rise of the nation-state ?', in *Review International of Political Economy*, **4** (3).

Marinetto, M. (2007), *Social Theory, The State and Modern Society*, Maidenhead: Open University Press McGraw Hill.

Mayntz, R. (1993), 'Governing failures and the problem of governability', in J. Kooiman, *Modern Governance*, London: Sage.

Meyer, J. (2000), 'Globalization. Sources and effects on states and societies', *International Sociology*, **15** (2), 233–48.

Migdal, J. (2009), 'Researching the state', in M.I. Lichbach, A.S. Zuckerman (eds), *Comparative Politics: Rationality, Culture and Structure*, Cambridge: Cambridge University Press.

Miller, P. and Rose, N., (2008), *Governing the present*, Cambridge: Polity Press.

Moran, M. (2003), *The British Regulatory State*, Oxford: Oxford University Press.

Peters, G. (1997), 'Can't Row, Shouldn't Steer: What's a Government to Do?', *Public Policy and Administration*.

Peters, G. (2008), 'The two futures of governing: decentering and recentering process in governing', Working paper 114, Political science series, Institute for Advanced Studies, Vienna.

Pierre J. and G. Peters (2005), *Governing Complex Societies*, Basingstoke: Palgrave Macmillan.

Poggi, G. (1983), *The Forms of the State*, Oxford: Polity Press.

Pollitt, C. (ed.) (2004), *Agencies: How Governments Do Things Through Semi-Autonomous Organizations*, Basingstoke: Palgrave Macmillan.

Porter, M. (1995), *Trust in Numbers: The Pursuit of Objectivity in Science and Public Life*, Princeton: Princeton University Press.

Pressman, J. and A. Wildavsky (1973), *Implementation*, Berkeley: University of California Press.

Power, M. (1999), *The Audit Society: Rituals of Self Verification*, Oxford: Oxford University Press, 1999.

Rhodes, R.A. (1994), 'The changing nature of the public service in Britain: the hollowing out of the State', *Political Quarterly*, **65** (2), 138–51.

Rothberg, R. (2004), *When States Fail*, Princeton: Princeton University Press.

Rose, R. and Davies, P. (1994), *Inheritance in Public Policy:Change without Choice in Britian*, Newhaven and London: Yale University Press.

Rose, N. and Miller, P. (2008) *Governing the Present*, Cambridge: Cambridge University Press.

Salamon, L. (eds) (2002), *The Tools of Government: A Guide to the New Governance*, New York: Oxford University Press.

Scott., J. (1998), *Seeing Like a State*, New Haven: Yale University Press.

Skinner, Q. (2009), 'A genealogy of the modern state', *Proceedings of the British Academy*, **162**, 325–70.

Skowronek, S. (1982), *Building a new American state: the expansion of national administrative capacities, 1877–1920*, Cambridge: Cambridge University Press.

Skowronek, S. (2009), *Conclusion*, in D.King, L.Jacobs, eds., *The ungovernable American state*, Oxford: Oxford University Press.

Skowronek, S. and M. Glassman (2007), eds, *Formative Acts, American Politics in the Making*, Philadelphia: University of Pennsylvania Press.

Stone, C. (1989) *Regime Politics: Governing Atlanta, 1946–1988*, Lawrence: University Press of Kansas.

Strange, S. (1996), *The Retreat of the State, the Diffusion of Power in the World Economy*, Cambridge: Cambridge University Press.

Streeck, W. (2010), 'The fiscal crisis continues: From liberalization to consolidation', *Comparative European Politics*, **8**, 505–14.

Thatcher, M. (2007), *Internationalisation and Economic Institutions: Comparing European Experiences* , Oxford: Oxford University Press.

Tilly, C. (2010), 'Cities, states and trust networks: Chapter one of cities and states in world history', *Theory and Society*, **39**, 265–80.

Vu, T. (2010), 'Studying the state through state formation', *World Politics*, **62** (1), 148–75.

Weber, M. (1978) *Economy and Society*, Berkeley: University of California Press.

9. Changing varieties of capitalism. Societal consequences of spatial and institutional fragmentation in Germany and Italy

Ulrich Glassmann

INTRODUCTION

How do firms in coordinated market economies (CMEs) stay competitive in an international environment that favours liberal market practices, such as temporary contracts or other flexible forms of worker assignment? Although firms in CMEs traditionally follow quality oriented modes of production which limit intense forms of price competition, international-ized markets confront these enterprises with a strong imperative for higher productivity gains. This has led many CME firms at the beginning of the 1990s to pursue new strategies regarding supply chain management and in-house efficiency. The crisis that affected core sectors in the German economy at that time was highly reinforced by a subsequent reorganiza-tion of large firms in the automobile and machinery industries aiming at a reduction of their bloated cost base and stimulating process innovation (Töpfer 1998). In an effort to restructure inter-firm relations effectively, many large firms implemented new global sourcing strategies, which exaggeratedly pressured domestic supplier businesses and forced many German *Mittelstand* firms to file for bankruptcy (Glassmann 2007).

These events represent a critical juncture for CMEs. Firms needed to develop effective counter strategies against severe price competition from low wage countries that endangered comparative advantages in estab-lished product markets. Quality production prevents an easy relocation of business activities. Instead, CME enterprises need to find a home-based solution to their problem. I will argue in this chapter that this was com-pleted by domestic deregulation furthering a dual labour market (institu-tional fragmentation) and a policy shift towards exclusive regional support of traditional manufacturers (spatial fragmentation). I will further argue that these two processes overlap, on the one hand stabilizing production in traditional markets and prosperous regions, on the other hand creating social exclusion reinforced by regional decline and downgrading of urban districts.

In many CMEs strong pressure in the open economy could not be compensated by supporting community, social, and personal services. Scharpf (2001) has labelled this lack of service sector growth the 'continental dilemma', because it mainly occurred in continental (conservative) welfare states (Esping-Andersen 1990). Liberal welfare states supported employment growth in private services. Flexible labour market regulations allowed for the development of a low wage economy, admittedly furthering the rise of the working-poor. In contrast, Scandinavian welfare states, though this strained public budgets tremendously, invested in public services supporting double earner households and community welfare. Because of the specific provisions of the conservative welfare state neither the one path nor the other appeared viable. A dynamic private service sector was blocked by strong corporatist labour arrangements, while a public service sector of the Scandinavian type was not created, because conservative welfare states – strengthening the male breadwinner model – primarily relied on transfer payments to sustain family welfare instead of providing real services to households (Esping-Andersen 1999). Thus, CMEs like Germany, which carry the features of conservative welfare states, deal with a twofold adversity – the consequences of de-industrialization and internationalization on the one hand and a slow growth of the service branch on the other. This however made the creation of higher labour market flexibility for traditional industries even more inevitable.

Despite these gloomy prospects, the Varieties of Capitalism (VoC) approach by Hall and Soskice (2001) reminded of the valuable institutional features and the remarkable comparative advantage CMEs created for traditional industries. VoC certainly developed a plausible organizing principle for the analysis of political economies, but at the time the study was published many CMEs had already undergone major institutional change. This was due to the above-mentioned crisis, which forced entrepreneurs in CMEs as well as public policy makers to adapt to new economic challenges.

In this chapter I will analyse how this was done in Germany and Italy. Of course, Italy is not a pure type CME, which is pointed out by Hall and Soskice in their introduction (Hall and Soskice 2001: 19–21), but it serves as a case in point for an economy that carries some features of a coordinated market economy; however, it lacks the spatial coordination devices to establish efficiency gains from national regulations. I will demonstrate that spatial homogeneity is an implicit assumption for the functioning of pure models in the logic of VoC, nevertheless an assumption that no longer obtains in Germany. In addition to this, I will show how institutional fragmentation leads to economic inequality, paradoxically stabilizing enterprise competitiveness.

The chapter is structured as follows: I will briefly discuss the VoC literature and various hypotheses on institutional change. The subsequent section deals with spatial homogeneity vs. heterogeneity of production patterns in Germany and Italy and the process of change. I will then discuss institutional fragmentation as well as societal consequences of this development and draw some conclusions.

THEORIES AND HYPOTHESIS ON CHANGES IN POLITICAL ECONOMIES

The VoC approach contrasts pure models of coordinated and liberal market economies as the two most successful institutional arrangements organizing capitalist production. It has been argued that this success is rooted in the complementarity of institutional sectors. Corporate governance structures, industrial relations institutions, vocational training systems, and so on, produce additional efficiency gains for the whole economy when they are closely interlocked. Encompassing institutions do not only solve coordination problems in one particular sphere of regulation, but have more far-reaching effects on other spheres of regulation as well (Hall and Soskice 2001: 17). For instance, if enterprises aim at the production of high quality goods and establish an adequate work organization they will also be highly dependent on a sophisticated vocational training system that qualifies workers for autonomous decisions on the shop-floor and allows them to acquire the necessary skills. This however creates a collective action dilemma. If workers are usually trained very well, it appears highly attractive for firms to poach these workers instead of contributing to the general skill base of the economy. If this negative incentive is not removed, it severely affects cooperative inter-firm relations and destabilizes the production regime (Hall and Soskice 2001: 24–5). Firms are thus in need of additional support from industrial relations regulations. Collective agreements that equalize wage structures across firms and industries make poaching unattractive and prevent firms from pursuing strong free-rider strategies.

Although this argument about the reinforcement mechanism of institutional arrangements appears quite intriguing, it implies controversial assumptions on the logic of historical institution building and the effectiveness of national regulations. Many discussions in the critical discourse on VoC evolved around the institutional complementarity thesis (Crouch et al. 2005). While this often led to the critique the approach may be too static, functionalist, apolitical, and equilibrium-biased (Hancké et al. 2007: 7f.), it has rarely been pointed out that an efficient system of national regulations in the VoC spheres is highly dependent on the spatial homogeneity of production and coordination by encompassing institutions across regions. Following the VoC logic, complementarity would be ruined if sub-national entities deviated from national arrangements by providing diverging services and regulations. I will demonstrate in the next section that a standardization of such services across regions was indeed typical of the German political economy in the past. However, this situation has changed, not only due to the reunification process.

In a long line of history, Italy always showed a much more diverse picture with respect to regional production and innovation (Putnam 1993) and local assets are central for the explanation of economic success and failure (Locke 1995; Burroni and Trigila 2001). For actors in the German political economy this emerges as a new and challenging process with far reaching consequences on production and social cohesion.

Moreover, VoC is a concept that explains why actors decide to pursue an equilibrium strategy. Hence, it is difficult for advocates of VoC to account for institutional change. Nevertheless, Hall and Thelen (2005) outline that even in the VoC perspective institutional rules can be modified. They reject the view, in which economic actors are only passive rule-takers. Instead, such actors use institutions as resources. For instance, the authors argue, German corporations have successfully watched out for new cross-shareholders when banks withdrew (Hall and Thelen 2005: 32). Actors change institutional rules incrementally by what the authors call defection or reinterpretation. Reinterpretation occurs when economic actors do not touch formal rules, but only 'change the content of the practices associated with it' (ibid.: 21). Defection describes the attitude of an uncooperative actor, for instance, when firms resign from employer federations (ibid.: 20), as has been frequently observed in the German machinery industry during the 1990s (Schroeder 1997). Although this account allows for describing *how* actors modify institutional rules, the question remains *why* they modify them, especially if an equilibrium strategy promises higher returns than most alternatives.

The convergence hypothesis assumes that CMEs will transform into liberal market economies (LMEs). However, liberalizing reforms are contrary to employers' interests in CMEs. Wood (2001: 268–72) gives interesting examples for this by analysing how the German liberal party (FDP) supported law initiatives in the 1980s that were supposed to weaken labour union power by changing the electoral laws of works councils. This initiative would have fragmented union representation on the enterprise level. Although, a moderate compromise was found owing to parliamentary opposition against the proposal and an explicit resistance by employers' federations, who feared that bargaining efficiency would be put at risk if works councils were to sustain a more heterogeneous composition. Politicization of the industrial relations system could have followed as a consequence, which was not desired by employer federations. In line with this argument Swank and Martin (2001) show that high centralization of employers' organizations, their strong cohesion as well as a high level of cooperation across firms, as typical for CMEs, is positively associated with entrepreneurial support for social policies. The reason is that employers in CMEs seek qualified and well protected personnel to achieve a stable framework of production. Therefore, it appears unlikely that employers coordinate on a merely liberal strategy.

Another hypothesis assumes that entrepreneurs enhance their scope of action by introducing an incremental process of liberalization. Public policy makers support this development leading to a profound transformation of CMEs (Streeck and Thelen 2005: 9). The authors explain that it is inherent to the logic of liberalization processes to occur gradually, because they do not require consensual collective action, but are completed through incremental forms of defection, the depletion and neglect of institutional rules, and so on (ibid.). In this case CMEs would transform into mixed market economies with a strong alignment towards LMEs. However, in a longer perspective this would create effects comparable to abrupt liberal reforms.

I assume a different restoration path in CMEs and countries like Italy. CMEs neither converge on LME strategies nor experience liberal alignments. Instead they experience a lasting fragmentation *within* institutional sectors, not *between* them. CME rules are no longer universally applied to capital and labour. Consequently, some firms maintain institutional rules, others not. Parts of the workforce remain highly protected while others suffer from low wages and deficient welfare entitlements. This allows actors to choose between liberal or coordinated solutions to their problems. However, what logic is assumed behind this process of change?

Increasing competition demands higher enterprise and employee efficiency, but it also furthers distributional conflicts among firms and employees. Shifting towards a free market environment makes distributional consequences rather unpredictable. Workers with permanent employment contracts and firms in traditional markets will thus attempt to keep as many advantages of the old regime and shift the costs of increasing competition on outsider groups. This logic is actually furthered by the power of labour unions, which primarily defend established workers rights, even if their clientele is decreasing (for the erosion-thesis, see Hassel 1999, 2002).

A society with privileges emerges that rather maintains the socio-economic status, income levels and qualification profiles of 'a core work-force', while these forms of protection are abandoned for temporary and hired-out workers. Nevertheless, the latter groups secure international price competitiveness for the old production regime. Although even the 'core workforce' experiences relative losses, these will mainly occur in the form of indirect measures such as wage restraints. As a result of this strategy, the world of labour becomes increasingly divided. In the German case, the emergence of a new and strong left party is the consequence of this bifurcation.

An important theoretical question remains: How can institutions rein-force opposite kinds of behaviour, if they exist to constrain deviance? Institutions in endangered CMEs work with amendments. These amend-ments define what qualifies individuals to receive privileged protection. Important criteria are age and acquired rights. However, amendments may also occur as neutral options to opt out of binding contracts, as in the case of exemption clauses in collective bargaining agreements which allow firms to undercut wage settlements. Reforms do not aim at a general decrease of transaction costs, but constrain labour market participation for outsider groups to assure competitiveness.

To sum up: I agree with advocates of VoC that processes of institutional change in political economies are characterized by an attempt of firms 'to modify their practices so as to sustain their competitive advantages' (Hall and Soskice 2001: 63). However, the explanation given here differs from VoC in the way the restoration path of comparative advantages is interpreted. In the logic of VoC public and private actors must restore an efficient equilibrium and seek ways to bridge evolving complementarity gaps. Instead I hypothesize that fragmentation within institutional sectors and across localities maintains complementarity where it is desired and abandons it where it leads to cost pressure and other limitations of com-petitiveness. As a result, declining regions no longer profit from efficiency gains of national regulations. In an effort to restructure, they will most likely follow new technology paths, which however exclude *older age cohorts* of the traditional workforce who cannot easily be re-qualified. Successful traditional industries will as well concentrate regionally, but exclude *younger age cohorts* as a consequence of a dual labour market strategy. As a result, this restoration path increases social and economic inequality across social strata between generations and finally between regions.

VARIETIES OF CAPITALISM AND SPATIAL PATTERNS OF PRODUCTION

In the following section I will demonstrate that Germany maintained a relatively homogeneous production order across regions until the 1990s. This was an important precondition for the efficiency of the German model, since frequent local or regional deviance from CME rules would have ruined the complementary framework of encompassing institutions. I will also demonstrate that Italy, which shows a less efficient institutional design according to VoC, failed to provide such a spatially balanced system of production. Instead, its regional and local productive specialization emerged as a secret of its economic success in some regions.

Many sectors in which Germany has gained comparative advantages for export markets are promoted under a nationwide regime for the provision of collective competition goods. Collective competition goods are real services for enterprises, such as technology transfer and training, but also collective regulations as agreed technical norms or wages (Le Galès and Voelzkow 2001). I have demonstrated elsewhere that specific federal and corporatist arrangements spatially reproduce and inter-regionally coordinate the provision of such goods in Germany (Glassmann 2007). A sectoral division of work (as opposed to a spatial division) emerged from this support infrastructure and prevented the downgrading of social and economic standards on a regional level for a long time. Not primarily regions, as to say their respective inter-firm networks as well as highly specialized public entities, developed exclusive and specialized knowledge on certain parts of the value chain; instead formal organizations such as technical schools, institutes for basic or applied research or R&D enterprise departments generated and stored specialized innovative knowledge. These formal organizations do not primarily operate on the basis of tacit knowledge which is so highly important for many small-firm networks in the Third Italy and are thus capable of making this knowledge disposable across regional confines. Sectorally specialized employment in Germany is thus concentrated to a lesser degree in local confines relative to other countries. Consequently, a rather polycentric industrial and innovative activity emerged in German regions, while a contrary image appears in the Italian case.

This analysis does not ignore the apparent social and economic divide between northern and southern parts of Germany as well as the striking differences between West and East German *Länder*. Neither does it deny the relevance of cluster processes for German local economies (Sternberg and Litzenberger 2004). The punch line of this argument is that in the past comparative advantages in the German economy did not depend as much

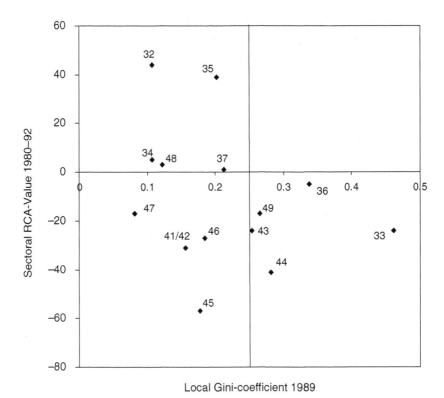

Source: Lau (1997), Glassmann (2007), own depiction, own calculation.

Figure 9.1   Sectoral, spatial concentration and revealed comparative advantage of NACE sectors in Germany

on exclusive spatial settings as this has been the case in other countries in Europe.

Figure 9.1 and Figure 9.2 give evidence for this by illustrating the sectoral and spatial concentration as well as comparative advantages for economic sectors in Germany and Italy. The most important difference between the two figures can be seen in the fact that the north-east quadrant of Figure 9.1 (Germany) is empty while in the Italian case (Figure 9.2) the NACE sectors 44, 45, 46 and 49 can be found in this quadrant – these are the economic sectors: leather manufacturing, shoes and clothing, wood processing and other manufacturing industries.

Many sectors in which the Italian industry has gained comparative advantages are thus highly concentrated in local confines. This rather

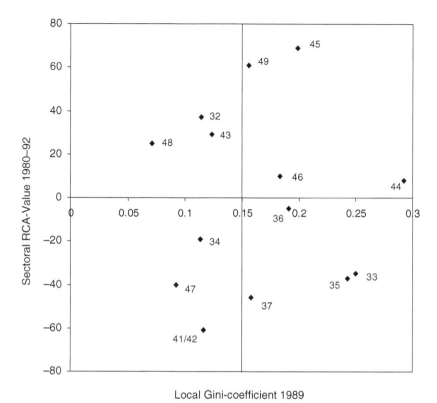

Source: Lau (1997), Glassmann (2007), own depiction

*Figure 9.2   Sectoral, spatial concentration and revealed comparative
advantage of NACE sectors in Italy*

unsurprising finding is in line with the traditional literature on the relevance of industrial districts in Italy (Becattini 1979, Brusco 1989). The
finding for the German case, however, appears less self-explanantory. In
fact, compared with Italy, Great Britain and France (Lau 1997), Germany
is the only political economy that displays a spatially polycentric feature
of its most successful industries.

Data for Figure 9.1 and Figure 9.2 are taken from approximately the
period for which Hall and Soskice (2001) measure patent specialization in
CMEs and LMEs demonstrating the different innovation paths (incremental
vs. radical) of these types. I argue that interlocked institutions in CMEs are
highly dependent on relative spatial de-concentration of business activities as
shown in Figure 9.1, because complementarity implies not only coordinated

action between institutional sectors but also between regions. Exclusive sectoral specialization by firms within regions create exclusive knowledge networks and reinforce deviant patterns of enterprise coordination which run counter to the logic of efficiency gains from national regulations.

Although Crouch et al. (2009) have shown that such deviance can be productive as well this has been demonstrated especially and interestingly for new economic sectors, such as the media industry, which demand different support structures than traditional CME industries. Taking a look at spatial patterns of patent applications in traditional economic sectors reveals the main difference between the country cases.

While in Italy each sector is represented in one particular region where firms have specialized in innovative capacities of the respective technological field and economic sector (with the exception of textile processes & paper) the German innovation system is dominated by a different spatial pattern (see Table 9.1). As in Italy strong and weak innovative regions coexist within the national innovation system (Greif 2000). Nevertheless, strong innovative regions are present in many different technological fields (Gehrke and Legler 1999). This polycentric innovation activity complements the conclusion drawn from Figure 9.1 which points to a relatively high level of employment de-concentration in the German political economy for the period analysed.

Theoretically *Länder* autonomy in education, economic support programmes, and so on, could have led to completely diverging support structures, and although diversity in performance exists between *Länder* (Bertelsmann-Stiftung 2001) and has dramatically increased over the recent years, in comparison with other countries this effect has been dampened by growing interventions of the federal level. Concurrent legislation allowed federal government to decide upon compensating social and economic policies in sub-national entities. This was justified on the basis of Art. 72 (meanwhile reformed) of the basic law, which lays down the principle of equal living conditions. A rather homogeneous infrastructure was also built with reference to guidelines set up in the regional planning act which defined equivalent living conditions as the main planning target. This definition was found in the 1960s when mass production and mass consumption were pillowed by Keynesian politics and expansive welfare support creating upward social mobility among most social strata (Rommelspacher 2004). The planning act was supposed to ensure that peripheral or declining regions could benefit from this process as well. Equalizing regional planning was thus an accordant welfare measure and exclusive spatial politics were rejected on the basis of this argument.

However, the formal institutional mechanism of unanimous consent on the *Länder* level, as described by Scharpf (1985) in his analysis of the

Table 9.1   *Innovative German* and Italian regions (NUTS II) in Europe – classified according to average patent applications per annum and 100 000 wage earners at the European Patent Office (1993–1995/96)*

Ø Patent intensity by sector (1993-95/96) NUTS II	Highly superior	Superior	Above average
Daily consumer needs		Rheinhessen-Pfalz	Köln, Stuttgart, **Veneto**
Manufacturing processes & transportation	Stuttgart	Rheinhessen-Pfalz Köln	**Emilia-Romagna**
Chemistry & metallurgy	Rheinhessen-Pfalz Köln		
Textile processes & paper	Stuttgart	Rheinhessen-Pfalz Köln, **Toscana**	**Lombardia, Friuli-Venezia Giulia, Marche, Umbria**
Construction engineering & mining		Stuttgart, Köln	
Machinery Industry, lighting, weapons etc.	Stuttgart	Köln	Rheinhessen-Pfalz, **Valle d´Aosta**
Physics		Stuttgart	Rheinhessen-Pfalz, Köln, **Liguria**
Electronics	Stuttgart		

Notes: * Only some German regions have been selected for this depiction demonstrating the polycentric feature of the innovation system. Above average = values may double EU average; Superior = values double EU average and reach margins beyond; Highly superior = values skyrocket beyond double EU average.

Source: Eurostat, New Cronos Regio-Data base, calculations NIW according to Gehrke and Legler (1999: 46, legend: 19–20), own depiction.

joint decision trap, also furthered sectoral instead of spatial support. Since compensating spatial policies would have privileged *Länder* with declining regions over others regarding the distribution of public grants, disadvantaged *Länder* governments did not agree on such measures and therefore blocked decisions on spatial policies. Instead, *Länder* governments voted unanimously for sectoral economic support measures, because this strategy allowed acting against the cyclical downswing of an industry as well. However, when compensating policies were implemented, these could be fairly distributed among regions. Consequently, vertical and horizontal coordination between *Länder* and the federal government implementing spatially equalizing sectoral support infrastructures led to a quick diffusion of innovation measures across regional confines.

The Italian innovation system is spatially divided (Malerba 1993). DeBresson et al. (1996) have demonstrated that the numerous production systems of the Third Italy often specialize in design-based innovation for niche products. Capital-intensive R&D-driven innovation more often stems from large firms and research institutes in Lombardy, where about one-third of all industrial patents in Italy originated in the mid-1990s (ISTAT 1995). Thus, as in Germany, an inter-regional exchange of competition goods is typical of the Italian political economy; however, the transfer is unidirectional. Economies of the Third Italy do not supply their cluster specific competences to firms in other regions. However, Lombardy emerges as a region that transfers sophisticated innovative knowledge to local economies elsewhere (DeBresson et al. 1996). Thus, the main actors of Italy's fragmented national innovation system have established a spatial division of work. Public entities were not able to coordinate the provision of these goods as in Germany, because the central state often used resources as a means for patronage politics and regional governments were endowed with too few competences and little budgetary discretion for effective inter-regional coordination. Consequently, localities provided tailor-made spatial support. Knowledge was often generated in a long historical process, but this knowledge was not powerfully diffused across territorial borders.

The VoC model cannot take account of this logic since it assumes national regulations as a framework for production. Nevertheless, such regulations are rather ineffective in the Italian case owing to the subnational logic of production and innovation. In contrast, this logic appeared intriguing in the German case, because enterprise support was standardized across regions creating stability and relative social cohesion throughout distinct regional economies. Efficiency gains from complementary institutional sectors were thus reinforced by inter-regional coordination. On the other hand, this system impeded new productive regional specializations and for many years it was badly armed for stimulating growth in new technology markets.

INSTITUTIONAL CHANGE AND SPATIAL FRAGMENTATION

The German reunification process was of course an exogenous factor affecting the inter-regional balance of the production system. Complete institutional transfer was the proclaimed formula for the restructuring of eastern *Länder*. This strategy caused unanticipated effects as in the science-driven economy of Dresden. The city was always a renowned place for creative inventions and again displays a dense network of university and research institutes in the natural sciences. Saxony was the most industrialized of all East German *Länder*. But traditional entrepreneurial activity severely declined after reunification. Today the local economy focuses on technological specializations typical of LMEs: life sciences & biotechnology, microelectronics & information as well as communications technology and finally new material- & nanotechnology. This success follows from the revitalization of an old historical path in research and development as this has been modelled theoretically by Crouch and Farrell (2004). In other regions of Germany, where this path is missing, only cumbersome economic development can be observed. More generally however, East German *Länder* specialized relatively early in R&D-intensive production. In the period between 1993 and 1997 East German industrial activity involving cutting-edge technology already held a share of 11.2 per cent of all industrial activity while West German industrial activity involving such technology only held a share of 4.9 per cent. Small and medium sized firms play an important role in furthering this research-intensive development path in East Germany. In 1997 only 16 per cent of R&D expenditure was generated in West German small and medium sized enterprises (SMEs), while East German SMEs reached a share of 65 per cent in private R&D expenditure. Many public and private actors have established a new innovation path in East Germany – and this seems to be the most promising route to success, because CME activity cannot effectively be transplanted to other regions. If Eastern labour standards and wages get ever more adapted to Western examples, East German firms will find it difficult to compete with renowned enterprises in the branch. Local economies are in need of support for new technological innovations, but the public infrastructure is designed to support production for traditional markets. Thus, local economies in backward regions such as the *Mezzogiorno* or East Germany must creatively deviate from national regulations. In any case, either decline or deviant entrepreneurial strategies lead to coexisting worlds of production and spatial fragmentation in both country cases.

Moreover, de-industrialization causes labour market decline in formerly prosperous regions. Because sub-national governments realized the meanwhile high failure rate of restructuring strategies for traditional markets and considered savings capacities under monetarist financial constraints, many *Länder* governments abandoned their equalizing spatial support measures at the end of the 1990s. For instance, North-Rhine Westphalia (NRW) began to turn its regional policy approach upside down: while in the past such policies were designed to stimulate growth and start-up activity everywhere across the territory, the new approach only supports already existing and successful economic clusters. In the year 2000 the Ministry of Economics, Mittelstand and Energy in NRW proclaimed a comprehensive reform, including its departmental structure and mode of policy operation. In 2005 cluster departments were established, which manage the cooperative support of inter-firm networks. This implies a redirection of former 'compensation measures' to already prospering regions by asking entrepreneurs to substantiate cooperative relations with other firms producing for the same value chain. But this keeps labour unions out of the game. Private entities are supposed to provide real service in accordance with the cluster concept disburdening overstrained public budgets (Interview MWME 2007). Thus, public actors intentionally support a process of spatial fragmentation by withdrawing funds from failing 'compensation strategies' in declining regions. Of course, structural policy initiatives are still deployed to combat economic demise. However, the new focus is put on existing comparative advantages. This will degrade CME infrastructures in declining regions.

Italian regional governments must approach the same problem from the other end of the scale. While territorial fragmentation is already a long-lasting social and economic reality, the Italian political economy suffers from a lack of coordination on the regional level. Because of this, various governments have pushed for a federalist reform which was supposed to empower the regions with more competences and budgetary discretion (Fabbrini and Brunazzo 2003). Owing to fiscal reforms, the share of exclusive regional taxes increased from 15 per cent in 1992 to 45 per cent in the year 2000 (Grasse and Gelli forthcoming); however, most of these resources are channelled into the decentralized health system. The emerging problem is that better performing regions gain a higher regional tax revenue and consequently invest much more into regional services and infrastructure than economically backward regions: in 2005 per capita expenditure from regional taxes varied between 1.201€ in Apulia and 4.587€ in Valle d'Aosta (ibid.). Provisions concerning regional autonomy, as they have been laid down in the constitutional reform in 2001, are surely desirable in increasing regional coordination capacities. Nevertheless, they will almost certainly increase or at least maintain infrastructural deficiencies in some regions if an effective system of inter-regional revenue sharing is not set up. Therefore, spatial fragmentation will not vanish but become an even more dominant development path. It appears interesting in this context that the *Lega Nord* not only fights against migration or attempts to push for federal reform, but mainly addresses small-firm entrepreneurs with neo-liberal policy statements. In fact, the *Lega*'s electoral programme can be taken as a symbol of all the fears traditional market actors face from international competition. The solution it offers consists of a (badly) exaggerated concept of spatial and institutional fragmentation.

INSTITUTIONAL FRAGMENTATION AND THE LABOUR MARKET

While it has long been assumed that associations would probably remain a more constant factor among the institutions of German capitalism, Anke Hassel (1999) has shown that industrial relations in Germany tend to erode. First, coverage declined, affecting both the works council system as well as wage agreements. Second, collective agreements appeared more and more decentralized. In particular decentralization, it is argued, destabilizes the balanced division of labour between company-level activities and associational bargaining. Unlike many other countries, Germany resisted decentralization in the 1980s (Hassel 1999), due to the capabilities of the industrial relations system to introduce flexible measures through labour representation on the firm level. Exactly this division of work was at stake in the 1990s.

As customer firms began to squeeze their suppliers in order to make them produce for lower costs, firms could no longer accept sectoral and nationwide agreements that did not suit counter-cyclical developments on the firm level. Because of this many firms resigned from employers' confederations in the 1990s (Schroeder 1997). As a result, collective wage agreements no longer covered the same number of firms and workers. As Hassel noted: 'Between 1995 and 1998 the coverage rates of West German plants shrank from 53.4 to 47.7 per cent. In East Germany the share of plants covered by a collective agreement fell from 27.6 to 25.8 per cent between 1996 and 1998' (Hassel 2002: 312). The same trend can be shown for the coverage rates of employees by collective agreements in the private sector. In West Germany coverage declined from 72.2 per cent to 67.8 per cent between 1995 and 1998 and in Eastern Germany from 56.2 to 50.5 per cent in the same period of time (ibid.).

However, the most important indicator for erosion is seen in the relation between company-level representation and associational bargaining, because the particular balance of these two spheres in the industrial relations system was responsible for 'social equality, industrial peace and economic performance' in Germany (ibid.: 309f.).

It can indeed be shown that company-level agreements, as a share of total agreements, continuously increased from 25 per cent up to 45

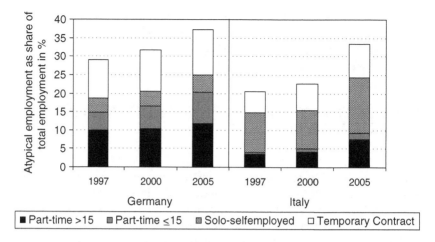

Source: Eurostat Labour Force Survey according to Brzinsky-Fay et al. (2007), own depiction

Figure 9.3   Atypical employment as a share of total employment in Germany and Italy

per cent between 1989 and 2004 in Germany. The main paradigm shift occurred in the West where the number of company-level agreements was rather low in 1989, but increased about 20 per cent until 2004. In the East the whole system was much more decentralized after reunification and quickly stabilized at around 50 per cent of company-level agreements as a share of total agreements.

This alone does not hint to the establishment of a dual labour market, because the growth of firm-level agreements may also mirror the fact that some firms use such agreements to install incentive structures within the firm that allow individual workers to earn salaries above the agreed wage scale. But decentralization emerged in combination with a liberalization of the framework for temporary work contracts (OECD 2008). The reform was initiated by the social democratic–green government in 2003 and allowed atypical employment to grow.

Figure 9.3 shows that atypical employment, defined as part-time, temporary or solo self-employment, has indeed increased both in Germany and Italy. A comparative analysis demonstrates that this trend also emerges in other CME countries; however, not in Great Britain or Denmark (Brzinsky-Fay et al. 2007). The reason is simple: in LMEs job protection rights are less developed. Therefore, employers need not fall back on temporary contracts to make sure they can get rid of employees. Scandinavian welfare states carry similar features with respect to job protection, but provide more generous unemployment benefits and active labour market policies to reintegrate unemployed workers. Germany and Italy however have created a rather problematic institutional mixture for atypically employed workers.

In both cases atypical employment has risen in all categories between 1997 and 2005. The youngest age cohort of between 15 and 29 years is affected the most by atypical contracts (ibid.). An interesting difference between the countries can be seen in the fact that Italy shows a much larger proportion of solo self-employed while in Germany growth emerges mainly from the other categories of atypical employment.

Surely, part-time work became a more desired form of contracting, but compared with regular employed workers, employees in all categories of atypical contracts face a much higher unemployment risk when contracts are terminated (ibid.). Hence, workers with atypical employment contracts are more at risk of falling back on public benefits. According to the German labour market and social security reform in 2003 this implies a quick decline of the individual living standard to the level of social assistance. Therefore, such contracting creates a severe outsider effect and reinforces a dual labour market structure. Meanwhile, the German production system relies heavily on atypical employment, not only in the service sector but in the traditional manufacturing industries. For temporary contracts in industrial jobs workers may have acquired a relatively high qualification level – thus irregular contracting is not only an exception for the assignment of unskilled legwork. More than one-third of the working population in Germany is employed on the basis of non-standard contracts. In the year 1996, 177935 hired-out workers were registered. In the year 2008 this number had mounted up to 793661 (Bundesagentur für Arbeit 2008). Moreover, Germany has only implemented an equal pay rule with exceptions which allows for wage differences up to 40 per cent for the same occupation.

Italy, in contrast, has implemented a general equal pay rule for hired-out workers. Unsurprisingly, its estimated percentage of hired-out workers (0.7%) as a share of total employment lay below the German share (1.3%) in 2006 (Mai 2008). Nevertheless, as Figure 9.3 shows, atypical employment has grown from 20.5 per cent in 1997 to 33.4 per cent in 2005. In addition to this, the employment quota of the youngest age cohort (15–29 years) only amounts to 40.9 per cent and thus is 10 per cent lower than in Germany. Italy faces a severe problem with respect to youth unemployment; at the same time, the relative share of atypical employment in the youngest age cohort is just as high as in Germany. These numbers mirror enormous difficulties for younger workers to achieve independence and an acceptable living standard at the beginning of their careers in Italy.

One way out of this dilemma seems to be informal and solo

self-employment. This strategy is not new within the Italian political economy. In fact, in his landmark article on the Emilian model, Brusco (1982) long ago described the functioning of decentralized production regimes in Emilia as collaboration between open and hidden enterprise activity. While open sector firms possessed bigger productive structures, larger numbers of employees and established union representation at the plant level, firms in the hidden sector consisted of self-employed or few-person subcontractors. Many used to be family firms and did not establish trade union representation, since the provisions of the Workers' Statute only apply for firms with more than 15 employees. Hidden sector firms were not covered by collective agreements either. As a result, wages in firms operating in the open sector were rather high while salaries in small family firms used to be much lower. Enterprises from both spheres closely collaborated. Subcontractors from the hidden sector functioned as an important flexibility resource for open sector firms because they did not demand long-term contracts, were not determined to produce for a specific production niche and allowed decreased production costs using low wage personnel. The stability of the informal economy stemmed from its independence of rigid and formal rules, its embeddedness in a larger social network and its quick reorientation towards potential collaborations with other manufacturers. When open sector firms ran into crisis informal subcontractors quickly adapted to new emerging demand. To sum up, in the 1980s solo self-employment served as an important pillar to the economy; however, its functionality depended a lot on supporting family ties and other social relations.

Interestingly, VoC cannot explain the efficiency generated by the Emilian model as it worked at the time, because actors mixed contradicting modes of regulation to achieve maximum efficiency. Thus, institutional fragmentation was already an important characteristic of the Italian political economy in the 1980s. Regini (1995) explains that labour unions and employers' federations set up decentralized agreements on the local and regional level in a process of 'micro-concertation'. Decentralized agreements were designed to support flexible production modes in successful industrial districts and amended or substituted national agreements.

Since then two important changes have been introduced to the Italian industrial relations system. The first one occurred in 1993 when an inter-confederal social accord was struck on the national level, which focused on a coordinated consensus regarding wage restraint. Italy needed to meet the convergence criteria of the Maastricht Treaty if it wanted to join the European Monetary Union. Hence, a recentralization of industrial relations appeared appropriate, since this allowed to implement an accordant policy to fight inflation. Nevertheless the accord of 1993 did not eliminate decentralized bargaining. In fact, local bargaining was explicitly provided as an alternative to company agreements or designed for firms that did not implement enterprise agreements. Therefore, the system remained institutionally fragmented despite a more formalized procedure in which collective agreements were reached on the national level and territorial or company agreements were supposed to amend these.

The second important institutional change in industrial relations occurred in 2009 when collective bargaining was again reformed. The new agreement altered validity periods of agreements, their synchronization etc. But the most relevant change consists of tax relief incentives for an intensified use of company agreements and exemption clauses. In addition to this, options to undercut collective agreements in times of crisis were enlarged.

This reform establishes a new quality of institutional fragmentation in the Italian political economy by allowing companies to further atypical and lower wage employment in the open and regulated sector. Of course, this trend has not been initiated by the 2009 reform. As shown by the data in Figure 9.3: atypical employment has already expanded between 1997 and 2005. This must not be bad news, if for instance the rise of part-time work results from modernized labour force participation. However, since youth unemployment has been growing recently and atypical employment rises especially in the youngest age cohort, this development seems to result from a new demand in flexible labour that is disproportionately shouldered by distinct generations. The latest reform of the industrial relations system will probably reinforce this trend and therefore endanger the old balance of cooperation between the open and hidden economy. In the past, dual labour market structures that resulted from institutional fragmentation often served as functional flexibility resource to the regional market. Labour flexibility and wage structures in the hidden sector were certainly debateable, but as long as this system kept separate spheres of protection and as long as unprotected workers and the self-employed were bolstered by family ties this production model reached high levels of productivity and social integration. However, if poor labour standards spread in the open economy and if solo self-employment becomes an ever more dominant survival strategy, Italy will pay a high price for international competitiveness. The same is true for Germany. In order to support competitiveness in traditional markets, German workers have made remarkable sacrifices with respect to labour rights and wages. Moreover, if the effects of such measures are distributed unequally among the workforce, a severe outsider problem emerges.

SOCIETAL CONSEQUENCES OF SPATIAL AND INSTITUTIONAL FRAGMENTATION

Institutional fragmentation leads to income inequality. While global income inequality has been decreasing during recent decades (Sala-i-Martin 2006), especially because of India's and China's performance, within many European countries income inequality has been rising since the 1990s (OECD 2005). Germany and Italy are no exceptions, although German society still remains more egalitarian than the Italian. Gini-coefficients indicating equivalized household disposable income for Germany just slightly increased from 26.5 in the mid-1980s to 27.7 in 2001. Italy showed a much larger increase: between the mid-1980s and the year 2000 Gini-coefficients rose from 30.6 to 34.7. However, a closer look at income differentials between low, middle and high incomes in Germany reveals that income differentials started to change only a little later, from 2001 onwards (see Figure 9.4). In particular the 90/10 decile ratio in West and East Germany as well as the 50/10 ratio in East Germany increased significantly. This indicates that especially households in the bottom decile of East Germany experienced the strongest depletion, while households in the highest income decile in West and East Germany recorded the highest accretion relative to the bottom deciles. A similar trend is visible in Italy.

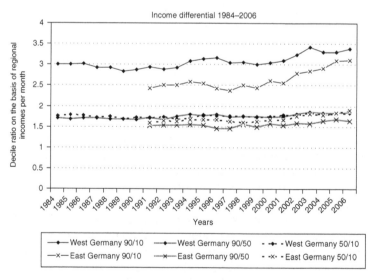

Source: DIW 2004, SOGP-Monitor

Figure 9.4   Income differential 1984–2006

Data quality for continuous inter-temporal comparison of Italian income differentials is rather poor. However, market income distribution between the three lowest, four middle, and the three top deciles show that 57.8 per cent of all market income in the year 2000 was earned in the three top deciles, which represents an above average OECD value (OECD = 55.1%). Market incomes in Germany's top three deciles, at least in 2001, only amounted to 54.4 per cent. Thus, among other things, inequality in Italy is due to above average income opportunities for the better of households.

Both Italian as well as German societies have become much more unequal. Although a number of different independent variables may drive this development, my main argument is that one causal mechanism can be found in the attempt to increase price competitiveness of firms in established product markets. West European CME firms must not fear losing their comparative advantage with regard to product quality, incremental innovation or market reputation. The most difficult challenge is to stay price competitive against low wage countries especially in Asia (Licht 2000).

High numbers of exported goods cannot be treated as the most relevant criterion to judge on market efficiency. Instead, the question occurs what enabled traditional manufacturers to achieve this goal. In both countries analysed an ever-growing dual labour market structure was the precondition for CME firms to win or keep international market shares. Unstable work relations, escalating job requirements and growing economic inequality can be described as emerging societal consequences. Although Italy and Germany exhibit very different political economies, they face the same challenges. Disregarding their diverging survival strategies, societal transformations are inevitable and coincide with spatial fragmentation in both cases.

In the Italian case, spatial fragmentation has a long history. However, institutional fragmentation reinforces this effect and leads to a further concentration of decline in old industrial and underdeveloped regions. Although one certainly needs to inquire more deeply into the reasons for success of newly emerging southern Italian industrial districts (Burroni and Trigilia 2001), the general under-provision of public goods poses an ever-growing threat to a real option for change. It would be tragic if the envisaged empowerment of regional governments were to aggravate this effect. However, prospering regions will experience spatial fragmentation as well, for instance, between urban districts, because hire-out work is a more urban phenomenon.

Germany faces a slightly different prospect. Public and private actors were used to relatively de-concentrated industrial activity, a polycentric innovation system, quick technological diffusion across spatial confines, equalizing public support, and, as a result of this, to a relatively homogeneous public infrastructure and egalitarian social texture. This has all changed dramatically. The incredible number of plant closures in East Germany after reunification cut off the traditional industrial path of manufacturing. New growth emerges from new technology industries where highly skilled labour is demanded. Institutional fragmentation allows regions to develop new specialization profiles, because compared with the past entrepreneurs can now revert on many more liberal coordination devices. Therefore, institutional and spatial fragmentation can be understood as an integrated concept for rescue and redevelopment. However, skills for new technology industries have not been acquired by workers in traditional East German firms. These workers migrated from their East German homes or faced a difficult future. Traditional firms in West Germany however, defend their comparative advantage by assigning these workers and younger age cohorts into atypical employment contracts. Owing to the diverging industrial structure and general employment situation, hired-out job contracts are overwhelmingly a West German phenomenon in absolute numbers (560 742 workers in West Germany as opposed to 139 407 workers in East Germany in 2008).

This stabilizes the production regime and allows the core workforce to maintain full protection and relatively high wages; however, a society with privileges emerges which is concentrated in West Germany. In the new *Länder*, however, regions decline either because of migratory effects or exclusion of the traditional workforce. In general, income inequality rises and overlaps with regional success and failure, creating boom towns as well as dreadfully underdeveloped and neglected spaces.

CONCLUSIONS

Many critics complained that VoC cannot take account of sub-national variations of the dominant production order and institutional change. This is true, because the approach focuses on national regulations and devises types of political economies which, by definition, cannot account for dynamic processes. Moreover, severe transformations of European political economies are certainly undeniable and sub-national variations of national regulations often hold the key to understanding successful strategies for innovation and new growth. Nevertheless, VoC provides an excellent approach to understanding how CMEs and LMEs might work and how they run into trouble. For instance, explaining efficiency gains from national regulations makes it easier to capture the role of homogeneous institutional support for collective competition goods. VoC very fruitfully describes the way in which spatial and social integration served as an important precondition for the economic success of CMEs. By highlighting the role of reinforcement mechanisms and efficiency gains stemming from a complementary institutional order, it also appears quite manifest how to explain new emerging problems: Problems occur if spatial and institutional coherence is put at risk. I argue that this is definitely the case in countries like Italy and Germany; however, spatial and institutional fragmentation may be interpreted as an attempt to rescue endangered traditional manufacturing systems. Thus, the positive consequence of this strategy is that it enables CMEs to survive. The negative consequences are that declining regions will fail completely if they cannot be restructured for new technology industries and many workers in the traditional industries will be poorly paid and protected.

Today empirical cases do not carry the typical features of pure models of capitalism. Nevertheless VoC establishes a valuable point of reference in understanding how individual countries lose coherent institutional orders. Scholars may picture the recent dynamic in CMEs as a complete transformation towards liberal strategies. In this chapter I argue instead that CMEs or countries that have specialized in traditional manufacturing rather create spatially and institutionally coexisting worlds of production. This cannot be interpreted as a process of liberalization. The German and Italian political economies will not fail in traditional manufacturing. Instead, production in these segments has come under extreme forms of price competition. Quality production hinders these firms in completely exiting the national territory. Instead, agents of change establish a dual labour market in their home countries and pursue an exclusive policy of spatial support to maintain comparative advantages. As a result of this, CMEs remain competitive and may sustain a quite remarkable trade balance regarding their traditional export goods. Nevertheless, this success rests on a process of fragmentation which causes unstable work relations, escalating job requirements and growing economic inequality, especially for outsider groups. The future of CMEs is thus uncertain, not necessarily regarding their economic capacities to keep up in international competition, but to find solutions for newly emerging distributional conflicts within Western societies. In order to find solutions one must study diverging patterns of socio-economic and political innovation. Thanks to the great works of scholars such as Colin Crouch intriguing and inspiring answers are already to hand.

REFERENCES

Becattini, G. (1979), 'Dal Settore Industriale al Distretto Industriale: Alcune Considerazioni sull' Unità d' Indagine dell' Economia Industriale', *Rivista di Economia e Politica Industriale*, 1, 7–21.

Bertelsmann-Stiftung (ed.) (2001), *Die Bundesländer im Standortwettbewerb*, Gütersloh: Verlag Bertelsmann-Stiftung.

Brusco, S. (1982), 'The Emilian model: Productive decentralisation and social integration', *Cambridge Journal of Economics,* 6 (2), 167–84.

Brusco, S. (ed.) (1989), *Piccole Imprese e distretti industriali*, Torino: Rosenberg & Sellier.

Brzinsky-Fay, C. et al. (2007), *Atypische Beschäftigung – Umfang, Dynamik und soziale Sicherung im europäischen Vergleich*, Paper presented at the 5. Internationale Forschungskonferenz über soziale Sicherheit, Warsaw, 5–7 March 2007.

Bundesagentur für Arbeit (2008), *Arbeitnehmerüberlassung: Bestand an Leiharbeitern nach Art der ausgeübten Tätigkeit*, Nürnberg: Statistik der Bundesagentur für Arbeit.

Burroni, L. and C. Trigilia (2001), *Italy: Economic Development through Local Economies*, in C. Crouch, P. Le Galès, C. Trigilia and H. Voelzkow (eds), *Local Production Systems in Europe. Rise or Demise?* Oxford: Oxford University Press, pp. 46–78.

Crouch, C. et al. (2005), 'Dialogue on 'Institutional complementarity and political economy', *Socio-Economic Review* 3 (2), 359–82.

Crouch, C. et al. (2009), *Innovation in Local Economies. Germany in Comparative Context*, Oxford: Oxford University Press.

Crouch, C. and H. Farrell (2004) 'Breaking the Path of Institutional Development? Alternatives to the New Determinism', *Rationality and Society*, 16 (1), 5–43.

DeBresson, Christian et al. (eds) (1996), *Economic Interdependence and Innovative Activity. An Input–Output Analysis*, Cheltenham, UK/ Brookfield, US: Edward Elgar.

Esping-Andersen, G. (1990), *The Three Worlds of Welfare Capitalism*, Princeton, New Jersey: Princeton University Press.

Esping-Andersen, G. (1999), *Social Foundations of Postindustrial Economies*, Oxford: Oxford University Press.

Fabbrini, S. and M. Brunazzo (2003), 'Federalizing Italy: The Convergent Effects of Europenization and Domestic Mobilization', *Regional and Federal Studies*, 13 (1), 100–120.

Gehrke, B. and Legler, H. (1999), *Innovationspotentiale in den Regionen. Niedersachsen im europäischen Vergleich*, Forschungsberichte des NIW, 27, Hannover: Niedersächsisches Institut für Wirtschaftsforschung e.V.

Glassmann, U. (2007), *Staatliche Ordnung und räumliche Wirtschaftspolitik: Eine Analyse lokaler Produktionssysteme in Italien und Deutschland*, Gesellschaftspolitik und Staatstätigkeit, Bd. 29. Wiesbaden: VS Verlag für Sozialwissenschaften.

Grasse, A. and F. Gelli (forthcoming), 'Föderalismus, Regionen und Territorialität in Italien: Governance-Konzepte zwischen Markt und Staat', in Ulrich Glassmann, Stefan Köppl and Karonline Rörig (eds), *Länderbericht Italien*, Bonn: Bundeszentrale für politische Bildung.

Greif, Siegfried (2000), 'Regionale Verteilung von Innovations- und Technologiepotentialen in Deutschland im Spiegel von Patenten', München: Online available at: www.isi.fhg.de/ir/regionalstudie/greif_text.pdf.

Hall, P.A., and D. Soskice (eds) (2001), 'An Introduction to Varieties of Capitalism', in *Varieties of Capitalism. The Institutional Foundations of Comparative Advantage,* Oxford: Oxford University Press, pp. 1–68.

Hall, P.A. and K. Thelen (2005), 'Institutional Change in the Varieties of Capitalism', Paper presented for the presentation of the Annual Meeting of the American Political Science Association, Washington DC, 1 September 2005.

Hancké, B., M. Rhodes and M. Thatcher (2007), 'Introduction: Beyond Varieties of Capitalism', in B. Hancké, Martin Rhodes and Mark Thatcher (eds), *Beyond Varieties of Capitalism. Conflict, Contradictions, and Complementarities in the European Economy.* Oxford: Oxford University Press, pp. 3–38.

Hassel, A. (1999), 'The Erosion of the German System of Industrial Relations', *British Journal of Industrial Relations,* **37** (3), 483–505.

Hassel, Anke (2002), 'The Erosion Continues: Reply', *British Journal of Industrial Relations,* **40** (2), 309–17.

Interview MWME (2007), Interview with ministerial officer in the department for cluster policies at the Ministerim für Wirtschaft, Mittelstand und Energie des Landes Nordrhein-Westfalen on 18 July 2007.

ISTAT (1995), *Statistics on Scientific Research and Innovation,* Roma: Istituto Nazionale di Statistica.

Lau, D. (1997), *Sektorale, räumliche Konzentration und ihre Bedeutung für die Industriepolitik,* Veröffentlichungen des HWWA-Institut für Wirtschaftsforschung-Hamburg, Band 34. Baden-Baden: Nomos Verlagsgesellschaft.

Le Galès, P. and Voelzkow, H. (2001), *Introduction: The Governance of Local Economies,* in Colin Crouch et al. (eds), *Local Production Systems in Europe. Rise or Demise?,* Oxford: Oxford University Press, pp.1–24.

Licht, G. et al. (2000), *Zur technologischen Leistungsfähigkeit Deutschlands. Zusammenfassender Endbericht 1999,* Mannheim: BMBF Bericht.

Locke, R.M. (1995), *Remaking the Italian Economy,* Ithaca/ London: Cornell University Press.

Mai, C. (2008), *Arbeitnehmerüberlassungen – Bestand und Entwicklungen.* Statistisches Bundesamt, Wirtschaft und Statistik 6/2008.

Malerba, F. (1993), 'The National System of Innovation: Italy', in Richard R. Nelson (ed.), *National Innovation Systems. A Comparative Analysis,* Oxford: Oxford University Press, pp. 230–59.

OECD (2005), M. Förster and M. D'Ercole, *Income Distribution and Poverty in OECD Countries in the Second Half of the 1990s,* Social, Employment and Migration Working Papers, Paris: OECD.

OECD (2008), *Economic survey of Germany 2008.*

Putnam, R.D. (1993), *Making Democracy Work. Civic Traditions in Modern Italy,* Princeton, New Jersey: Princeton University Press.

Regini, M. (1995), *Uncertain Boundaries. The Social and Political Construction of European Economies,* Cambridge: Cambridge University Press.

Rommelspacher, T. (2004), 'Die "Gleichwertigkeit der Lebensverhältnisse" ist nicht mehr zeitgemäß', available at www.kommunale-info.de/infothek/2320 (accessed 04.05.2010).

Sala-i-Martin, X. (2006), 'Global Inequality Fades as the Global Economy Grows', in 2007 Index of Economic Freedom: Washington: Heritage Foundation, *Wall Street Journal*, pp. 15–25.

Scharpf, F.W. (1985), 'Die Politikverflechtungs-Falle. Europäische Integration und deutscher Föderalismus im Vergleich', in *Politische Vierteljahresschrift*, **26** (4), 323–56.

Scharpf, F.W. (2001), 'Employment and the welfare state. A continental dilemma', in B. Ebbinghaus and P. Manow (eds), *Comparing Welfare Capitalism. Social policy and political economy in Europe, Japan, and the USA*, London/New York: Routledge, pp. 270–83.

Schroeder, W. (1997), 'Loyalty and Exit – Austritte aus regionalen Arbeitgeberverbänden der Metall- und Elektroindustrie im Vergleich', in Ulrich von Alemann and Bernhard Weßels (eds), *Verbände in vergleichender Perspektive. Beiträge zu einem vernachlässigten Feld*, Berlin: Edition Sigma, pp. 225–52.

Sternberg, R. and Litzenberger, T. (2004), 'Regional Clusters in Germany – Their Geography and Their Relevance for Entrepreneurial Activities', *European Planning Studies*, **12** (6), 767–91.

Streeck, W. and K. Thelen (2005), 'Introduction: Institutional Change in Advanced Political Economies', in W. Streeck and K. Thelen (eds), *Beyond Continuity. Institutional Change in Advanced Political Economies*, Oxford: Oxford University Press, pp. 1–39.

Swank, Duane H., and C. Jo Martin (2001), 'Employers and the Welfare State. The Political Economic Organization of Firms and Social Policy in Contemporary Capitalist Democracies', *Comparative Political Studies* **34** (8), 889–923.

Töpfer, A. (1998), *Die Restrukturierung des Daimler-Benz Konzerns 1995–1997: Portfoliobereinigung, Prozeßoptimierung, Profitables Wachstum*, Neuwied/Kriftel: Luchterhand.

Wood, S. (2001), 'Business, Government, and Patterns of Labour Market Policy in Britain and the Federal Republic of Germany', in P. Hall and D. Soskice (eds), *Varieties of Capitalism. The Institutional Foundations of Comparative Advantage*, Oxford: Oxford University Press, pp. 247–74.

10. The boundaries between economy and society in European cities[1]

Luigi Burroni

ECONOMY, SOCIETY AND GOVERNANCE AT LOCAL LEVEL

During recent years a growing strand of research has focused on the so-called globalization paradox: the global competitiveness of firms and economic systems is increasingly rooted in the local institutional endowment and it depends on how effective local actors are in boosting external economies and creating stable locational advantages. This means that globalization increases the territorial mobility of companies but at the same time it renders them more dependent on their external context: the institutional context plays a key role in reinforcing the competitive advantage of a place thanks to contextual resources that have been recently defined as 'local collective competition goods' (Crouch et al. 2001, 2004). They include tangible elements such as infrastructure, logistics, services, the availability of qualified employees, the presence of research and development centres, the provision of information on new markets, the availability of specific transport infrastructures, but also intangible components such as cooperation relationships, that is, social networks, trust, skills and tacit knowledge. This paradox has been emphasized also by the recent financial crisis that since 2007 has interested all EU countries: a large number of cities are facing important processes of economic restructuring, and the outcomes of these processes seem to be strongly influenced by the quality of collective resources available in each city.

The analysis of local governance modes, based on the study of the role played by organizations, institutions and actors in the production/provision of local competition goods, is a valid research path in studying the reciprocal influence between economy and society at local level and to better understand the above-mentioned paradox. The definition of governance adopted here is rooted in the economic sociology tradition and refers to the set of mechanisms, devices and institutional arrangements that coordinate the economic actions of actors and organizations, regulate the distribution of resources and structure conflicts. For this reason I find particularly useful the distinction between *forms of governance* and *models of governance* (Crouch 2005). Forms of governance are the *market*, for example, that is, a regulatory mechanism based on the exchange between supply and demand and regulated by the price of goods or services. The *state* represents another form of governance: in this case, the mechanism of regulation is based on public authority and power and on the action of the governments at their various levels (local, regional, national, European). The *community* is a third form of governance based on mutual trust, reciprocity and the presence of shared identity and values that can contribute in various ways to regulating the economy. The *hierarchy* refers to those arrangements that are underpinned by organizational authority, on both internal (the large firm) and external (the networked firm) lines. The *associative* form refers to the way in which associations (mainly employers' associations and trade unions) contribute to the regulation of the economy. Finally, the mechanism of *regulatory agency*, traditionally neglected by social sciences, is related to the role played by intermediate agencies – often consisting of non-elected technicians and often appointed directly by central government.

Naturally, as Crouch has emphasized, when we analyse empirical cases it emerges that these above-mentioned forms of governance are not mutually exclusive: a huge variety of combinations of them exists. For this reason the concept of *models of governance* is important: different models of governance are, in fact, produced by different combinations and interactions of forms of governance. Thus, dichotomic approaches are not so useful in explaining empirical cases. For example, focusing on the dichotomy state *vs* market, it is possible to note that there are blurring boundaries between state and market regulation and that many mixes of these two forms can be found. Therefore, forms of governance are useful conceptual tools, but in order to understand empirical cases, it is useful to focus on specific models of governance (Crouch et al. 2004, Crouch 2005).

I will concentrate on local modes of governance in three countries, France, the United Kingdom and Italy to emphasize how the competitiveness of cities – one of the key drivers of Western capitalism (Le Galès 2002) – is related to the action of a plethora of local actors and institutions that contribute to the creation of local competitive advantage. We will see that local institutional architecture differs among the three countries and this emphazises the existence of multiple path to economic competitiveness that has already been underlined by many comparative studies on Western capitalism (see Berger and Dore 1996; Crouch et al. 2001, 2004; Trigilia 2002).

STATE AND LARGE FIRMS: THE FRENCH CASE

Urban policies have always had an extreme importance in France, and this is obvious in a country where more than 80 per cent of the national population lives in cities. At the same time, this country is characterized by a relevant polarization between one large metropolitan area and the rest of the country characterized by cities of smaller dimensions: Lyon the second French city is seven times smaller than Paris; there are only 36 municipalities in France with more than 100 000 and about 25 000 municipalities with less than 700 inhabitants. These demographic disparities go hand in hand with economic differentiation: the Paris region represents about 75 per cent of the headquarters of the 500 largest French companies, 58 per cent of national employment in the field of research, 39 per cent in the field of services and 46 per cent in the field of finance.

For this reason, the importance of the Paris region has always been absolutely relevant for the entire French economy and the role played by the central level of regulation has been predominant. This centralism has diminished during recent years, with the rise of a process of administrative decentralization. However, this recent change has not modified the prevalent role of the state, which continues to be the most important form of governance in France: central and local administrations identify the needs and priorities of local firms and plan and implement the appropriate measures in order to fulfil those priorities. The promotion of the urban economy and the provision of local competition goods are still top priorities of the national and local political agenda and public forms of regulation continue to steer local economies, influencing the rise or decline of productive specializations, promoting the emergence of a certain organizative model among companies and attracting specific external investments.

Local coalitions of actors/organizations that characterize this governance architecture tend to be mono-centric, with the local state monopolizing the 'political space' devoted to the creation of local competition goods and with the other actors tending to be excluded. An eventual participation of local associations or private organizations is promoted directly by the local government and regulated by formal instruments (such as contracts and plans).

The recent process of decentralization and devolution of competencies reinforced local councils and emphasized the shift of authority from central to local bureaucracies. Many policy instruments reinforced the room for manoeuvre within the French local state, such as the new direction of urban policies which started at the beginning of the 1990s, with the *Chartés d'Objectifs*, the *Contrats de villes*, the *Programmes d'Aménagement Concerté du Territoire*. What is interesting is that in all these instruments the role played by local public organizations is reinforced and in many cases the central level of regulation continues to play an important role. At the same time, it seems possible to affirm that the importance of public-led regulation founds its roots in the evolution of urban policy instruments which began at the beginning of the 1980s.

Examples are given by the promotion of the so-called public agencies of local authority cooperation (*Etablissement Public de Cooperation Intercommunale*, EPCI), public bodies (such as the *Communautés urbaines*, the *Communautés de Villes*, the *Syndacats d'agglomeration*) that carry out a huge number of duties, often related to the promotion of the local economy. They have spread throughout France, where at the end of the 1990s about 19 000 EPCIs were active. Another interesting policy instrument introduced during the 1990s was the large city charters (*Chartés d'Objectifs*): their aim was to reinforce the tie between the central and local levels of regulation and to promote specific urban productive specialization, identifying a specific productive vocation for each urban area. Here the link between the local level of regulation and the ministers in charge of the related field assures major integration with other policies, such as the planning contracts (*Contrats de plan*).

The role of the public actor has also been emphasized by the town contracts (*Contrat de Villes*) and the programmes for negotiated local development – PACT (*Programmes d'Aménagement Concerté du Territoire*). In this case too, they are instruments of multilevel governance that bind the various levels of public administration. In the *Contrats de Villes*, in fact, central, regional, departmental and local levels of government decide a long-term development programme together, aiming at favouring both economic dynamism and social cohesion. The PACT *urbaines*, instead, are directed at those areas facing processes of industrial restructuring, with the aim of favouring a diversification of the local economies, promoting the rise of a local system of small companies, offering professional training and promoting the recovery of industrial areas.

In all these cases the relation between the central and the decentralized level of regulation is quite formalized: notwithstanding the ongoing process of administrative decentralization, the relations among different public actors (regions, departments, communes) take the form of contractual funding agreements among different levels of territorial regulation (Sellers 2002). This sort of state-led governance confirms that even in these days 'in France, the broad conception of the state as a definer of values and a purposive policy actor creates a set of values in which a self-conscious bureaucracy sustains a conception of the state as the leading force in development and provides the technical resources to allow the public authorities to dominate the process' (Keating 1991: 71).

It is true that the above-mentioned process of reform modified the institutional architecture of local governance introducing new tools and increasing the room for manoeuvre for local actors. However, some authors emphasized that this long-standing process of reforms did not modify the main pillar of the French model, namely the strong role of coordination and regulation played by the central state (Jessop 2000). These authors stress that despite the above-mentioned reforms the difference between the 'old' and 'new' models is not so strong: there are more elements of continuity than rupture even if the objectives of national policies are more focused towards local development than in the past. In other words, there is still a traditional French central government preponderance compared with the role of local public actors.

Although with decentralization reform regions should have had a key role in planning economic development, central government has continued to manage policies and to define priorities in this field. This can explain why in 2003 the Constitutional Reform included regions in the list of *collectivités territoriales* and ordinary law in 2004 defined them as *chefs de file* economic development; but then in 2005 the Centre-right Villepin government set up and implemented the *poles de compétitivité* through the DGCIS (*Direction Générale à la Compétitivité, l'Innovation et les rhewtoricServices*) without the official participation of regional and local administrations.

Another indicator of change is given by the growing importance of the role played by agency for local development, both at national and at local level. For example, the *L'Agence Nationale pour la Rénovation Urbaine* (ANRU) is the national agency in charge of financing projects of public and private actors aimed at making programmes of urban renovation and regeneration for poor urban areas – the *Zones Urbaines Sensibles* (ZUS) or areas with the same economic background. At the same time, many cities are creating their own local agencies to deal with economic and social local development programs (Cole 2008).

At the same time, the role of local political individual actors should not be overlooked. The French case, in fact, continues to be characterized by the role played by local notables, and a particular role is played by mayors: they have a relevant autonomy at local level and the link between urban mayors and the national political arena shows the increasing power of these local actors (Le Galès 2002, Cole 2008).

The territorial structure of the interests' organizations also favours this dominant role played by the state. Trade unions in France are characterized by a very low level of membership and maintain a strong antagonistic and conflictual approach: they are able to mobilize a large part of the population for contestation but they are rarely involved in proactive policies for local development. Employers' organizations (especially Medef) are highly fragmented, weak and dominated by large companies. This is why they are not interested in the promotion of local economic development, being more focused upon national strategies and concerns. Nevertheless, the involvement of this organization in local public/private bodies has recently grown, even if it remains far from the model of involvement that characterizes other European countries; as Sellers noted, although business organizations increased the role in the promotion of local economic development, local political leaders continue to exercise a strong guiding hand over regime agendas and policies (Sellers 2002).

It is also important to note that according to some authors, large companies have had a central place in the recent restructuring of the French political economy, being able also to 'exploit their pilot role by aligning the action of other relevant actors – state and regional authorities as well as small firms – with their interests' (Hancké 2002, 2003). Thus, on the one hand large companies contribute directly to the provision of local competition goods and, on the other hand, they influence the outcome of the action of local authorities and government.

Many recent researches seem to corroborate this path. John and Cole, for example, show that in the case of Rennes, which has recently achieved much success in attracting specialized public and private enterprises in ICT, it is possible to find a clear break between public and private actors, with a clear dominance of public regulation of the local economy (John and Cole 2000, Cole 2008). Another example is given by Grenoble, where the role played by the public actor has been of primary importance in order to explain the local increase of high-tech activities but also the scarce ability of these enterprises to compete in international markets (Aniello 2004, Novarina 2010). Or, again, the case of Lille, where a large project of urban restructuring, promoting the city as an international transport node that also included the revitalization of the local economy, was mainly public based (Couch et al., 2003).

Thus, looking at recent changes and features of the French model of local governance it seems possible to say that this model is characterized by the role of local and central state and by large firms.

An empirical example of this model of governance is given by the city of Lyon, one of the most important French urban economies. It is located in the Rhône-Alpes, the city has around 450 000 inhabitants and the metropolitan area around 1.5 million people. The metropolitan area is characterized by a diversified local economy, with services activities that represent a large part of total employment: at the end of the 1990s industrial activities represented around 25 per cent of local employment while services accounted for about 65 per cent. Information and Communication

Technology is one of the most important local specializations: more than 450 research laboratories are located in this area, together with a huge amount of the most important French large firms.

As for the local governance model, it is worth noting the so-called experience of strategic planning that started about 25 years ago with the process of reorganization of the *Schéma directeur d'aménagement et d'urbanisme* (Sdau). This process led to the local plan for development called 'Lyon 2010', with which the local public administration wanted to promote a process of modernization of the local economy. The main aim of the plan was to promote the competitive city, to attract new enterprises and to strengthen the position of Lyon in the international competition regime. This process of territorial reorganization represented a radical break with the previous practice of traditional and technocratic planning based on the regulation of land use promoting a precise model of socio-economic development, pursued via the reinforcement of already available assets (such as local research centres funded by public funds) or the setting up of new organizations devoted to the provision of local public services. As for the method of policy making, the attempt to involve the local society characterized the Lyon 2010 plan, even if this sort of local concertation was strongly dominated by local public authorities and associations as unions or employers' organizations played a minor role.

In 1997 a first group of experts started to draw a plan of the city agglomeration consisting of the greater Lyon area, made up of 55 municipalities of the metropolitan area of Lyon. This was the first phase of the so-called *Demarche Millenaire*. Later, five task forces were set up in order to develop five strategic thematic areas (urban ecology, reorganization of urban development, territory and governance, social cohesion and the cities and the global economy). The second phase of the *Demarche* started in November 1999, when the priorities and aims of the process of strategic planning were related to the adoption of a *Contrat de Plan et de Villas* and of one *Contrat d'agglomeration*, underlining once again the importance of central–local contractual instruments for French urban development that has continued up to 2010.

As for local development agencies, an important role is played by the Lyon Area Economic Development Agency (ADERLY), which identifies and provides support for projects involving investment and the setting up of new companies and national or international public organizations. It welcomes and supports companies and helps the people in charge of local economic projects to achieve positive results in the Lyon region. ADERLY has 60 public and private sector members who are among the major players in the economic life of Lyon; but in contrast with the British cases of local agencies presented below the strategy of this organization, the services it offers and its political action is driven by public actors.

The case of Lyon also emphasizes the important role of large firms in local urban governance. In the Lyon area there is a large number of firms (62) with more than 500 employees, and many of them play a very important role in the promotion of the local economy. Many of them are very important firms in chemical production, such as Brenntag, Biomerieux, Basf. Local and regional public actors are the other important pole of the governance of this sector. The *Communaute Urbaine*, ADERLY, the region of Rhône Alpes and the central state strongly support this sector, thanks to a massive amount of public funding devoted to the attraction of external firms, the creation of new local firms, and the support to the already existing companies. Furthermore, these actors, and especially the *Communaute*, are stimulating the territorial concentration of these activities in two areas, Gerland and the eastern suburb, Lyon Bron. Finally, Raymond Barre (mayor of Lyon, 1995–2001) promoted Biovision, an international biennial conference and trade fair that aims at being a World Life Sciences Forum able to promote internationally the image of Lyon as a hub of excellence in life sciences.

Summing up, notwithstanding some changes, the French model of urban governance continues to be characterized by the role of the state, at both central and local levels. In fact, in spite of recent processes of administrative decentralization, the new urban policy-making instruments are mainly public led and one of the most important coordinating mechanisms is the contract between different territorial levels of public administration. This is why, contrary to the English case, public–public partnerships are predominant in this case. Together with the state, large firms play a very important role in the provision of collective competition goods providing them directly and influencing the strategies of local and regional governments.

MARKET, AGENCIES AND PARTNERSHIP-LED GOVERNANCE: THE UK CASE

The model of urban governance that has emerged in the United Kingdom since the beginning of the 1980s has been characterized by three keywords: partnerships, regulatory agencies and market. Intermediate organizations (quasi non-governmental organizations – *quangos*) and firms play, in fact, the pivotal role in this model within private–public partnership.

The contracting out of public activities and the distribution of national public funds to local private or semi-public non-elected bodies that began during the 1980s favoured the proliferation of these kinds of intermediate organizations, so that there are in Britain now about 4500 quangos financed directly by the central government, with senior staff appointed directly by the government (Le Galès 2002). Training and Enterprise Councils (TECs) and Local Enterprise Councils (LECs) established in the early 1990s were examples of these intermediate bodies. From the 1990s TECs and LECs have played a key role in any public policy for company networking and for a general commitment to 'enterprise' encouragement, even if their primary point of reference was vocational training (Crouch et al. 1998, Crouch et al. 2001, 2004); they were abolished with the Learning and Skills Act in 2000 and were replaced by another quango funded by the government, the Learning and Skills Councils, aimed at improving adults' and young people's education and training.

Other examples of intermediate bodies are provided by Urban Development Corporations, created to regenerate urban areas through policies aimed at stimulating property development and local firms' dynamism, by Urban Regeneration Companies, created to stimulate new investment into areas of economic decline and to coordinate plans for their regeneration and redevelopment engaging the private sector in a sustainable regeneration strategy, and by Local Development Agencies with their relevant functions of steering and promoting economic growth and local development.

The rise of the role of these intermediate organizations went hand in hand with the growth of public–private partnership arrangements in the making of many local competition goods such as training or support for small and medium companies (Pierre 1999). Thus, it seems reasonable to say that the recent restructuring of urban governance in the United Kingdom was characterized by the growing importance of a specific form of governance, that of agency, based on public–private partnership. At the same time, thanks to this process of partnership, many large firms started to contribute directly to the provision of important local services and play an important role in local governance.

If we want to understand the rise of this model of urban governance it is important to focus on the relationship between the central and the decentralized level of regulation. In particular, it is important to focus on the attempts of central governments to weaken the role of local government. The importance of regulatory agencies and the rising role of partnership arrangement found their roots in the evolution of urban policy instruments for the promotion of economic development and social cohesion that started at the beginning of the 1980s. In this period, Conservative governments introduced some extremely important innovations for urban political frameworks that have been gathered under the definition of *private sector-led urban entrepreneurialism.* On the one hand, there was a process of reorganization of city governance instruments that strengthened a wide range of instruments like City Action Teams, Enterprises Zones, Development Corporations and English partnerships. On the other hand, the central government decreased the quantity of funds managed directly by local governments, weakening the role played by this level of regulation. Thus, governmental strategy was in a certain sense contradictory: it claimed to reinforce the decentralized level of regulation but at the same time, it undermined its spending autonomy.

A second line of policies emerged during the period 1991–97, when there was a change of direction undertaken by the Conservative government of John Major in order to answer the growing criticism of the institutional framework developed during previous governments (Hill 2000). What is interesting is that, paradoxically, this change reinforced the above-mentioned features, promoting a further territorial competition, the carrying out of private–public partnership and the involvement of private actors in delivering local public services. This 'new road' has turned out instruments such as the City Challenge, with the idea of integrating many different interventions including city regeneration, the promotion of economic competitiveness and policies for human resources and skills. At the same time, these local plans had to compete with each other in order to raise public money (Hill 2000). This twofold logic of integration, private protagonism and competition characterized many of the policy instruments that emerged during this period, such as City Pride.

After 1997, with the election of the Labour government, another approach emerged (Stoker 2004). The Labour government's 'New deal', in fact, just continued considering public–private partnership and territorial competition as two essential components for the promotion of urban dynamism. The main difference with the past was that with the 'New Deal' major attention was devoted to the reinforcement of social cohesion, aiming at balancing economic growth and competitiveness with the reduction of disparities and with a sustainable model of local development. But looking at the way in which collective competition goods are provided it emerges that intermediate agencies and firms have continued to increase their role.

Thus, even if later relevant changes in urban policies occurred in the last 20 years, it is possible to identify some pillars that continue to characterize the UK model during this period: the promotion of competition in the provision of local services, the reinforcement of local and regional agencies and the encouragement of private–public partnership.

These changes were also related to the emerging view that progressive marketization of some public activities would improve the delivery and the effectiveness of these services manifestly took shape. As underlined by Gerry Stoker, in order to understand changes in urban governance in the UK it is important to focus on the ideology and political thought that emerged with the so-called New Right that resulted in a rolling back of the state in search of new forms of intervention and control; and the main pillars of this view and a sort of anti-statist thought also fascinated the Left (Stoker 1998, 2004, see also King 1987). Thus, it is not surprising that the philosophy of the *New Public Management* had in the UK a relevant success, with its encouragement of new processes of governing in an entrepreneurial style and with major attention to competition, markets, customers and results (Centre for Regional Economic and Social Research, 2004).

The role played by the market and agencies has also been favoured by the particular configuration of business interest organizations and trade unions. The Confederation of British Industry (CBI), for example, is dominated by large companies with close links to national governments and institutions, but even though it has a regional organization, it has little to do with local governments: the process of involvement of business organizations in the process of urban policy making is still relatively rare. As for trade unions, their action at the decentralized level is mainly related to workplace activities, while they usually take their 'political' concerns to the national level, mobilizing at local-territorial level mainly for the solution of disputes. This is why the involvement of interest organizations in the making of local proactive and pro-growth coalitions is less important in Britain than in Italy, as we shall see.

Many examples of the main features of the above-mentioned local governance model can be found in some large and small UK cities. The city of Manchester is a good example of this model characterized by the important role of local agencies. Here the Urban Regeneration Company was founded in 1999 as a partnership between national (English Partnerships), regional (the North West Development Agency) and local government (Manchester City Council). It had the key role in the local regeneration project, *New East Manchester – A New Town in the City*, which provides the basis for how the regeneration of East Manchester will be carried out over a ten-year period. The Manchester Partnership (the Local Strategic Partnership – LSP), which brings together the main local public service providers, is another important local organization. The LSP was set up in January 2002 and charged with the identification of the priorities of local neighbourhoods, diagnosing their problems and designing appropriate responses and integrating activities already undertaken in the areas concerned. Its purpose is to coordinate improvements in public services that support local economic, social and physical regeneration and, in order to fulfil this aim, the LSP backed a series of services for the promotion of local economic development. The structure of the LSP is organized around five Thematic Partnerships and among them the partnership on Economic and Local Employment, which is in charge of the promotion of local economic development, is especially important for our topic. At the same time, the Manchester Digital Development Agency, founded in 2003, is responsible for coordinating the Digital Strategy for the Manchester city region and has a number of key roles in supporting growth, employment and skills, in the digital business sector, with specific support to small and medium firms. MIDAS – the Manchester Investment and Development Agency – was founded in 1997: it was established to provide an ensemble of services for companies moving into or within the area, ensuring access to information and assistance, including access to grants and support for companies in recruiting and training their workforces; now it is in charge of developing the improvement of the city in order to attract investments.

In many cases, these agencies are built of large partnerships of local public and private stakeholders, such as the local government and large firms, and contribute to the making of various urban programmes. This is the case of Manchester City Pride, an urban programme started in the second half of the 1990s that took shape at central government level in the early period of the Conservative administration of 1992–97, when Manchester City Council received a government invitation to produce a first prospectus for City Pride, a long-term process of strategic planning. This is why Manchester City Council had the leadership of this project and has invited the neighbouring authorities of Salford and Trafford to participate in this programme. Later, the Metropolitan Borough of Tameside also joined the partnership making the City Pride area coterminous with that of Manchester's Training and Enterprise Council and with the Chamber of Commerce. In 2001 an Economic Development Plan was prepared by the four City Pride Authorities, working in partnership together through Manchester Enterprises, the newly-established economic development agency for the area. The first prospectus for the Manchester City Pride area was presented to the government in 1994. In 1999, following local consultation between the local authorities and the private sector, City Pride partners signed a statement of intent to establish the Manchester Enterprises Group as the local agency dedicated to the continuing economic development of the City Pride area, through business support, training and jobs. More recently, the 2008 Local Area Agreement – a three-year agreement that identifies the priorities for the development of the city – has been developed and agreed among all the partners of Manchester Partnership. Furthermore, the Statement of Community

Involvement (2007) sets out the rules and methods of involvements of the local community and of local stakeholders in planning processes in Manchester aimed at producing the Local Development Framework for the period 2010–13.

Some authors have emphasized that this model based on plans for development, local agencies and on the role of local political entrepreneurs such as Graham Stringer, mayor of the city from 1984 to 1996 (and then from 1997 to 2010 member of Parliament for Manchester Blackley), promoted a shift from what has been defined as *municipal socialism* to the *entrepreneurial city* (Quilley 2000).

Summing up, it is possible to find specificities that characterize the urban governance architecture in the United Kingdom: firms and development agencies are the dominant forms of governance and public–private partnership is the prevailing coordinating mechanism. The rise and the recent reinforcement of this model finds its roots in a process of reorganization of public policies aimed at weakening the power and the autonomy of local councils and in the growing legitimization of new public management practices. At the same time, the reinforcement of development agencies was also favoured by the weakness of 'functional alternatives', such as regional and local interests' organizations.

NEO-VOLUNTARISM AND NEGOTIATED LOCAL DEVELOPMENT: THE ITALIAN CASE

Internal differentiation in the organization of local economies and in models of governance have strongly characterized Italy for the entire postwar period (Trigilia and Burroni 2009). However, in this case it seems possible also to identify a national core of urban governance that characterizes many Italian cities. Here associations and local government, together with the role of communitarian arrangements, define the prevailing form of governance. As for the coordinating mechanism, a wide use of negotiation on a voluntary basis among private and public actors can be found. These negotiations may result in a local plan/pact or in more informal agreements that lead to a sort of rationalization of the private and public effort in promoting local development and providing local competition goods.

A specific kind of this local negotiation characterizes many small and medium cities with a high specialization in manufacturing and industrial districts. In these cases, a sort of local neo-corporatism can be found, in which a development-oriented coalition gathers together local government, trade unions and employers' associations. The kind of local competition goods produced by this model are mainly sectoral and targeted at the promotion of economic development, even if sometimes more collective goods related to the quality of life and the environment may be found. There is usually a medium-high degree of coordination in the provision of these goods, given by the internal cohesion and limited extension of the group of actors that take part in social negotiation practices. The coordinating mechanism is social concertation that deals with such topics as labour flexibility, promotion of local entrepreneurship, employment and training.

Examples of this model can be found among the industrial districts of the so-called Third Italy, and especially in the 'red regions', such as Emilia Romagna and Tuscany. Here local governments, employers' associations and trade unions share a long-standing tradition of cooperation that has led to many experiments of what has been defined as 'hidden micro-concertation' (Regini 1991). The production of local competition goods supported by this model has created and reinforced local competitive advantages that have been defined as external economies (Trigilia and Burroni 2009, Burroni 2001).

The industrial district of Prato represents the more well-known example of this kind of local governance: it is a local production system located in central Tuscany, and has a population of about 240 000 with almost 50 000 employees in the manufacturing sector. This is one of the most important Italian industrial districts: the textile industry accounts for 80 per cent of manufacturing companies, employs 83 per cent of occupation in manufacturing activities, and produces 10.8 per cent of the total national amount of textile exportation. In this local production system, production is highly fragmented in its various stages with many companies specializing at each stage of production. Recently there has been a growth in business services, tied to the de-localization of the more labour-intensive stages of production (Burroni et al. 2008; Burroni and Trigilia 2011).

The governance of this productive structure has been both of the communitarian type as well as formalized: in fact, the behaviour of the economic actors has often been regulated by 'implicit' rules. People who behave opportunistically are excluded from the 'group'; this mechanism of living up to one's own reputation has been and still is of considerable importance in regulating inter-firm activity (Dei Ottati 1995). It has also been emphasized that agreements between suppliers and customers are informal, and that in case of any disagreement this would be settled by mutual accord, informally and by 'meeting each other half way'. Yet, alongside this sphere of governance based on communitarian mechanisms, involving informal reciprocity, there is a formalized regulation, with a strong role played by local political institutions and associations.

In fact, one has to take into account that in Prato union density is particularly high, that the employers' associations (both artisan and industrial) provide services for their members and that local government is active in sustaining local economic development.

An important agreement signed in 1997 by the employers' associations (Unione Industriale, CNA, and Confartigianato), is a good example of this tendency. It aims at improving the relations between customers and suppliers and at preventing opportunistic behaviour by both sides. The agreement provides a replacement of the so-called 'oral contracts' with a standard written document in which quantity, price and terms of payment are well specified, establishing a model that will be readopted in the national law 192/98 which regulates customer and supplier relations. It had two main objectives: first, the institutionalization of social partnership, as the regulation agreed on by the social partners ought to reduce disputes and stabilize prices. Second, the agreement attempts to raise the quality of production in the area through greater coordination between the partners, which should improve the quality of the production system. It is, thus, an agreement that confirms a collective involvement in the creation of local competition goods, and the gradual coordination of relations between individual and collective actors. Another interesting example of competition goods provided by local institutions through more formalized regulation is provided by local collective bargaining during periods of crisis; in this case, unions and employers' associations shared the view that 'favouring the restructuring of firms in difficulties and promoting the change necessary to restore efficiency and foster local development' were unavoidable measures to pursue; for this reason trade unions accepted company plans that involved dismissal, requiring at the same time a reorganization of overtime (Dei Ottati 2002). In this sense, local bargaining favoured a consensual reorganization of the local labour force with positive outcomes on local economic dynamism. Finally, the last example can be given by the intense activity of local concertation that led to the proposal to the national government of a derogation for the extension of a social shock absorber to small scale firms: in this case, local employers' associations, trade unions and the local government worked together to make a proposal that was then adopted by the national government in the 2004 Financial Act.

A diverse model of social negotiation is recently influencing governance architecture of some large cities and metropolitan areas. It has been influenced by the relative scarcity of policy instruments dedicated at promoting local development in Italian urban and metropolitan contexts. Even if since the beginning of the 1990s new territorial tools such as Provincial Plans, Basin Plans, Park Plans, Wide Area Plans and Environmental

Plans have been introduced, all these instruments were mainly aimed at land use control. And the same is true for the PRUSST (*Programmi di Riqualificazione Urbana e Sviluppo Sostenibile del Territorio*) and PRU (*Programmi di Riqualificazione Urbana*), that are adopted to redefine urban planning processes and spatial re-organization. At the same time, the strand of policy instruments for local development that has been gathered under the definition of negotiated planning (*Programmazione negoziata*), such as territorial pacts or area contract, was mainly addressed to small cities and not metropolitan areas.

This second model of local negotiation is a more dialogic and incremental process that promotes the rise of an heterogeneous group of actors composed of experts, politicians and practitioners who start to share a 'common vision of the world'. It is a neo-voluntaristic instrument. The output of this process is a plan that delivers a 'vision for the city', based on the identification of long-term needs, priorities, objectives and measures.

A good example of this trend can be found in Turin, one of the former centres of Italian Fordism, where the presence of the FIAT Company influenced the social and economic fabric of the city for a long period. From the end of the 1980s FIAT met considerable difficulties and began a long-term process of restructuring. This process led to a radical decline in the role played by this large company in the economy of the city: massive re-localization of manufacturing activities and the attempt to diversify the FIAT group activities towards more tertiary functions have modified the economic structure of the city. Thus, after a long period of the identification of Turin as an industrial city, alternative pathways for local development became necessary. Starting from this period, local actors (local government, associations, unions) began to think in terms of productive diversification, and much effort was directed at the promotion of 'new' activity, such as tourism, information and communication technology (ICT). The successful application for the 2006 Winter Olympic Games boosted this diversification effort, introducing a strong need to rationalize local policy making together with a strong re-orientation of the local economy towards a more service-based urban society.

The so-called process of strategic planning emerged in this framework. In 1998 Mayor Valentino Castellani promoted a new planning process for the city of Turin, with a project called Torino Internazionale. The first step was to involve a large number of local and extra-local experts to carry out a diagnosis of the advantages, shortcomings and needs of the city. The outcome of this first stage was a document containing fundamental data on the present and future situation of the city. About a thousand people took part in the preliminary round of debates and participated with different relative weight to the setting up of the plan of action for promoting the city that contained six strategic lines of action, 20 more detailed aims and 84 specific actions or interventions. A pact on the development of Turin was signed by a large number of local actors/organizations and the Torino Internazionale association, dedicated to controlling and monitoring the implementation of the specific projects of the Plan, was founded.

The strategic planning experience is important because of its effort to coordinate the actions of various local organizations and firms devoted to set up collective competition goods: LCGs are identified through a process of deliberative negotiation among many local actors, and many of them are also involved in the implementation and provision of these goods. It is worth noting that this complex process of planning contributes directly to the creation of local competition goods devoted to new sectors. One example is Torino Wireless, a project for stimulating the development of the Turin area in the field of information and communication technologies.

While the case of Prato could be defined as local neo-corporatism, with unions, employers' associations and local government working together to support the economy of the city still based largely on textiles, the case of Turin shares more similarities with a model of local deliberative democracy, with a wide range of local actors – unions, employers' associations but also the 'civic society' – involved in promoting a process of diversification of the local economy.

Summing up, the Italian case is characterized by a relative scarcity of policy instruments aimed at triggering local development in urban contexts, and it seems reasonable to hypothesize that this scarcity has indirectly promoted a mobilization of local actors to find some sort of functional equivalent. A model of local neo-corporatism prevailed in industrial districts, in which development-oriented coalitions gather together local governments, trade unions and employers' associations. The kind of local competition goods produced by this model are mainly sectoral and targeted at the promotion of economic development, even if sometimes more collective goods related to the quality of life and the environment can be found. The dominant coordinating mechanism is the so-called social concertation that deals with topics as labour flexibility, the promotion of local entrepreneurship and employment and training. At the same time a more deliberative process of planning has emerged in some metropolitan area such as Turin, where an incremental negotiation promotes the rise of an heterogeneous group of actors composed of experts, politicians and practitioners who have started to share a 'common vision of the world'. The output of this process is a plan that delivers a 'vision for the city', based on the identification of long-term needs, priorities, objectives and measures. In this case, the plan is flexible and may be implemented continuously and the process of negotiation is more similar to a sort of experiment of deliberative democracy than to the above-mentioned local corporatist pact.

CONCLUSIONS. DIFFERENCES AND SIMILARITIES IN LOCAL GOVERNANCE

Summarizing the results of this analysis it is possible to say that the three countries are characterized by different models of local governance. In the French case large firms and the state continue to be the two prevailing forms of governance, while contractual policy instruments promoting partnership between different levels of public administration are the most important coordinating mechanism. A diverse asset characterizes urban governance models in the UK, where market and regulatory agencies are two dominant forms of governance, while partnership arrangements between public and private actors are the main coordinating mechanisms for the provision of local competition goods. Finally, social negotiation characterizes both the Italian cases, but in a very different way. The model of governance in industrial districts is similar to a sort of local neo-corporatism, with a rooted social concertation between economic associations and the local government, aimed at producing local competition goods with a sectoral character, directed at promoting the competitiveness of the textile sector. Communitarian mechanisms of regulation are more active in industrial districts than in metropolitan areas. In contrast, in the case of large cities there is a diverse type of social negotiation, based on deliberative practices with inter-sectoral results targeted at local economic competitiveness.

However, despite these differences some relevant similarities can be found. A first common process is the already mentioned process of devolution that reinforced the role of regional and local actors and organizations. This process of decentralization does not imply 'the end of the national state': the central level of regulation continues to play an important role in a) setting the general rule of room for manouvre of local actors, b) identifying the logic under and priorities pursued by local actors (especially in France), and c) carrying out some forms of control and monitoring of the action of local actors. A second similarity is related to actors and governance forms involved in these local experiments to reduce uncertainty: in all three countries new actors are emerging. Environmental organizations as well as other forms of organization related to the local society are more and more involved in the local governance even is their real weight in the decision-making process should not be overestimated.

Regional and local agencies are playing a growing role in all three countries. In some cases the emerging of new actors leads to 'hybrid' forms of governance: for example, the voluntary sector in the United Kingdom is a mix between a communitarian mechanism of regulation and associational governance; or regional development agencies fall between state, associations and networks. A third similarity is related to the kind of relations among local actors. In the three cases, local organizations tend to act in partnership, with formalized mechanism of cooperation, in which the role and the contribution of single actors is well specified. Different partnerships may be located in the same territory, and their composition may be variable according to their objectives. This is also related to the importance of negotiation as a method of decision making: local actors – sometimes with regional and national actors – bargain measures and strategies and mediate different interests. Finally, it is possible to find a common language among cases and countries based on a similar 'rhetoric' that influences the actions of local public and private actors. European political integration favoured the diffusion of keywords such as regeneration, privatization, territorial competitiveness, socio-economic sustainability, and so on, that can be found in the large majority of local experiments in the three countries.

All this shows that in three countries there is an important relationship between economy and society at local level: single firms, local political actors such as the local government, local organizations such as unions or employers' associations and organization representing the 'civic society' contribute directly to the set-up and distribution of local competitive advantages that influence the competitiveness of local firms. For this reason the analysis of models of local governance is a valid methodological tool in studying how places are facing the pressures of globalization and are promoting processes of restructuring to deal with the impacts of economic crisis. Paraphrasing Roger Hollingsworth (1998), one of the great challenges for contemporary sociology is to create a new theory for governance able to grasp processes and trends that are embedded in a world in which individual actors, organizations, localities, sub-national regions and nation-states are all intricately linked.

NOTE

1. The research on which this chapter is based has been partly funded by the FP7 project 'Meeting the challenges of economic uncertainty and sustainability through employment, industrial relations, social and environmental policies in Europe' (GUSTO); I acknowledge the financial support of the European Commission.

REFERENCES

Aniello, V. (2004), *Grenouble*, in C. Crouch, P. Le Galès, C. Trigilia and H. Voelzkow, *Changing governance of Local Economies. Responses of European Local Production Systems*, Oxford: Oxford University Press.

Berger, S. and R. Dore (1996), *National Diversity and Global Capitalism*, Cornell: Cornell University Press.

Burroni, L. (2001), *Allontanarsi crescendo. Politica ed economia in Veneto e Toscana*, Turin: Rosenberg & Sellier.

Burroni, L. and Trigilia, C. (eds) (2011), *Le città dell'innovazione. Dove e perché cresce l'alta tecnologia in Italia*, Bologna: Il Mulino.

Burroni, L., G. Dei Ottati and C. Trigilia (eds) (2008), *Innovazione nella continuità. Meccanismi di cambiamento nelle aree distrettuali della Toscana*, Pisa: Edizioni Plus.

Centre for Regional Economic and Social Research (2004), *New Deal for Communities National Evaluation. Annual report 2003–4*, London.

Cole, A. (1998), *Governing and Governance in France*, Cambridge: Cambridge University Press.

Cole, A. (2008) *Governing and Governance in France* Cambridge: Cambridge University Press.

Crouch, C. (2005), *Capitalist Diversity and Change. Recombinant Governance and Institutional Entrepreneurs*, Oxford: Oxford University Press.

Couch, C., C. Fraser and S. Percy (1993), *Urban Regeneration in Europe*, Oxford: Blackwell.

Crouch, C., D. Finegold and M. Sako (1999), *Are Skills the Answer? The Political Economy of Skill Creation in Advanced Industrial Countries*, Oxford: Oxford University Press.

Crouch, C., P. Le Galès, C. Trigilia and H. Voelzkow (2001), *Local Production Systems in Europe. Rise or Demise?*, Oxford: Oxford University Press.

Crouch, C., P. Le Galès, C. Trigilia and H. Voelzkow (2004), *Changing governance of Local Economies. Responses of European Local Production Systems*, Oxford: Oxford University Press.

Dei Ottati, G. (1995), *Tra mercato e comunità: aspetti concettuali e ricerche empiriche sul distretto industriale*, Milano: Angeli.

Dei Ottati, G. (2002), 'Social concertation and local development: The case of industrial districts', *European Planning Studies*, **10** (4), pp. 449–66.

Hancké, B. (2002), *Large Firms and Institutional Change. Industrial Renewal and Economic Restructuring in France*, Oxford: Oxford University Press.

Hancké, B. (2003), 'Many roads to flexibility. How large firms built autarchic regional production systems in France', *International Journal of Urban and Regional Research*, **27** (3), 510–26.

Hill, D.M. (2000), *Urban Policy and Politics in Britain Contemporary Political Studies*, Basingstoke: Palgrave.

Hollingsworth, R.J. (1998), 'New Perspective on the Spatial Dimension of Economic Coordination: Tension between Globalization and Social Systems of Production', *Review of International Political Economy*, **5** (3), 482–507.

Jessop, B. (2000), 'The Crisis of the National Spatio-Temporal Fix and the Tendential Ecological Dominance of Globalizing Capitalism', *International Journal of Urban and Regional Research*, **24** (2), 321–60.

John, P. and A. Cole (2000), 'When do institutions, policy sectors and cities matter? Comparing networks of local policy makers in Britain and France', *Comparative Political Studies*, **33** (2), 248–68.

Keating, M. (1991), *Comparative Urban Politics. Power and the City in the United States, Canada, Britain and France*, Edward Elgar: Aldershot.

King, D.S. (1987), *The New Right*, London Macmillan.

Le Galès, P. (2002), *European cities. Social conflicts and governance*, Oxford: Oxford University Press.

Novarina, G. (2010), 'Ville et innovation scientifique. Le cas de l'aire métropolitaine de Grenoble', in Luigi Burroni and Carlo Trigilia, *Le città dell'innovazione in Italia e in Europa, Rapporto di Artimino 2010*.

Pierre, J. (1999), 'Models of urban governance. The institutional dimension of urban politics', *Urban Affairs Review*, **34** (3), 372–96.

Quilley, S. (2000), 'Manchester First. From Municipal Socialism to the Entrepreneurial City', *European Journal of Urban and Regional Research*, **24** (3), 610–15.

Regini, M. (1991), *Confini mobili. La costruzione dell'economia fra politica e società*, Bologna: Il Mulino.

Sellers, J.M. (2002), *Governing from Below. Urban Regions in a Global Economy*, Cambridge: Cambridge University Press.

Stoker, G. (2004), *Transforming Local Governance. From Thatcherism to New Labour*, Basingstoke: Palgrave Macmillan.

Stoker, G. (1998), 'Governance: Five Prepositions', in *International Social Science Journal*, **50** (155), 17–28.

Trigilia, C. (2002), *Economic Sociology. State, Market and Society in Modern Capitalism*, Laden Mass: Blackwell.

Trigilia, C. and L. Burroni (2009), 'Italy: rise, decline and restructuring of a regionalized capitalism', *Economy and Society*, **38** (4), 630–53.

11. Social institutions among economists in the wake of the financial crisis

Henry Farrell

Much of Colin Crouch's recent work focuses on the relationship between institutional diversity and change. It argues against overly ideal-typical (Varieties of Capitalism) and deterministic (crude path dependence) accounts of how economies and societies function. Instead, Crouch (2005) argues for the importance of diversity and redundancy in explaining institutional adaptation. Actors who have access to diverse institutional frames, whether because these institutions exist (in suppressed or occasional form) among them, or because they have access to the lessons of others, are likely to adapt better to unexpected change than actors who do not have such access. Moreover, Crouch offers the beginnings of an account of the order in which actors are likely to draw on diverse resources. Drawing an analogy with cognitive misers, Crouch's actors are cognitively lazy. They are likely to adopt the institutional form that (a) provides some solution to the problem posed by the existing environment, while (b) being easy to access, even if other solutions would be superior. In the language of heuristic science, they are likely to converge on local optima and stick there – even when there might be better global optima available if only they searched harder and more extensively.

This set of arguments stands in sharp distinction to those of economists (although see Bednar and Page (2007) for an interesting reconciliation of game theory with learning across different cultural contexts), who typically discount heuristics in favor of assumptions about optimizing actors in a world of complete information. However, even while economists' *theories* may emphasize optimizing behavior, their own *actions* may not be optimizing. Economists operate within their own universe of institutions and heuristics. An interesting research program in sociology has begun to try to identify the assumptions and institutions underlying the field of economics both cross-nationally and within national contexts (Fourcade 2009).

In this chapter, I argue that Crouch's framework (Crouch 2005, Crouch and Farrell 2004) provides us with a very useful way of understanding adaptation and change among economists.

As the larger economic crisis of 2008–2010 worked itself out, the economics profession found itself enjoying its own miniature crisis of faith (Eichengreen 2009, Krugman 2009b). Dominant approaches to macroeconomics (the rational expectations approach; a watered down neo-Keynesianism) did not predict the crisis, and had little useful to say about it in its early stages. Some of the underlying causes of the crisis were identifiably the direct result of dominant forms of economic theorizing (Fox 2009). Efficient markets arguments that were first advanced within the academy had become the basis for both complex risk management instruments and a laissez-faire approach to regulating market behavior. Even if, as Eichengreen (2009) argued, regulators had selectively cherry-picked 'the theories [within economics] that supported excessive risk taking,' those theories were also the ones that enjoyed most purchase within the academy.

Economists' response to the crisis was to return to a more traditional form of Keynesian economics that advocated demand management. While some economists remained convinced (Fama 2010) that rational expectations and efficient market hypotheses still worked and that demand stimulation would be a disaster (Barro and Redlick 2009), they became an embattled minority within the profession. Several well-known right-wing economists and fellow travellers publicly converted to Keynesianism. This turn poses three interesting puzzles. First – why did academic economics find itself in crisis in the first place? In other words, why were there insufficient resources within mainstream economics circa 2008 to provide compelling insights into the crisis's origins and consequences? Second – why did economists converge on Keynesianism, rather than some other approach? It was not because Keynesianism was necessarily right. As Quiggin (2010) observes, Keynesian approaches were poorly suited to understanding the roots of the crisis.

Third, why did the various alternative approaches receive next-to-no consideration among prestigious economists? Furthermore, other alternative approaches to economics – which might have provided better insights – received next-to-no public debate.

In the remainder of this chapter I argue that Crouch's arguments provide a compelling answer to these questions. To answer the first question, it is necessary to examine how economics had reconstructed itself to become the intellectual equivalent of a monocrop economy. While this provided economists with enormous intellectual advantages (a unified approach to explanation; a simple, powerful and coherent set of intellectual tools), it also meant that economics was less well suited to deal with changing conditions that did not fit easily with prior conceptions. In particular, mainstream economics' impoverished view of institutions made it very difficult for economists to explain the recent financial crisis. To answer the second, it is necessary to look at how Keynesianism became a redundant capacity within economic theory. Even if Keynes had fallen from graduate student syllabi, and economists did not frequently cite his work, he was nonetheless recognized as a major economist, and his ideas were familiar at least to middle-aged economists who had done their training before the rational expectations revolution.

Finally, economists' willingness to turn to Keynes rather than to heterodox economists or to insights from other fields (economic sociology, comparative and international political economy) can be explained by cognitive laziness. Even if, as both Ronald Dore and Crouch himself have argued in recent articles, an institutional approach would have better explained the underlying causal mechanisms of the crisis, and possible solutions to it, economists (like other academics) were more likely to turn to the 'good' explanation that was closest to their previously held priors, than to look to more distant explanatory frameworks for insight.

The next section discusses how mainstream economic analysis became highly path dependent, with a submerged path that occasionally re-emerged (Keynesian analysis). The section following examines the social processes through which economists came to converge on Keynes. The penultimate section examines why economists failed to pay any attention to alternative approaches that might have helped them understand the roots of the crisis. The final section provides an overview both of how Crouch's approach helps explain economists' responses to the crisis, and what this approach should incorporate to better understand the mechanisms of change (specifically: closer attention to the relationship between organizing ideas and political contention).

HARVESTING THE MONOCROP: ECONOMICS AND INTELLECTUAL HOMOGENEITY

The story of economics' increasing convergence on a unified intellectual approach emphasizing a specific set of mathematical models is frequently told, both by those who celebrate (Krugman 1998) and deplore (Hodgson 2001) it. Rather than recapitulating this debate at length, I seek to understand it within Crouch's analytic framework.[1]

In Crouch's most simple account of path dependence theory, an actor has to match her actions to changes in the environment. As in Arthur

(1994), the environment draws balls which may be either red or white, with the probability of a red draw (or a white one) being a positive function of the number of red (or white) draws that have been made in the past. However, Crouch's twist on Arthur is that an actor exists independently of the environment, who can also draw red or white balls – but may pay a cost to try for a new draw if she does not like the ball she has drawn. If the actor succeeds in matching the ball that the environment has drawn, she wins a reward.

This provides a useful shorthand account of how actors may seek to respond to an ergodic environment with a tendency towards path dependence (e.g. an environment in which the frequency of future events of a particular kind is a positive function of how often these events have occurred in the past). Actors – in seeking to respond to such an environment – will use institutional tools that have path-dependent qualities themselves As institutions develop over time, they too will make some actions easier and cheaper than others. Most importantly, this theoretical innovation draws a clear distinction between (a) the external environment, and (b) actors' institutionalized responses to that environment. It thus allows us to think more clearly about what happens when the environment changes for exogenous reasons (e.g. an environment with a strong path dependency on producing red balls suddenly switches over so that it tends to produce white balls instead). Under these circumstances, we might expect that institutional misfits and inefficiencies, which prevented actors' responses from conforming perfectly to their environment by, for example, requiring them occasionally to choose white balls in the past, can become a source of strength. Heterogeneity increases adaptability, by providing actors with resources that make it easier to switch to a new path. However, actors – especially those most strongly committed to the dominant path at a particular moment – may have a strong incentive to seek to eliminate these apparent maladaptations, since they lead to substantial short-term inefficiency.

Such a process – path-dependent adaptation to an existing environment – provides a remarkably good understanding of the development of the field of economics since the 'marginalist revolution' of the late nineteenth century, and of the more recent eclipse of Keynesian theory within macroeconomics. There is bitter controversy between the enthusiasts and detractors of modern economic theory and rational expectations macroeconomics. However, both agree that economics has over time come to be defined in terms of a specific – and highly formal – set of understandings of how the economy works.

Assumptions of rationality and of complete (although not necessarily perfect) information allowed economists to engage in equilibrium analysis and hence to use a unifying set of conceptual tools that could be employed to analyze the economy. For many economists (but not all), these tools went together with assumptions about the superiority of markets vis-à-vis other forms of social organization, and consequent limits on the appropriate role of government. Critics of the 'neo-classical' approach to economics (which sought to rebuild many of the arguments of classical economics on sounder microfoundations) pointed to the many heroic assumptions which were required to make these arguments work. Real life economic actors did not have the cognitive capacities and ability to look down decision trees that economists attributed to them (Simon 1979). They were also prone to systematic cognitive biases (Tversky 2000).

Both skeptics and adherents agree that economics has become increasingly unified over time as a field based on a core set of formalized microfoundations. Very recent developments (the emphasis on econometrics, and efforts to capture causal relationships through instrumental variables, experiments and natural experiments) are layered over these core microfoundations, but as yet show no signs of replacing it. Economists who are trained at first tier and second tier US institutions share a common training in a very specific set of techniques and intellectual assumptions. This theoretic unity contrasts with other social sciences (political science, sociology, anthropology) which display considerably greater internal diversity.[2]

This search for increasing formalization has strong aspects of path dependence. The specific mechanisms that induce path dependence are a matter of dispute. Scholars who favor formalization point to the positive network externalities associated with a unified approach. For example Krugman (1998) argues that 'professional economists also have another task: to communicate with each other, and in so doing to help economics as a discipline progress. In this task it is important for your colleagues (and students) to understand how you arrived at your conclusions, partly so that they can look for weak points, partly so that they may find other uses for the technical tricks you used to think an issue through. . . . publication in professional journals is or at least should be a form of education: it is how economists teach each other about their work. Tjalling Koopmans (1957) once complained about Marshall's "diplomatic style" – his emphasis on persuasion, his mingling of theory and evidence, his willingness to sweep awkward points under the rug. I am a great admirer of Marshall, yet Koopmans had a point. Marshall's style – the style some insider critics think we need to recapture – was entirely appropriate for a general audience, even a highly educated and intellectual one. But Marshall adopted the same style when writing for economists and their students. To do so is in effect to turn professional economics into the repetition of received truths rather than a continual process of exploration.'

The claim is straightforward – the more economists adopt formal techniques, the easier it is for them to communicate with each other, learn from each other, critique each other and contribute to a mutually intelligible body of theory. These network externalities provide economists with strong incentives to coordinate on a common set of microfoundations and theoretical tools. One can also (as Krugman does not – though he perhaps hints at this) extrapolate an argument about how this can provide the basis for economics' success vis-à-vis other social sciences. Under this argument, economists are indeed matching their environment – but in a largely benign fashion. By employing formal theory, economists' significantly advance their understanding of economic interactions in ways that are externally validated by the outside world. They hence receive collective and individual rewards (greater prestige, more resources) than other social sciences which have failed to achieve this benign feedback loop, and convert these rewards into yet further progress.

Skeptics point to a quite different set of mechanisms inducing path dependence at the level of the discipline. Very frequently, they refer to control of hiring and publication resources by formally inclined economists (Hodgson and Rothman 1999, Dunn 2000). Here, the argument is not that convergence on a common framework of analysis creates positive network effects. Rather, it is that sociological institutional forces and power relations create incentives for actors to converge on the perceived 'mainstream' of the profession, punishing individual economists (and indeed economics departments) which deviate significantly.

Some of these skeptics have pointed to decisions over time by the University of Notre Dame effectively to close down its heterodox program in economics. Originally, Notre Dame had sought to specialize in areas of economic theory (post-Keynesianism, Marxism) which had been marginalized in the discipline as a whole. It had become the most prominent department in these areas in the country. However, over time, the university grew to regret this decision, and to roll it back (Glenn 2009). In 2003 the department of economics was split so as to sideline its heterodox members into a separate department of economics and social studies. Then in 2009 this department (which had not been allowed to take on new graduate students or to fill vacant faculty positions) was dissolved. There is strong evidence that the university's decision was driven by the desire to conform to the demands of other, more prestigious departments elsewhere in the country. 'Another recent alumnus says that the university's turn toward econometrics and the neoclassical model has been the right move. The economics program as a whole "is in a far better place than it was 10 years ago before the split," says Matt Gunden, a 2004 graduate who is now a doctoral student in economics at Northwestern University, in an e-mail message. "I feel that had I graduated even three or four years earlier than I did, that I would not have had the opportunities I now have to pursue graduate study." Mr. Gunden is exactly the kind of student that the founders of the econometrics department wanted to cultivate: mathematically inclined students who could win admission into highly-ranked doctoral programs. Mr. McGreevy, the dean, says that this development has been a great success. "Economics is our fastest-growing major," he says. "And we've had several students move into top-20 departments"' (Glenn 2009).

Under this argument, the mechanism underlying path dependence is less benign. Rather than reflecting positive externalities, it reflects environmental pressures to converge on a common approach regardless of its intellectual merits. If heterodox economists are punished by being unable to send their students to prestigious programs, to publish in prestigious journals, to receive significant grants, and so on, then we may expect them either to converge, or (as in this case) to have their programs eliminated by universities that wish to have prestigious economics departments. Similarly, it leads to isolation between economists and practitioners of other social sciences (although economists do not bear all of the blame for this isolation, see Farrell and Knight 2010).

In this chapter, I do not propose to adjudicate between these two mechanisms. It is quite plausible that both of them apply. That is – convergence on a coherent formal methodology may be driven *both* by positive network externalities *and* by unattractive social pressures. Actors may invest ever more heavily in formal techniques both because they have scientific benefits, and because they worry about being excluded from the rewards of the profession if they do not. Instead, I simply point out that both these putative mechanisms point in the same direction. They both lead to convergence on a single path of development, and towards the gradual elimination of 'inefficiencies' – insights that are not readily formalizable, programs that tend toward heterodoxy rather than orthodoxy, and linkages with other social sciences which invoke different mechanisms of explanation. Such inefficiencies were not eliminated entirely – as Crouch observes, white balls will continue to appear very occasionally even when red balls dominate. There remains some degree of internal heterogeneity within economics. But even so, in comparison with other social scientific disciplines, it appears to be quite homogeneous.

This carries intellectual advantages and disadvantages. Its advantages are most apparent in 'normal' times, where there is a high degree of stability over time, where actors understand their interests reasonably well (and in self-interested terms), and where there is reasonable concordance between actual economic relations (as best society understands them) and the theoretical tools that economists can apply to them. Under such circumstances, economic theory (like other theories) is clearly likely to neglect many interesting facets of the economy, but may nonetheless provide a plausible account of major aspects of economic life. Over time, economic theory may itself become more 'efficient,' ironing out arguments, theories and models that do not accord well with perceived experience. Such efficiencies are more realizable precisely to the extent that economists share common formalizable assumptions. Fields without such a common language (such as sociology, and, to a lesser extent, political science) are less well able to achieve such efficiencies, and hence retain internal heterogeneity.

However, conventional economic theory is likely to do considerably less well in times of unexpected economic crises. In such situations, academic fields are going to be less well suited to explain the crisis exactly to the extent that they are 'overfitted' to the previous situation of 'normality.' Heterogeneous fields of inquiry, in contrast, are likely to find it easier to respond, *ceteris paribus*. As Page (2008) argues, groups of actors with highly diverse heuristics are better able to find attractive local optima in search over rugged landscapes than even 'smart' actors with less diverse heuristics.

This helps us understand why economics has had such difficulty in dealing with the crisis (which very few academic economists indeed foresaw, even if some of them predicted a somewhat different crisis resulting from global imbalances). Economists – when they look at the world – draw upon a very specific set of intellectual tools and assumptions. These tools and assumptions are well suited to understanding the operation of the economy in 'normal' times. Over time, the intellectual assumptions became more and more wed to a set of assumptions about continued stability (the 'Great Moderation'). Both reinforced each other – the intellectual assumptions provided underpinnings for claims about continued stability, which in turn justified the intellectual assumptions. However, when the crisis exploded – from a set of relationships that economists had either paid no sustained attention to, or had assumed to be stability-inducing (Fox 2009) – economists had few initial tools to work with. As the next section discusses in greater detail, this does not mean that they had *no* useful tools. However, they had to work from assumptions that did not always fit very well with observed data, and only now are beginning to address the actual origins of the crisis, and what these origins mean for economic theory.

THE RETURN OF KEYNESIAN ECONOMICS

The arguments above should not be taken to suggest that there was *no* internal diversity within economics. Instead, it suggests that economics was an unusually homogeneous discipline among the social sciences, and that its internal diversity (along certain axes at least) had substantially diminished over time. A specific path dominated (red balls, in Crouch's analogy), but occasional white balls appeared. Although a new generation of economists in the 2000s had begun to focus their attention on econometrics rather than formal theory, and on trying to capture causal relations with better tools, their efforts did not so much overturn existing theories as add new empirical flavor to them. Within economic theory itself, viewpoints that had once had a significant place in debate (certain varieties of Keynesianism) were now relegated to the margins. Economics increasingly sought to become a normal science seeking to make progress on the basis of shared assumptions rather than engagement with grand theoretical debates. While economics was no longer as sterile and abstract as it had once been (Colander 2007), it still largely proceeded on assumptions of optimizing rational actors, complete information and relatively efficient equilibria.

Economists forsook study of the past in the hope of future progress. As described by one prominent game theorist: 'you can emerge from your graduate studies in economics without having read any of the classics, or indeed, without having anything other than a vague notion of what the great thinkers of the past had written. The modern economist doesn't even try to legitimize her inquiry by linking it to questions addressed in the canon; she typically begins her article by referring to something in the literature a few months old. . . . In order to do creative work, there is a further advantage in not being knowledgeable about the intellectual concerns and struggles of bygone eras; there would be a lower risk that the past was setting the present's research agenda' (Partha Dasgupta; quoted in Hodgson 2009).

This lack of interest in the past obviously reinforces the path dependence described in the previous section. If actors systematically ignore the choices not taken in previous historical conjunctures, they make it harder for themselves to travel back 'up the tree' of exfoliating choices when it becomes apparent that they have chosen a dead end. Knowledge of historical alternatives can allow actors to extract themselves from intellectual traps of their own devising.

However, economics did have some internal diversity – at least *in potentia*. Macroeconomics had always been a partial outlier in economic theory. Forged by the necessities of the Great Depression, it had initially eschewed rigorous microfoundations in favor of a broad understanding of the major forces shaping the macroeconomy. As time went on, intellectual entrepreneurs began to try to reintegrate it within economics as a whole, by providing it with microfoundations that mirrored those of microeconomics and which would hence perhaps allow for a unification of microeconomics and macroeconomics over the longer term. Even so, earlier strains of macroeconomics remained as a hidden resource within economics, which could be drawn on again in times of intellectual crisis. In particular, a specific form of Keynesianism, which emphasized the importance of inefficient equilibria, was preserved by some economists who had trained under the old system. This redundant path – which was partly rediscovered, partly reinvented – provided the basis for economists' major response to the crisis.

It is important, however, to clarify how deeply that resource was buried. Over the 1970s, 1980s and 1990s, a school variously dubbed 'New Classical Macroeconomics', 'Rational Expectations' or, more colloquially, freshwater economics (its sources of strength were in the Great Lakes region, as opposed to saltwater economics on the East and West coasts) fundamentally reshaped macroeconomic theory. This school did not entirely prevail – some of its starting assumptions proved to be untenable. But it did succeed in obliging its intellectual opponents to remake themselves so as better to meet its critiques. Keynesian economics had considerable difficulty in explaining the economic circumstances of the late 1960s and early 1970s. Relationships such as the Phillips Curve (which had been grafted on to Keynesian theory in the 1960s) broke down quite dramatically.

Macroeconomists became far more careful about microfoundations, but also far more limited in their theoretical aspirations. Ideas about uncertainty which had animated Keynes and some of his immediate disciples were relegated to obscure journals and peripheral departments (Skidelsky 2009). 'Neo-Keynesianism', which absorbed some of the arguments of the rational expectations revolution (Blinder and Snowdon 2001), fared rather better, but at the expense of losing much of what had made Keynes's initial arguments provocative and interesting.

The results were emphatic. Traditional Keynesianism more or less disappeared from economics syllabi. Traditional Keynesians did not quite disappear, but they certainly found themselves beleaguered. In the (likely deliberately provocative) description of Robert Lucas, the most important pioneer of rational expectations economics: 'one cannot find good, under-forty economists who identify themselves or their work as "Keynesian". Indeed, people even take offense if referred to as "Keynesians". At research seminars, people don't take Keynesian theorizing seriously anymore; the audience starts to whisper and giggle to one another.'

Although neo-Keynesianism had a significant revival in the 1990s, Keynes himself was much revered, but more or less unstudied. In his two surveys of economics graduate students at several elite US departments, Colander (2007: 63) found that Keynesianism had 'faded from the teaching of economics'. More generally, Colander reports that that macroeconomics has become a specialized version of advanced dynamic general equilibrium price theory (ibid.). Most courses did not discuss macroeconomic policy. As described by one student interviewed by Colander, 'monetary and fiscal policy are not abstract enough to be a question that would be answered in a macro course' (Colander 2007: 46).

Geoffrey Hodgson reports (Hodgson 2009: 1208) that 'I tried without success to find the work of Keynes or Minsky on any reading list available on the web of any macroeconomics or compulsory economic theory course in any of the top universities in the world. Instead, there is ample evidence of student proficiency requirements in mathematics' (Hodgson 2009: 1208).

Nonetheless, even if Keynesian theory was no longer taught, it still remained a submerged path 'within' the path of mainstream economics. Despite the above, Colander found that Keynes (together with Adam Smith) was the only economist to be listed by respondents as one of the five most respected economists, dead or alive. Even if graduate students were not acquainted with his work, they were surely aware of his name. More importantly, scholars of an earlier generation retained direct familiarity with his work, either because they had themselves been prominent Keynesians (Robert Solow), or had been exposed to his work (Paul Krugman, Brad DeLong). Krugman most notably had come to a new appreciation of Keynesianism as a result of his interest in Japan's 'lost decade'. This meant that when economics experienced its own intellectual crisis, they were able to draw on Keynes as an intellectual resource, in their arguments over both economic policy and the internal politics of the academy. Indeed, Keynesians were unusually well equipped to engage in these debates – in contrast to rational expectations scholars, prominent Keynesians and neo-Keynesians had directly involved themselves in policy debates, and indeed in policy making.

Keynesian theory – at least as these scholars employed it – did not provide a very satisfactory account of the sources of the Great Recession. As a policy-inclined macroeconomist observes, neither neo-Keynesians nor their theoretical rivals really tried to model financial markets. 'As I have discussed, many modern macro models incorporate financial market frictions. However, these models generally allow households and firms to trade one or two financial assets in a single market. They do not capture an intermediate messy reality in which market participants can trade multiple assets in a wide array of somewhat segmented markets. As a consequence, the models do not reveal much about the benefits of the massive amount of daily or quarterly reallocations of wealth within financial markets. The models also say nothing about the relevant costs and benefits of resulting fluctuations in financial structure (across bank loans, corporate debt, and equity). . . . Macroeconomists abstracted from these features of financial markets for two reasons. First, prior to December 2007, such details seemed largely irrelevant to understanding post-World War II business cycle fluctuations in the United States (although maybe not in other countries, such as Japan). This argument is certainly less compelling today. Second, embedding such features in modern macro models is difficult. . . . private information about key economic attributes, such as future asset payoffs or firm prospects . . . is hard to incorporate into the kind of dynamic economic models used by macroeconomists' (Kocherlakota 2010).

As Paul Krugman describes it: 'the self-described New Keynesian economists weren't immune to the charms of rational individuals and perfect markets. They tried to keep their deviations from neoclassical orthodoxy as limited as possible. This meant that there was no room in the prevailing models for such things as bubbles and banking-system collapse. The fact that such things continued to happen in the real world – there was a terrible financial and macroeconomic crisis in much of Asia in 1997–8 and a depression-level slump in Argentina in 2002 – wasn't reflected in the mainstream of New Keynesian thinking. . . . new Keynesians, unlike the original Keynesians, didn't think fiscal policy – changes in government spending or taxes – was needed to fight recessions. They believed that monetary policy, administered by the technocrats at the Fed, could provide whatever remedies the economy needed' (Krugman 2009b).

Thus, Keynesian (and other) macroeconomics models were remarkably poorly suited to provide any explanation of the 2008–2009 economic crisis (which originated in financial markets). They did, nonetheless, have a conspicuous advantage over rational expectations arguments, which claimed in contradiction to widely available evidence that the crisis (to the extent that there was a crisis) was not the result of any underlying problems in financial markets. Eugene Fama, when asked in an interview whether financial markets had gotten it systematically wrong, responded: '(pauses) A lot of mortgages went bad. A lot of corporate debt went bad. A lot of debt of all sorts went bad. I don't see how this is a special case. This is a problem created by a general decline in asset prices. Whenever you get a recession, it turns out that you invested too much before that. But that was unpredictable at the time' (Fama 2010).

Instead, he claimed that the initial problems in the housing market (provision of bad loans) had their origins in government intervention: 'that was government policy; that was not a failure of the market. The government decided that it wanted to expand home ownership. Fannie Mae and Freddie Mac were instructed to buy lower grade mortgages' (Fama 2010).

This claim seems starkly at odds with the available empirical evidence (Kroszner 2008). John Cochrane of the University of Chicago claimed 'it's fun to say we didn't see the crisis coming, but the central empirical prediction of the efficient markets hypothesis is precisely that nobody can tell where markets are going – neither benevolent government bureaucrats, nor crafty hedge-fund managers, nor ivory-tower academics. This is probably the best-tested proposition in all the social sciences' (Cochrane 2009).

While Cochrane allowed that some unspecified tinkering with the incentives of banks and other actors could have beneficial effects, he retained faith in the validity and usefulness of the efficient markets argument.

The evident failure of financial markets led some unlikely economists and economic commentators to declare themselves Keynesians (Posner 2010). It also led to a pitched rhetorical battle between Keynesians (whether long established or newly converted) and rational expectations economists over policy. Rational expectations arguments suggested that government intervention – even (and perhaps especially) in crisis situations – was more likely to hurt than to help.

Keynesian models in contrast, suggested that in situations of real and persistent economic crisis ('liquidity traps'), monetary tools would have no useful effect. Instead, activist fiscal policy (substantial spending by government) was needed to boost aggregate demand, and hence allow the economy to escape from its trap. Thus, Keynesians like Paul Krugman argued that the US government, and other governments in the developed world, should create large and substantial stimuluses to help the economy recover (Krugman 2008).

Rational expectations economists and conservatives retorted that Keynesian prescriptions for fiscal stimulus were based on outdated and exploded economic theories: 'nothing in the incoming data has removed the inconsistencies that plagued Keynesian economics for forty years until it was thrown out. I mean, we threw it out for a reason. It didn't work in the data. When inflation came in the nineteen-seventies that was a major failure of Keynesian economics. It was logically incoherent. What happened is the government wanted to spend a lot of money. They said "Keynesian stimulus" and people got excited. What event, what data says we've got to go back to Keynesianism? Again, I'm going to throw it back on you. What about it other than that Paul Krugman thinks we need another stimulus tells us that this is an idea to be rehabilitated?' (Cochrane 2010).

They further argued that empirical evidence suggested that stimulus spending doesn't work (Barro and Redlick 2009). Keynesians, for their part, argued that the data was suspect, and that critics of stimulus spending were recapitulating the fallacious 'Treasury View' of Montagu Norman and other economic decision makers who had contributed to the Great Depression (Delong 2009).

These arguments were bitter and quite personalized. Rational expectations economists accused Paul Krugman, a prominent defender of Keynes, of 'mak[ing] stuff up' and wanting to become the 'Rush Limbaugh of the Left' (Cochrane 2009). Krugman, for his part, suggested that economists like Fama and Cochrane were 'barbarians in the grip of an obscurantist faith' (Krugman 2009a). However, at least in the short run, the Keynesians appeared to prevail. They succeeded in persuading the US government, and the governments of many other industrialized countries, to adopt stimulus packages, albeit smaller packages than they would have liked (Farrell and Quiggin 2010). They also succeeded in converting many economists who were previously opposed to Keynesianism, or neutral regarding its merits, to an active belief in Keynesian economics.

This conversion is best seen as the revival (at least for the moment) of a previously suppressed path within economics as a response to changed environmental circumstances. Rational expectations economics and the efficient market hypothesis both seemed tenable in a world of relative economic stability. They successfully supplanted a previously existing tradition of 'strong' Keynesianism, both because they seemed to offer a better explanation of that world, and because they fit better with the dominant approach within economics as a whole, which stressed rationality, quantifiable risk and strong microfoundations. However, they fit remarkably poorly with the changed circumstances of the economy during the crisis. As Richard Posner, one of the unlikely converts to Keynesianism described it, the crisis: 'called into question a whole approach to economics – one that is very formal, making very austere assumptions about human rationality: people have a lot of information, a lot of foresight. They look ahead. It is very difficult for the government to affect behavior, because the market will offset what it does. The more informal economics of Keynes has made a big comeback because people realize that even though it is kind of loose and it doesn't cross all the "t"s and dot all the "i"s, it seems to have more of a grasp of what is going on in the economy' (Posner 2010).

It is important to note though that the transition from the one path to the other (should it take over the longer term) was not a smooth or easy process of intellectual adjustment. Instead, it was highly conflictual. Actors with a strong stake in the continuation of the existing path bitterly resisted the efforts of Keynesian heretics to change it. Rhetorical struggles affected government policy, and also likely affected the allocation of less visible resources (hiring decisions, placement of articles in prominent journals). I return to this point in the chapter's conclusions.

WHY NOT A MORE RADICAL CHANGE OF PATH?

Mainstream economists – to the extent that they have changed their minds – appear to have done so by re-embracing Keynesianism. This raises an important question, given that Keynesian thought does not offer any-where near a complete account of the recent crisis, and is unlikely to do so, at least in the near future. Why have economists not opted for a more sub-stantial change in path, to an approach that might offer a better account of how the crisis arose? Paul Krugman – who is more associated than any other individual with the revival of Keynesianism – acknowledges that: 'a few economists challenged the assumption of rational behavior, questioned the belief that financial markets can be trusted and pointed to the long history of financial crises that had devastating economic conse-quences. But they were swimming against the tide, unable to make much headway against a pervasive and, in retrospect, foolish complacency' (Krugman 2009b).

However, as Galbraith (2009) notes, these economists remain just as far from the mainstream as they were previously. They 'are not named. Their work is not cited. Their story remains untold. Despite having been right on the greatest economic question of a generation – they are unpersons in the tale.'

Krugman depicts the major struggle within macroeconomics as taking place between saltwater economists (who bought too heavily into rational expectations arguments, but, as pragmatists, were willing to change their minds) and freshwater economists (who cling to their belief in efficient markets). His prescriptions for the future development of economics argue for greater pragmatism and recognition of the limitations of economic theory.

'It's much harder to say where the economics profession goes from here. But what's almost certain is that economists will have to learn to live with messiness. That is, they will have to acknowledge the importance of irra-tional and often unpredictable behavior, face up to the often idiosyncratic imperfections of markets and accept that an elegant economic "theory of everything" is a long way off. In practical terms, this will translate into more cautious policy advice – and a reduced willingness to dismantle economic safeguards in the faith that markets will solve all problems' (Krugman 2009b).

However, he does not argue for any concerted effort to integrate the views of heterodox economists who arguably got the crisis 'right' into the mainstream. Krugman at least recognizes the existence of these alternative paths. Other economists, as a whole, do not. Galbraith summarizes the contribution of a number of heterodox approaches to economics. These range from Marxism (which did not provide specific indicators) through the work of Dean Baker and the Keynesian economist Wynne Godley (who both focused on the unsustainability of an economic bubble), neo-Minskyans such as Barkley Rosser and Ping Chen to neo-Galbraithians who focused on the degree of fraud and corruption in the existing system. He notes that none of these ideas has received serious attention within the literature.

One might ask similar questions about why economists have failed to take up insights from non-economists, such as for example economic sociologists. Bruce Carruthers' work on risk and bubbles (Carruthers 2009) and Donald MacKenzie's work on how financial models shape markets (Mackenzie 2008) are just two prominent examples of scholars whose insights seem relevant to understanding the financial crisis.

There are a number of possible reasons why economists have failed to take up these insights. It is, for example, possible that some analyses, which were correct in predicting the crisis, are wrong most of the time. It is also possible that some of these approaches (as Galbraith suggests with respect to e.g., Marxism) are of limited predictive ability – while they predict that crisis is endemic to capitalism, they do not have any very specific insights into when crises will happen and what will precipitate them.

Nonetheless, there are also good reasons to believe that *even when* heterodox economists or non-economists have ideas that have direct bearing on the understanding of economic relations, their contributions are likely to go unacknowledged. Everyday empiricism suggests that the high degree of intellectual homogeneity within the economics profession goes together with high barriers to entry for ideas that do not directly address core propositions of economic theory. These barriers do not merely involve economists' distaste for non-formal expositions of theory, but also certain kinds of theoretic assumptions. In general, economists prefer models that involve some form of equilibrium, and provide us with insights about the circumstances under which this or that equilibrium can be reached or maintained. They tend to be uncomfortable with accounts that do not produce equilibrium predictions; this may be one reason why, for example, we have seen a revival of Keynes's thought among economists, but no revival of Minsky's. Despite some recent improvement, there is still scant intellectual exchange between for instance economists and economic sociologists, despite a clear overlap in interests.[3]

Again, Crouch's arguments provide us with a useful shorthand means of understanding how economists are likely to respond to external changes. Even more than other social scientists, they are likely to have a structurally induced tendency towards cognitive 'laziness' (this term is not here meant in a pejorative sense). Their relative disconnection from other fields of inquiry, together with the powerful short-term advantages of their own preferred path of research, means that they are less likely than other social scientists to seek to import ideas from other fields, or from economists whose work has been defined as heterodox. They are less easily able to borrow ideas from other players who are playing other games with different balls, precisely because these other players are more 'distant' from them in terms of the accessibility of their theories and portability of their arguments back over the borders of economics. Higher search costs mean that economists *ceteris paribus* are less likely to seek alternative ideas outside their own discipline than other social scientists. Those who do so successfully are likely to win substantial rewards (a brief perusal of winners of the Economics Nobel and the John Clark Bates medal suggests that there is an unusually high number of border-crossers among them) – but require unusual ingenuity to translate the insights of other disciplines into terms that economists can understand.

As Crouch's argument suggests, economists converged on a solution that was 'good enough' (Keynesianism), even if it did not provide a clear understanding of the origins of the crisis, instead of engaging in a costly, difficult, and perhaps fruitless search for alternative explanatory frameworks. This is unsurprising, given the distance between economics and other fields in the social sciences that might have had different solutions to bring to bear on the problem. Crouch's argument would furthermore suggest that other disciplines' responses to the crisis are likely to be more diverse, and draw more directly on cross-disciplinary resources, precisely to the extent that these disciplines are less isolated from each other than economics is from any of them.

CONCLUSIONS

In this chapter, I have argued that Crouch's arguments about path dependence provide us with a good understanding of how academic economists have responded to the recent economics crisis. First, they help to explain the processes of path dependence through which economists came to converge on one 'path' of intellectual inquiry to the exclusion of others. Second, they explain why economists drew on Keynes's thought when their models were faced with serious empirical challenge from an entirely unexpected crisis. Keynes's ideas were a suppressed path within economics proper – and one that appeared directly relevant to a situation of world-wide economic crisis. Finally, they help us understand why economists are happy at the time of writing to stick with Keynes's explanation rather than searching further afield (among the ideas of heterodox economists or other social scientists). The intellectual distance between economics and these other fields is sufficiently large that economists have less incentive than other social scientists to engage in costly search.

Clearly, this chapter is deliberately impertinent in its analysis of the field of neo-classical economics through decidedly non-classical means. It suggests that even if economists are not interested in economic sociology, economic sociology is surely interested in them. Nonetheless, it does not try to adjudicate the question of whether economics' very specific intellectual orientation is 'good' or 'bad' (here, it may differ from Crouch's own views on economics, which are, as best as I can discern from many conversations, politely skeptical). Instead, it uses Crouch's ideas to identify more clearly the methodological bet that economists have taken. If economics is like classical physics – that is, its subject matter involves relatively mathematically tractable relationships, where simple models have high explanatory power, then it may be that economists' collective bet is a good one. There may be high returns over the long run as well as the short to formalization and concentration on tractable models with determinate equilibria. If, in contrast, economics has a subject matter without such convenient relationships, then economics is likely to find itself in trouble not only as a result of a temporary crisis, but increasingly over the longer run.

Finally, the chapter points to some important ways in which Crouch's arguments can be extended. The changes – such as they were – within economics in the wake of the recent crisis, were neither smooth nor non-conflictual. Instead, they emerged through bitter contestation between actors with starkly different interests and ideas regarding the proper role of economic theory. Crouch's arguments do very clearly have some room for power relations. However, they do not (in contrast to much of Crouch's work elsewhere) treat contestation as a core dynamic of institutional change. Future work – which may unite Crouch's work on path dependence with his work on processes of social contestation – may plausibly provide a richer and more accurate theory of how real institutions change.

NOTES

1. I note that I helped Colin to develop these ideas in their original formulation, but should make it quite explicit that the inspiration behind them was Colin's, not mine (I provided initial readings and worked on some of the technical aspects of the paper).

2. The reasons for these differences between fields are beyond the scope of this chapter.
3. However, as (Fourcade 2007) notes, economic sociologists have created their field in direct competition with economics – overlap may not always have benign consequences for intellectual exchange.

REFERENCES

Arthur, William Brian (1994), *Increasing Returns and Path Dependence in the Economy*, Ann Arbor, MI: University of Michigan Press.

Barro, R.J. and C. Redlick (2009), 'Stimulus spending doesn't work', available at http://online.wsj.com/article/SB10001424052748704471504574440723298786 310.html (accessed 1 October 2009).

Bednar, J. and S. Page (2007), 'Can Game(s) Theory Explain Culture? The Emergence of Cultural Behavior within Multiple Games', *Rationality and Society*, **19** (1), 65–97.

Blinder, A. and B. Snowdon (2001), 'Keeping the Keynesian Faith', *World Economics*, **2** (2), 105–40.

Carruthers, B.G. (2009), 'A sociology of bubbles', *Contexts*, **8** (3), 22–6.

Cochrane, J.H. (2009), 'How did Paul Krugman get it so wrong?', available at http://faculty.chicagobooth.edu/john.cochrane/research/papers/krugman_response.htm (accessed 16 September 2009).

Cochrane, J. (2010), 'Interview with John Cochrane', available at http://www.newyorker.com/online/blogs/johncassidy/2010/01/interview-with-john-cochrane.html (accessed 13 January 2010).

Colander, David (2007), *The Making of an Economist, Redux*, Princeton: Princeton University Press.

Crouch, Colin (2005), *Capitalist Diversity and Change. Recombinant Governance and Institutional Entrepreneurs*, New York: Oxford University Press.

Crouch, C. and H. Farrell (2004), 'Breaking the path of institutional development? Alternatives to the new determinism', *Rationality and Society*, **16** (1), 5–43.

DeLong, B. (2009), 'Fama's fallacy, take i: Eugene Fama rederives the "Treasury view"', available at http://delong.typepad.com/sdj/2009/01/eugene-fama-rederives-the-treasury-view-a-guestpost-from-montagu-norman.html (accessed 14 January 2010).

Dunn, S.P. (2000), 'Wither post keynesianism?', *Journal of Post Keynesian Economics*, **22** (3), 343–64.

Eichengreen, B. (2009), 'The last temptation of risk', *The National Interest*, 101, 7–14.

Fama, E. (2010), 'Interview with Eugene Fama', available at http://www.newyorker.com/online/blogs/johncassidy/2010/01/interview-with-eugene-fama.html (accessed 13 January 2009).

Farrell, H. and Knight, J. (2010). *Rational Choice as Sociological Theory: A Pragmatist Account*.

Farrell, H. and Quiggin, J. (2010). *The Revenge of Defunct Economists: Fiscal Policy in the 2008–2010 Recession*.

Fourcade, M. (2007), 'Theories of markets and theories of society', *American Behavioral Scientist*, **50** (8), 1015–34.

Fourcade, Marion (2009), *Economists and societies. Discipline and profession in the United States, Britain, and France, 1890s to 1990s*, Princeton: Princeton University Press.

Fox, Justin (2009), *The Myth of the Rational Market. A History of Risk, and Delusion on Wall Street*, New York: Harper Business.

Galbraith, J.K. (2009), 'Who are these economists anyway?', *Thought and Action*, Fall, 85–97.

Glenn, D. (2009), 'Notre dame plans to dissolve the "Heterodox" side of its split economics department', available at http://chronicle.com/article/Notre-Dame-to-Dissolve/48460/ (accessed 16 September 2009).

Hodgson, Geoffrey M. (2001), *How Economics Forgot History. The Problem of Historical Specificity in Social Science*, New York: Routledge.

Hodgson, G.M. (2009), 'The great crash of 2008 and the reform of economics', *Cambridge Journal of Economics*, **33** (6), 1205–21.

Hodgson, G.M. and H. Rothman (1999), 'The editors and authors of economics journals. A case of institutional oligopoly?', *Economic Journal*, **109** (453), 165–86.

Kocherlakota, N. (2010), 'Modern macroeconomic models as tools for economic policy. 2009 annual report', *The Region*, May, 5–21.

Kroszner, R.S. (2008), 'The community reinvestment act and the recent mortgage crisis', available at http://www.federalreserve.gov/newsevents/speech/kroszner20081203a.htm (accessed 3 December 2008).

Krugman, P. (1998), 'Two cheers for formalism', *Economic Journal*, **108** (451), 1829–36.

Krugman, P. (2008), 'Let's get fiscal', available at http://www.nytimes.com/2008/10/17/opinion/17krugman.html?partner=perma (accessed 16 October 2008).

Krugman, P. (2009a), 'A dark age of macroeconomics (wonkish)', available at http://krugman.blogs.nytimes.com/2009/01/27/a-dark-age-of-macroeconomics-wonkish/ (accessed 27 January 2009).

Krugman, P. (2009b), 'How did economists get it so wrong?', available at http://www.nytimes.com/2009/09/06/magazine/06Economic-t.html (accessed 2 September 2009).

MacKenzie, Donald (2008), *An Engine, Not a camera. How Financial Models Shape Markets*, Cambridge, MA: MIT Press Books.

Page, Scott (2008), *The Difference: How the Power of Diversity Creates Better Groups, Firms, Schools, and Societies*, Princeton: Princeton University Press.

Posner, R. (2010), 'Interview with Richard Posner', available at http://www.newyorker.com/online/blogs/johncassidy/2010/01/interview-with-richard-posner.html (accessed 13 January 2010).

Quiggin, John (2010), *Zombie Economics. How Dead Ideas Walk Among Us*, Princeton: Princeton University Press.

Simon, H.A. (1979), 'Rational decision making in business organizations', *The American Economic Review*, **69** (4), 493–513.

Skidelsky, Robert (2009), *Keynes. The Return of the Master*, New York: Public Affairs.

Tversky, A. and D. Kahneman (2000), 1. Judgment under Uncertainty: Heuristics and Biases. Judgment and Decision making: An Interdisciplinary Reader, p. 35.

Index